Sport
A Critical Sociology

Second Edition

Richard Giulianotti

polity

The right of Richard Giulianotti to be identified as Author of this Work has been asserted in accordance with the UK Copyright, Designs and Patents Act 1988.

First edition published in 2005 by Polity Press
This second edition first published in 2016 by Polity Press

Polity Press
65 Bridge Street
Cambridge CB2 1UR, UK

Polity Press
350 Main Street
Malden, MA 02148, USA

ISBN-13: 978-0-7456-6992-2
ISBN-13: 978-0-7456-6993-9 (pb)

A catalogue record for this book is available from the British Library.

Library of Congress Cataloging-in-Publication Data

Giulianotti, Richard, 1966-
  Sport : a critical sociology / Richard Giulianotti. -- Second edition.
    pages cm
  Includes bibliographical references and index.
  ISBN 978-0-7456-6992-2 (hardback : alk. paper) -- ISBN 978-0-7456-6993-9
  (pbk. : alk. paper) 1. Sports--Sociological aspects. I. Title.
  GV706.5.G533 2015
  306.4'83--dc23
                                        2015003523

Typeset in 10.5 on 12 pt Plantin by
Servis Filmsetting Ltd, Stockport, Cheshire
Printed and bound in the UK by Clays Ltd, St Ives plc

The publisher has used its best endeavours to ensure that the URLs for external websites referred to in this book are correct and active at the time of going to press. However, the publisher has no responsibility for the websites and can make no guarantee that a site will remain live or that the content is or will remain appropriate.

Every effort has been made to trace all copyright holders, but if any have been inadvertently overlooked the publisher will be pleased to include any necessary credits in any subsequent reprint or edition.

For further information on Polity, visit our website: www.politybooks.com

Contents

Contents

Acknowledgements

The writing of this book has benefited greatly from my working in the School of Sport, Exercise and Health Sciences at Loughborough University. I would particularly like to thank my colleagues in the school's social science section, with whom I have undertaken collaborative research and writing, and my postgraduate students for their sharp analysis, enthusiasm and endeavour in researching diverse sport topics. I would also like to thank my many colleagues in Bø, at Telemark University College, Norway, for the opportunity to participate in many stimulating and instructive conversations and collaborations in the fields of sport, culture and outdoor life.

Over the years I have immensely enjoyed undertaking different collaborative projects with Gary Armstrong and Roland Robertson, which have led to the publication of various books and many articles. The influence of these joint activities is evidenced in different parts of this book, most obviously in discussions on sport subcultures and security issues (with Gary) and on the complex interplay of sport and globalization (with Roland). In regard to assisting my work on specific passages in the book, I thank Ansgar Thiel and Jan Ove Tangen for providing very helpful comments on an earlier discussion of Niklas Luhmann's theories, Tommy Langseth for pointing me to very useful literature on snowboarding and surfing, and David Howe for insightful discussions on sport and disability.

Finally, I owe a great deal to the expertise, support and patience of my publishing team at Polity, specifically Jonathan Skerrett for inviting me to write the revised edition of this book, Clare Ansell for supervising production, and Caroline Richmond for copyediting.

Abbreviations

ABC	Australian Broadcasting Corporation
AFL	Australian Football League (elite Australian Rules football league)
AGIL	adaptation, goal attainment, integration, latency (sociological model)
ATP	Association of Tennis Professionals
BBC	British Broadcasting Corporation
BIRG	basking in reflected glory
BRICS	Brazil, Russia, India, China and South Africa
CBC	Canadian Broadcasting Corporation
CCCS	Centre for Contemporary Cultural Studies
CCTV	closed-circuit television
CNN	Cable News Network
CORF	cutting off reflected failure
EGLSF	European Gay and Lesbian Sport Federation
EPL	English Premier League
EU	European Union
FARE	Football against Racism in Europe
FIFA	Fédération Internationale de Football Association (world football governing body)
FIS	Fédération Internationale de Ski (world skiing governing body)
FIVB	Fédération Internationale de Volleyball (world volleyball governing body)
ICC	International Cricket Council (world cricket governing body)
ILO	International Labour Organization
IMF	International Monetary Fund

IOC	International Olympic Committee (Olympic sport governing body)
IPC	International Paralympic Committee (world governing body of paralympic sport)
IPL	Indian Premier League (cricket tournament)
IRB	International Rugby Board (world rugby union governing body; rebranded as World Rugby in 2014)
ISF	International Snowboard Federation
LGBT	lesbian, gay, bisexual, transgender
LPGA	Ladies' Professional Golf Association (North American)
MLB	Major League Baseball (elite North American baseball league)
NBA	National Basketball Association (elite North American basketball league)
NCAA	National Collegiate Athletic Association (US college sport association)
NFL	National Football League (elite US American football league)
NGO	non-governmental organization
NHL	National Hockey League (elite North American hockey league)
NRL	National Rugby League (elite Australasian rugby league)
PCS	Physical Cultural Studies
PED	performance-enhancing drugs
RFID	radio-frequency identification
SDP	sport for development and peace
TCC	transnational capitalist class
TNC	transnational corporation
UEFA	Union Associations of European Football (European football governing body)
UN	United Nations
UNESCO	United Nations Educational, Scientific and Cultural Organization
UNOSDP	United Nations Office on Sport for Development and Peace
WADA	World Anti-Doping Agency
WAGs	wives and girlfriends
WHO	World Health Organization

Prologue

This book seeks to advance a critical sociological interpretation of modern sport. Throughout, I examine and engage critically with core theories and substantive research themes within the sociology of sport. Other disciplines – notably anthropology, history, human geography, political science and political philosophy – contribute substantially towards broadening the book's interpretive horizons.

Sport is a vast global field of social, cultural, economic and political activity which cannot be ignored by sociologists. Consider the scale of the world's leading sport mega-events. The 2012 London Olympic Games involved 204 nations competing in 302 events, assisted by around 70,000 volunteer staff, reported on by 21,000 accredited media workers, and watched live by hundreds of millions of television viewers. In the United States, American football's NFL Super Bowl is watched on television by increasing numbers, peaking for the 2012 game with an average of 113 million viewers – the highest ever US audience for any television broadcast. At the other end of sport, at grassroots level, tens of millions of people participate in sporting pastimes, notably the football codes,* skiing, basketball, gymnastics, track and field athletics, and volleyball.

There is no single reason for sport's huge cross-cultural appeal. Like love, truth and art, sport is a kind of human medium that conjoins people. Modern sport promises playful pleasures to players and spectators; new skills are tutored and learnt. Different sports facilitate

---

* These football codes include association football (soccer), American football (or gridiron), Australian Rules football, rugby union and rugby league, and Gaelic football. Unless otherwise indicated, 'football' designates the sport of soccer alone.

controlled, pleasurable interaction with particular landscapes. In our increasingly 'performative' consumer culture, the physical endeavour of sport compensates for our sedentary work and leisure practices.

All sports are rule-governed, thereby enabling their easy transmission across different cultures; yet the rules and techniques of sports are not followed in totally uniform ways and thus tend to be transformed to suit local needs. Sport allows different cultures to explore old and new identities and conflicts, in particular concerning community, gender, social class and ethnicity. The ideals that tend to surround sport – for example, with reference to 'sportsmanship' and 'fair play' – reflect dominant, liberal-democratic and masculine ideologies within the West. Institutionally, sport has been a normative training ground for young elites, notably the English aristocracy and international business leaders. The multi-billion-dollar economics of sport are now dominated by a power matrix that features top sports governing bodies, transnational corporations and global media networks. And the global appeal and growth of sport are reflected in the continuing expansion of 'sport studies' as an interdisciplinary field of academic inquiry. New departments and schools, courses and programmes have evolved with a diversity of names and disciplinary emphases. One broad intention for this text is to contribute fully and critically to this expanding social scientific field of inquiry on sport.

This book represents a fully revised version of an earlier edition published by Polity in 2005. My aims in making these complete revisions have been threefold: first, to update the earlier book in order to take account of developments in sport, and in the sociology of sport, over the intervening decade; second, to make the text more accessible to a wider audience, particularly a broader cohort of students at different levels of study; and, third, to inspire further debate among readers, notably through the listing of questions for discussion at the end of each chapter.

Towards a sociological definition of sport

To begin this sociological analysis of sport, I turn first to the issue of how sport might be defined. Of course, the meaning of any keyword will be contested and subject to significant historical and cultural variations. The definition of 'sport' is thus somewhat slippery and, to our modern eyes, in the context of the English language, carries some unusual and archaic ties to pre-industrial aristocratic leisure pursuits, such as hunting and shooting. Indeed, for *Chambers Twentieth Century Dictionary*, the verb 'to sport' is to 'frolic', 'make merry' or 'amuse', as well as to 'wear' and 'exhibit'; as a noun, 'sport' denotes 'recreation', 'games' and 'play', and even 'amorous behaviour', 'mirth', 'jest' and 'dalliance'.

The modern sociological definition of sport is more specific and systematic. Adapting McPherson, Curtis and Loy (1989: 15–17), I suggest that sport may be defined by the following five properties:

1 *structured*, by rules and codes of conduct, spatial and temporal frameworks (playing fields and time limits on games), and institutions of government;
2 *goal-oriented*, as sport is aimed at achieving particular objectives – e.g., scoring goals, winning contests, increasing averages – thus winners and losers are identifiable;
3 *competitive*, as rivals are defeated, records are broken;
4 *ludic*, enabling playful experiences, which germinate excitement;
5 *culturally situated*, in that 1–4 are intertwined with the value-systems and power relations within the host society.

Criteria 1–4 enable us to distinguish sport from other practices such as walking or exercising that lack, for example, competition. Criterion 5 enables us to recognize that any transformation of the social context in which sport is played may well lead to the transformation of the sport *per se*. Hence, to enable its sociological understanding, we need to examine sport with reference to its historical and cultural contexts; its underlying power relations, social structures and cultural values; and the diverse meanings, practices and identities associated with sport by different social groups.

The above criteria enable an inclusive approach in the classification of 'sports'. Despite their comparatively low requirements in terms of physical activity or fitness, this definition does stretch to include competitive games such as darts, bowling, snooker, pool and motor-racing. Each discipline requires intensive physical engagement and proficiency in hand–eye co-ordination and is structured, goal-oriented, competitive and ludic. Moreover, the officials, participants and spectators within these activities tend to advocate their sport status; their associated sport equipment is retailed by 'sports' shops; and significant events and incidents within these disciplines are reported by 'sports' media.

The historical and international dimensions of sport

The sociological definition of sport raises issues regarding the historical and international dimensions of sporting practices. To consider in a little detail, it might be noted first that the field of modern sports has a very extensive historical backdrop. Indeed, prehistoric societies were believed to have contested ball games and blood sports as part of their religious cosmologies, often as rituals 'to placate the unknown powers that people called gods' (Baker 1988: 6). The modern Olympic Games inherited sporting disciplines from the original ancient Greek games, including sprinting, the long-jump, javelin-throwing and wrestling. Yet it was the British, particularly in the late nineteenth century, who were instrumental in transforming folk games and medieval pastimes into modern codified sports. In part, this endeavour was driven by the attempt to secure order and to inculcate 'muscular Christianity' among young men. British schoolboys had been adept in 'hard-drinking, horse-racing, gambling, blood sports, prize fighting and sexual indulgence' (Mangan 1998: 179), but these unruly energies were gradually dissipated in schools, as sports such as football, rugby, field hockey, boxing, lawn tennis, squash, and track and field athletics were systematically institutionalized (Mangan 1981: 15–18). In turn, these sports underwent international diffusion through the diverse routes of trade and empire. As Perkin (1989: 217) noted,

> where the public-school boys went in large numbers, inside or outside the Empire, there cricket and rugby prevailed, and where the horny-handed sons of toil, or at least of the counting house, predominated, there soccer fever tended to infect the locals and become endemic.

British dominions such as Australia, New Zealand and South Africa embraced the old school 'games cult'. The Australians were the first to codify football, as their sport of Australian Rules, in 1859; the sports of rugby union, rugby league and cricket were subsequently seized upon to different degrees by the dominant white communities. In the Indian subcontinent and the Caribbean, cricket was favoured, although local publics came to transform the sport's colonial culture. After Indian national independence in 1947, *kabaddi* underwent forms of modern sportification as different local codes of play were harmonized and playing procedures were standardized.

North America's aristocracy and upper middle classes may have enjoyed tennis, polo and cricket but, up to 1914, new American sporting traditions were established. Baseball, spread initially by the army in the mid-nineteenth century, gained mass popularity among the lower classes; young males at leading universities took up American football; later, the Christian movement established basketball and volleyball as alternatives to existent sports. In Canada, ice-hockey and lacrosse were founded as national sports, the latter being derived from the game played by First Nation peoples.

In central Europe, gymnastic forms of physical culture were also inculcated. In Germany in the early nineteenth century, Friedrich Jahn founded the *Turnverein*, a set of nationalistic disciplines combining gymnastic drill with military training (notably fencing). The Czech equivalent, *sokol*, spread across East and Central Europe. 'Swedish gymnastics' were founded by Pehr Henrik Ling in the early nineteenth century and were quickly spread internationally, for example by being practised by middle-class English women from the 1830s onwards. Beyond gymnastic activities, to meet competitive demands among German sportspeople, handball was invented and popularized after the First World War to challenge football's popularity. France's major contribution to the development of early sport was largely political and administrative. Baron Pierre de Coubertin founded the modern Olympic Games, first contested in Athens in 1896, and the French were also catalysts in establishing football's governing body, FIFA, in 1904. France's distinctive sporting event remains the Tour de France, the world's most prestigious cycling race, first contested in 1903. While football's European hegemony remains intense, shooting and the alpine sports continue to be strong across the Alps and Nordic nations. In Ireland, hurling and Gaelic football, established to counteract perceived British cultural imperialism, maintained strong grassroots support. In Latin America, there are no noteworthy indigenous sports; football dominates, but baseball is hugely popular in Central America. In East Asia, notably Japan and Korea, different martial arts were gradually transformed into such modern international, competitive sports as judo, kendo and taekwondo. In China, the ancient games of *cuju* (a form of football) and dragon-boat racing were contested more than 2,000 years ago; in modern times, table-tennis has been particularly popular, while there has been mass interest in volleyball, basketball and, latterly, football. Thus, overall, while notwithstanding the transnational appeal of such 'global games' as football, this short look at the modern history of the diffusion and development of sport points to the significant variety of sporting traditions, tastes and cultures prevalent across different nations and regions.

Book contents

This book is committed to providing a critical sociological analysis of sport that engages fully with historical and cultural issues and questions. The discipline of sociology may be viewed as the inquisitive child of modernity, as its focus is traditionally directed at examining industrialized and industrializing societies. The explanatory influence of sociology has certainly expanded throughout the twentieth century, particularly towards and after the millennium, to become a kind of master discipline within the social sciences that often encompasses the themes, theories and methods drawn from history, anthropology, economics, geography, politics and international relations, and social psychology.

In this sociological study of sport, I argue that historical and anthropological standpoints are particularly valuable. They enable sociologists to provide crucial comparative perspectives both on the categorical range of sporting practices and on the interconnections between these practices and power relations, community identities, codes of social conduct and wider belief systems. Historical and anthropological approaches also help to reveal, on the one hand, the centrality of power relations and, on the other, the important socio-cultural creativity and agency of human actors in making modern sport. This sociological dichotomy – of structured power relations and elements of cultural vitality and agency – constitutes a key theme throughout the book.

I seek to provide a *critical* sociological analysis of sport. By critical, in broad terms, I am referring, first, to the endeavour to expose errors and misrepresentations, and to correct misunderstandings, concerning sport; second, to the commitment to highlight the power interests, divisions and inequalities that lie behind social relations and organizations within sport; and, third, to principles of democracy, social inclusion and social justice, and the concern to explore alternative ways in which sport may be organized and experienced. In that sense, my approach to the sociology of sport accords with the critical theoretical traditions within social science, particularly those that draw on neo-Marxist (especially neo-Gramscian) and Foucauldian standpoints (cf. Calhoun 1995).

To provide this critical sociological analysis of sport, the book is separated into twelve chapters. This distribution of intellectual labour is intended to make for diverse, concise discussions, although, given the constraint of contemporary academic publishing, they cannot be encyclopaedic. I have endeavoured to deploy a reasonable range of sociological texts, taking account of likely readership interests and, of course, my disciplinary research concerns and theoretical commitments. Each chapter also concludes with several questions on the relevant issues and subjects that warrant further consideration by readers.

The opening three chapters explore the broad influence of three founding fathers of sociology, namely Emile Durkheim, Max Weber and Karl Marx, in relation to sport. In the first chapter, I explore functionalist and system theories of sport that draw particularly from the Durkheimian tradition in sociology. These approaches emphasize sport's functional utility in promoting social cohesion and solidarity through quasi-religious rituals. Sport may be seen to strengthen social order at two levels: at the systemic level, as claimed by structural functionalists, through the interconnections between sport and other institutions; and at the everyday level, as indicated for example by Goffman, through particular interaction rituals that protect the 'face' of social actors.

Second, Weberian sociologies facilitate deeper understanding of sport's interpretive and rationalized aspects. Interpretive sociology focuses on the complex, varying meanings and identities of social actors within sport. Weber, Guttmann and Ritzer point us towards considering the impact upon sport of our highly rationalized, bureaucratized modern society. Despite significant respective strengths, I argue that Durkheimian and Weberian perspectives underplay the key political-economic factors that shape sport at structural and everyday levels.

Conversely, and third, Marxist and neo-Marxist theories address the political-economic divisions and underlying conflicts within sport in the context of modern capitalism. According to different neo-Marxist positions, sport reproduces the signature iniquities of industrial capitalism, such as in exploiting workers/athletes and manipulating consumers/spectators. However, such arguments may oversimplify Marx's understanding of the complexity of power relations at particular historical conjunctures and underplay how sport (and other cultural fields) may become key sites of social and symbolic conflict.

These discussions lead into an analysis of 'Cultural Studies' and wider neo-Marxist approaches in chapter 4. More plausible Cultural Studies approaches draw on sustained fieldwork and theory (notably from Gramsci and Williams) to examine how culture (including sport) is a site of struggle for subordinated social groups, notably the working classes, young women and ethnic minorities. Key concepts here relate to hegemony, resistance, transgression and the carnivalesque. I also consider how two further perspectives – drawing on the work of the Habermas and the recent 'Physical Cultural Studies' movement – may be deployed critically to examine sport.

These four, more theoretical opening chapters provide the crucial conceptual bases for examining four more substantive themes in the next chapters, relating specifically to 'race', gender, the body and space. The first two of these, on 'race' and gender, have become key research domains within Cultural Studies and the sociology of sport. I examine each theme with substantial reference to their modern sporting histories, highlighting the long-term social construction and cross-cultural complexity of these respective research fields. I explore how sport has contributed to racist mythologies and assess whether it offers alternative social mobility for non-white social groups. I examine sport's role in shaping distinctive and contested norms, identities and experiences in relation to gender and sexuality.

The subsequent two chapters examine, respectively, the body and sport spaces as two key sites of sporting practice. Foucault's theories on the corporeal and spatial disciplining of populations feature prominently. I explore the body in sport with reference to phenomenological experiences and the appeal of voluntary risk-taking but also with regard to the disciplining and governing of bodies and more problematic bodily risks. In the next chapter, I examine sport spaces with regard to deep emotional attachments, political economic issues, the increasingly extensive securing of stadiums, and processes of postmodernization.

The following two chapters examine the sport-centred contributions of two major international sociologists, Norbert Elias and Pierre Bourdieu. Elias's 'process sociological' standpoint examined society as a game wherein participants, spectators and governing bodies are 'interdependent' and caught in the constant flux of play. His theory of the civilizing process has been employed to trace sport's social history and, more problematically, to explain sports-related violence. Bourdieu forwarded a more critical, concerted sociological standpoint that connects sporting 'tastes' to intergroup classifications and social struggles. His later work became more overtly politicized through trenchant critiques of social inequality and the dominance of neoliberal government policies.

The final pair of chapters, on the postmodern and globalization, examine two of the most important debates within social science over the last two to three decades. Postmodern trends in sport are identifiable in the growing significance of media, the interpenetration of sporting codes and disciplines, the reorientation of stadiums towards fantasy consumption, more fluid forms of sports identification, and the collapse of sports-defined distinctions between high and low culture. Latterly, globalization has become the key research theme within contemporary sociology. I examine how modern sport illustrates *par excellence* the globalization of cultural practices and social relations, as well as the deep-seated divisions and inequalities in global politics and economics. As a whole, these chapters, and the short epilogue that follows, are intended to provide the reader with a critical sociological understanding of sport and to inspire reflection on how sport might be reformed and transformed according to principles that are rooted in democracy, social inclusion and participation, and social justice.

1
Functionalist Theories of Sport: Social Orders, Solidarities and Systems

Functionalist social theories, and their variants of structural functionalism and neo-functionalism, highlight the maintenance of social consensus and social order and downplay the role of conflict in social life. Although they were highly influential in sociology and social science in the early and mid-twentieth century, functionalist approaches lost most of their impact from the 1960s onwards to more attractive conflict-based theories, notably Marxist perspectives. Today, functionalist sociologies of sport tend to appear as historical artefacts that provide little of contemporary explanatory value.

While not ignoring their weaknesses, I seek to indicate here that the functionalist sociologies of Durkheim, Merton and Parsons help us to understand key issues in sport, notably with regard to social integration, solidarity, order, rituals and anomie. Aspects of functionalist sociology have been evidenced particularly by Central and North European scholars in applying the systems theory of the German sociologist Niklas Luhmann to sport. Goffman's more microsociological work also provides intriguing insights into the fragile social order that underpins everyday social interaction.

Durkheimian sociology: social order, solidarity and religion

Emile Durkheim (1858–1917), who advanced the first comprehensive functionalist standpoint in sociology, lived through periods of great social change in his native France – notably growing industrialization, urbanization and secularization, as well as the first global war. In partial consequence, his sociological focus was relatively conservative and concerned the nature and problem of how social order was to be maintained when faced with these kinds of major transformation.

In terms of his scientific method, Durkheim advocated the study of 'social facts' – that is, those social forces which shape our destinies and are independent of individual control (Durkheim [1895] 1938: 13). For example, in studying suicide, Durkheim ([1897] 1970) revealed the social fact that people who are more integrated within communities, families and religious orders (such as Catholics rather than Protestants) are more likely to be constrained from committing suicide than those in more individualistic social circumstances.

In theory, social facts might be harnessed to examine sport participation – for example, to study which social groups are most likely to join sport clubs or to play particular sports. However, if we look more deeply at social facts, the different social forces may be cross-cutting and thus difficult to disentangle. In exploring the social facts behind sport participation, Lüschen (1967) found that Protestants are more likely than other religious groups to participate in organized sport, especially individual-based ones. This 'social fact' might fit the argument that modern sports emphasize such Protestant values as asceticism and individualism. But non-religious factors may also account for higher levels of sport participation; for instance, lower levels of class inequality may explain why more (Lutheran Protestant) Scandinavians than (Catholic) Spaniards join sport clubs. Further complications are added by the point that joining a sports club is in itself surely a collectivist act, irrespective of whether that club favours individual sports (Bottenburg 2001: 33–4).

The conservative aspects within Durkheim's approach are best reflected in his functionalist perspective. Functionalist theories in social science assume that any social system is made up of different social parts that are functionally interconnected and work together to maintain that system. These functioning parts might include institutions that deal with family life, religion, politics and work. The social system is thus comparable to the human body, with organs that are required to function effectively in themselves and in accordance with other organs in order for that body to survive. The functionalist perspective therefore may be viewed as emphasizing social agreement, consensus, order and harmony, features of society which all help to maintain social 'equilibrium' – in other words, the smooth running of the social system. As a result, this approach is sometimes considered to be overly conservative, in terms of implicitly favouring the smooth running and status quo within any existing society, no matter how unjust, immoral or regressive that social system may appear to be for many of its members. A further criticism is that the functionalist approach pays too much attention to social order and too little attention to the social conflicts and divisions within a society. These weaknesses have serious implications for any functionalist analysis of sport.

For Durkheim, pre-modern and modern societies function in different ways as they have different social bonds or types of social solidarity. Pre-modern societies have a 'mechanical' social solidarity, featuring a simple division of labour, strong socialization forces, powerful forms of collective authority, low levels of individualism, and a strong basis for the reproduction of social roles and the common moral order (or 'conscience collective'). Conversely, modern societies have 'organic' forms of solidarity that feature a more complex division of labour, with stronger interdependency and specialization of work roles and greater space for individual decision-making.

For Durkheim ([1915] 1961), religion plays a strong functional role in reproducing mechanical solidarity and the conscience collective within pre-industrial societies. Religious ceremonies assist communal self-worship and thus function to bond the 'clan' socially and morally. The scope of the clan's religiosity is total: all aspects of the natural and social world acquire religious meaning. Clan members value and protect objects that are classified as 'sacred' against those that are classified as 'profane'; religious 'rituals' feature 'rules of conduct' that instruct and guide people in how to act in relation to sacred objects (Birrell 1981: 357). Positive rites set out the procedures of religious ceremonies, thereby maintaining the commitment of clan members to important social norms (Giddens 1971: 108–11). Negative rites serve to prohibit particular behaviours such as 'profane' language or touching sacred objects. At the individual level in religious life, the body is classified as profane and the soul as sacred. 'Totems' are objects, usually in the natural world (notably animals), that become sacred when they are represented in emblematic form. For Durkheim, the totem symbolizes the clan; thus, in worshipping the totem during religious ceremonies, the clan members are also in effect worshipping themselves.

Durkheim introduced the concept of 'collective effervescence' to explain the intense states of excitement and feelings of common solidarity that clan members experience when they come together to practise religious rituals. The anthropologist Victor Turner (1974) later developed the comparable concept of *communitas* to explain the intense forms of solidarity, unity and equality that members of a social group may feel, particularly when sharing a common experience or a socially significant 'rite of passage'.

For Durkheim, the functional influence of religion falls significantly within industrial societies, hence the old forms of solidarity and conscience collective also decline in influence. The question thus arises as to whether new belief systems or institutions are able to emerge in order for the social system to function smoothly. For Durkheim, social solidarity might be re-established through the 'cult of the individual', which he referred to as a 'religion in which man [*sic*] is at once the worshipper and the god' (Durkheim [1898] 1973: 46). However, an individualistic moral framework is problematic for maintaining social bonds and cohesion (Durkheim [1893] 1964: 170–2). Thus, for Durkheim, industrial societies are challenged socially by the rise of anomie – that is, the sense of normlessness and reduced levels of moral regulation that are to be found among individuals in these circumstances. Significant levels of class conflict and crime within industrial societies also point to weakening in the conscience collective.

Sport, social solidarity and religion

Durkheim's functionalist analysis of religious life and his model of mechanical and organic solidarity may be used to understand sport in a variety of ways.[1]

First, we may note that, in line with Durkheim's broad observation, many physical games had close ties to, or emerged out of, religious ceremonies (Giddens 1971: 111n). For example, across the Americas as far back as 3000 BC, the indigenous peoples played ball games that symbolized the fateful battle of life and death, often quite literally when the team leaders on losing sides were sacrificed. Many ball games originated from pre-Christian, pagan rituals that sought to harness natural forces in order to secure good harvests or communal well-being (Henderson 2001: 32–3). In medieval times, games were played during holidays such as Shrove Tuesday; like religious ceremonies, these activities functioned to forge social bonds and were also intended to ward off material, military and spiritual dangers (Muchembled 1985).

A Durkheimian standpoint may be adopted to examine the strong parallels between modern sports events and quasi-religious ceremonies. The French anthropologist Christian Bromberger (1995: 306–9) made this association in regard to seven aspects of modern football matches. First, football games occur in 'particular spatial configurations' (the stadium) which generate intense emotional states among fans; playing fields possess sacred qualities and are 'polluted' if they are invaded by ordinary members of the public. Second, as in religious ceremonies, spectators are spatially organized according to the social distribution of power; thus political leaders and other VIPs are given the best viewing positions. Third, football has distinctive temporal and rhythmic structures, as matches, cup finals and championship seasons follow established procedures and a regular calendar. Fourth, the roles of different groups on match day are highly ceremonial; for example, football supporters, while specially 'robed' in team colours, engage in intense ritual acts. Fifth, like the church, football has its own organizational framework, from local to global levels. Sixth, the football match ritual possesses a sequential order that guides the actions of participants, including pre-match preparations, the warm-up period, player entry onto the field, playing the game according to set procedures, and the game's conclusion, followed by supporter exit. Seventh, the football ritual generates *communitas*, a 'communion of minds', as strong forms of social solidarity are established between strangers through the sharing of common causes and identifications. While Bromberger's Durkheimian observations hold for football, they may also be applied to explain many other sports rituals in different nations.

Taking this approach further, we may explore how modern sport functions to promote social solidarity. Such an argument is particularly significant when we recall Durkheim's observation that, in contexts of organic solidarity, the social influence of religion falls into decline, hence alternative social institutions are needed to build a common moral order and conscience collective.

Sporting events may be seen as advancing social integration through much of the twentieth century and beyond, and in diverse political and cultural contexts. Riordan (1987: 391) examined modern sport in the old Soviet Union and concluded that 'sport has come closest to religious ritual in serving to provide what Durkheim saw as cohesion, solidarity, integration, discipline, and emotional euphoria'. In the United States, Serazio (2013) systematically applied Durkheim's theory of religion to study the fans of the victorious Philadelphia Phillies baseball team at the 2008 World Series. He argued that the baseball team represented a 'civic totem' of the city of Philadelphia and held a 'sacred capacity' to promote intense social solidarity among strangers, notably at a time when other integrative institutions were in decline. The Phillies' World Series victory engendered a powerful sense of *communitas* and enabled the club, media and supporters to celebrate idealized images of Philadelphian history and identity.

Similar arguments may be made on the social functions of many other sport teams and events. To take these analogies further, we may note how, within sport, the totemic symbols of the club and its 'clan' of fans may be derived from the natural world: think, for example, of the Toronto Maple Leafs in ice-hockey, the Indianapolis Colts in gridiron, or the 'vultures' of Flamengo in Brazilian football. Durkheimian moral codes are also evidenced in sport's popular culture among players and fans. Particular status tends to be accorded to teams that have a special 'spirit', 'heart' or 'soul', where players 'play for the jersey' – all of which points to a powerful collective solidarity. Conversely, 'passionless' clubs or 'mercenary' players are the subject of criticism, contempt or abuse from sports followers and communities. Supporters publicly express love for the club through positive rites of worship, such as stadium songs, wearing team colours or seeking player autographs. Match days are sacred occasions which are celebrated through feasting, heavy drinking and other forms of carnival behaviour that promote forms of collective effervescence. Negative rites serve to prohibit spectators from encroaching on the pitch or the verbal abuse of totemic players. Negative rites also include superstitious practices, for example as players avoid injured athletes or women for fear of being polluted and losing energy, or as athletes and spectators often carry charms and amulets into games. Such rituals have strong continuities with immanentist religious beliefs which highlight the transfer of spiritual powers between objects or persons. The songs, chants and choreographic displays among some spectator groups may be interpreted as immanentist ceremonies whereby the fan clan works to transfer its strong spiritual powers and energies into the team (Robertson 1970: 50–1).

We may also explore how sport functions as a 'civil religion' or 'secular religion' to strengthen social solidarity, particularly at national level (Bellah 1975). In this sense, sport events may be viewed as one of many modern civil and secular occasions – such as national holidays, royal weddings, military parades and remembrance gatherings – that function periodically to bind communities and nations. For example, Australian Rules football has been interpreted as a 'secular religion' that pervades many aspects of social life (Alomes 1994). The game is central to the construction of particular kinds of Australian identity and offers both possible transcendence to its followers and an apparent antidote to concerns about the 'loss of community' in fast-paced modern societies. Similarly, in the United States, the 'national sports' of American football, baseball and basketball may be interpreted as national civil religions that provide a common social and cultural anchor for Americans and a focus for collective solidarity and *communitas* (Bain-Selbo 2009; Forney 2007).

The civil religious aspects of sport may focus particularly on promoting national solidarity, for example through the singing of national anthems, the unfurling of national flags, the attendance of leading government figures, and various celebrations of military forces. Sport's role here highlights the broader importance of nationalism in the building of social cohesion through much of the nineteenth and twentieth century. State-driven nationalist ideologies were promoted throughout this time via the education system, mass media and other cultural institutions, including sport.

Overall, the functionalist approaches of Durkheim and others may be used to explain how sport serves to bind social groups, particularly through events that are highly charged in emotional terms. However, the most obvious weakness of these perspectives concerns the underplaying of social conflicts between different groups, institutions and belief systems. Thus, in sport, we may point to major conflicts involving different religious belief systems. For example, in the new American territories in the seventeenth and eighteenth centuries, Puritan and Quaker religious movements sought, against the rising urban male culture centred on such amusement and diversion, to prohibit sport and games (Gorn and Goldstein 1993: 34–41). In modern times, religion's disruptive influence within sport is commonly identified in the traditional 'sectarian' rivalry and violence between fans of two Scottish football clubs based in Glasgow: Rangers, with a strong Protestant-Unionist and anti-Catholic history, and Celtic, founded by Irish-Catholic migrants and with many Irish nationalist followers. In addition, we may point to numerous instances in sport in which conflicts have been underpinned by strong nationalism: consider, for example, the Cold War boycotts of the Olympic Games, first by the United States in relation to the 1980 Moscow games and then by the Soviet Union and some allies for the 1984 Los Angeles games, and incidents of violence surrounding international football fixtures between England and Scotland, Argentina and Brazil, Serbian and Croatian teams, China and Japan, and the so-called soccer war in 1969 between Honduras and El Salvador. Finally, the functionalist explanation of religious life or civil religions applies only to 'believers' who identify with the relevant institutions; this perspective does not hold for non-believers. In this context, we may note that functionalist arguments on the 'civil religious' or community-building power of sport cannot account for populations within cities and nations who have little or no interest in sport. If these outside populations are sufficiently large, it is difficult to make the argument that such sports events function to bind the wider society.

In the post-war period, functionalist and social system approaches in sociology were taken in three notable directions. The first, more prominent approach, pursued by the American sociologist Talcott Parsons, provided the dominant sociological paradigm in North America and Europe until conflict theories gained greater influence in the 1960s and onwards. The second approach, advanced by the German social scientist Niklas Luhmann, developed a distinctive systems theory which has been particularly influential in Central and Northern Europe. The third approach, from Erving Goffman, is usually associated with interpretive standpoints, but it did seek to build directly upon key Durkheimian themes on the making of social order. It is to a consideration of these different approaches that I now turn.

Structural functionalism: Parsons and Merton

The 'structural-functionalist' theoretical framework of Talcott Parsons substantially elaborated Durkheimian themes regarding social order and social systems. Parsons was particularly interested in broader systems and cybernetic theories across the social sciences. He thus sought to develop grand theories for explaining all kinds of system, ranging from systems of action at the everyday level through to the full social system. He focused on the constituent parts of systems and on how these systems seek to maintain their functional balance or equilibrium (Parsons 1951). Parsons (1966) argued that, in order to function effectively, all systems need to meet four 'functional prerequisites'; when applied to social systems, each prerequisite is linked to a particular part of the social structure. The fourfold model is captured by the famous Parsonian acronym AGIL and may be outlined as follows.

- *Adaptation*: where the system responds effectively to the environment; this is linked to the social system's economy.
- *Goal attainment*: where the system uses resources and establishes goals for its members; this is linked to the social system's political structures.
- *Integration*: where the system establishes social coordination and cohesion; this is linked to socialization and legal authority in the social system.

- *Latency or pattern maintenance*: where the system sustains and transmits cohesive values, such as through the generations; this is linked to community and culture within the social system.

The AGIL model might be used to examine how sport systems function. Consider, for example, sport's national governing bodies: they must adapt to economic circumstances through effective financial planning; they must consult members to clarify and then pursue their goals; they must promote cohesion by training and developing young athletes and having regulations in place to punish offenders; and they must promote common values and community standards, for example by educating young athletes on 'fair play' and balanced competition.

Parsons developed several other sociological models and categories for explaining social life. One important model concerns the 'pattern variables' and provides an ideal-type model that differentiates between expressive or instrumental types of interaction within society. These oppositions are as follows.

Expressive	*Instrumental*
Ascription	Achievement
Diffuseness	Specificity
Particularism	Universalism
Affectivity	Affective neutrality
Collective orientation	Self-orientation

Expressive types of interaction are associated with relatively close and small-scale social relationships, for example in families, local sport clubs and community groups. Conversely, instrumental types of interaction are more likely to be found in complex social groups, such as companies and large bureaucracies.

To apply the pattern variables to sport, we may see that sport federations present their competitions as being underpinned by instrumental qualities: for example, event officials are appointed on the basis of their achievements rather than their personal connections; engage with competitors in these specific roles rather than by having a wider or more diffuse set of possible relationships to these participants (such as family relations, friends, or joint members of other societies); engage with all competitors in the same way, on the basis of universal norms and standards, rather than developing special, particular ties to individual participants; are themselves neutral and do not have affective ties to any participant or teams of participants; and are personally responsible for individual decisions and actions during play. In passing, we might note that, in pointing to how particular social formations should or claim to be structured, rather than revealing how they are actually organized, these pattern variables actually appear as idealized models. However, in terms of highlighting possible flaws or weaknesses that need to be addressed by relevant social groups, the perceived gap between the model and reality does provide a useful basis for critical reflection and comment. For example, major weaknesses in some professional sport organizations may involve appointing people on the basis of their gender identity or family ties (ascription) rather than their professional competence (achievement). Among football fans in many nations, there is constant speculation that event officials favour particular players (particularism, not universalism) or one team over the other (and so are not 'affective neutral'). Hence, one potential benefit of the pattern variables lies in making the underlying principles of a social relationship or social organization more explicit, thus promoting the expectation that individuals and social groups should act according to these standards.

Parsons's work has been subjected to a wide range of criticisms over the years. Some of the strongest criticisms are that his theories are excessively ambitious, and cannot account for all types of social interaction, organization, institution or system, especially within complex modern systems; overly evolutionist, and take the biased, ideological position that post-war American society is the most advanced social system; are built on idealized representations of bourgeois American society; and greatly underplay the deep conflicts, divisions and opposing interests within social systems (in other words, he overemphasizes the functional 'consensus' within such systems).

Thus, in the sport context, the Parsonian approach would draw us into making too little of social conflicts, such as over the sexist and racist treatment of women and ethnic minorities or industrial action by professional athletes. It may also lead sociologists into accepting (rather than critically examining) the proposition that American sports function effectively, fit the modern pattern variables, and thus provide the most advanced and sophisticated type of sport system to which others should aspire.

One of Parsons's former students, Robert Merton (1968), in order to recommend a more cautious approach, provided a sympathetic modification of structural-functionalist theories. Merton favoured 'middle-range' theories that enable exploration of how different features within the overall social system may or may not work in ways that are 'functional'.

Merton (1968: 105) made a useful distinction between different types of function within social actions. *Manifest* functions are intended by social actors to produce positive adaptation within the social system, whereas *latent* functions 'are neither intended nor recognized' by social actors. In addition, Merton argued that *dysfunctional* actions may actually harm the social system, although they may be functional for the survival and development of specific social groups, while *eufunctional* actions are neutral and have no positive or negative impact on the system.

Thus, to illustrate this approach, we might consider how sport is used to publicize anti-smoking messages: the manifest function of the campaign is to raise public awareness of the dangers of smoking, while the latent functions might include promoting public concern with health or assisting in wider community-building; a eufunctional aspect might be that the campaign is meaningless to foreign visitors, and among the possible dysfunctions might be that smokers are put off from sport participation.

Merton (1938) recognized that, in complex social systems, significant levels of dysfunctional activity might occur, particularly among social groups that experience tensions or divisions between cultural goals and social structures (or 'institutional means') in that society. One such dysfunctional feature is urban crime, including (in the United States, during the mid-twentieth century) organized crime. To explain crime through Merton's concepts, we may point to how poor urban communities may share the cultural aims of wealthy communities but lack the social structures (institutional means) for achieving these goals. This thesis helped Merton to explain how, in the United States in the early twentieth century, Italian immigrants identified with American cultural goals (wealth creation) but lacked the institutional means (access to education, good employment and promotion prospects) in order to achieve those goals in the conventional way. Hence, some Italian Americans turned to crime in order to achieve their cultural goals: such action was dysfunctional for the wider social system but functional for those individuals and families who gained financial security and success.

Merton (1968) later indicated that there are five ways in which individuals might respond to the different relationships between their cultural goals and the institutional means. We may illustrate these five responses with reference to how young male students in the United States engage with American college football. Here, we understand American college football as a sport that promotes a particular set of cultural values (a tough, aggressive form of masculinity) through a specific set of institutions (notably high schools and colleges). Individuals may thus engage with American college football in the following ways:

1 *Conformism* Individuals conform to specific cultural aims that are pursued through recognized institutions – e.g., young male students play American football in colleges in aggressive, highly competitive ways.
2 *Innovation* Individuals follow cultural goals but employ their own means of attainment – e.g., young male students play American football and other sports outside college in aggressive, highly competitive ways.
3 *Ritualism* Individuals lose track of cultural goals and follow institutional rules out of blind habit – e.g., young male students have a routine involvement in their college football team and an intense knowledge of its rules and procedures, which they follow without thinking.
4 *Retreatism* Individuals reject both cultural goals and institutional means – e.g., young male students do not participate in American college football teams.
5 *Rebellion* Individuals reject cultural goals and institutional means, replacing these with radical alternatives – e.g., in opposition to college football, young male students in American colleges promote alternative sports with different values.

Clearly, conformism is the most explicitly functional strategy for sustaining the American football system in its current condition within the wider education system. The other four strategies have functional characteristics for specific groups of individuals, while also having different dysfunctional consequences for that sport system.

Merton's theories allow for greater structural differentiation in modern society and also possible deviations from functional roles (despite potentially dysfunctional consequences for the social system). However, in the final analysis, I would argue that both Merton and Parsons primarily *describe* rather than *explain* social systems – that is, they fail to account fully for power relations, for the underlying causes and complexity of social life, and also, as I have indicated earlier, the extent to which conflicts and deep divisions may take hold within the social system.

Luhmann and social systems

The second set of theories relating to the social order and social systems to be examined here centres on the German social scientist Niklas Luhmann (1995, 2000), whose work became significantly influential among sociologists of sport from the late 1980s onwards, particularly in Germany, Denmark and Norway (see Bette 1999; Cachay and Thiel 2000; Schimank 2005; Stichweh 1990; Tangen 2004, 2010; Wagner, Storm and Hoberman 2010). Luhmann's work – with its cybernetic understanding of systems as self-generating and self-regulating – was substantially influenced by the structural functionalism of Talcott Parsons, his former teacher at Harvard University.[2] Sport was not explored by Luhmann in his many publications, yet several key aspects of his theory may be fruitfully applied to explain this subject.

Luhmann's main goal was to provide a comprehensive, rigorous theory that sets out the complexity of modern society in regard to its constituent systems and subsystems. Systems undergo forms of functional differentiation and adaptation; accordingly, subsystems emerge, and contribute to the system as a whole, while also having a strong inherent impetus to grow and to 'progress' (Tangen 2010: 138–9). Luhmann (1986) borrows the term *autopoiesis* to explain how systems and subsystems create and re-create their logics, structures and components out of their own elements and operations. Autopoietic systems are understood as operating autonomously: they gain energy from their environment but are closed in terms of their organization and communication.

Social systems are to be found at the levels of interaction, social organization and society. Crucially, social systems are constituted not by persons, but by communication, and are structured by expectations. Actions are specific forms of communication that are attributable to persons. All systems and subsystems are underpinned by their own basic binary code of communication, which serves to establish difference as well as positive and negative identities, and by their own 'symbolic generalized medium', which enables communication to take place. In the economic subsystem, for example, the binary code is profit/loss, while the symbolic generalized medium is money.

To apply these theories to sport, we might begin by observing that sport is one subsystem – along with others such as education, law, politics and science – within the overall social system ('society'). Over the past few centuries, the sport subsystem has experienced increasing differentiation from its external environment and continual processes of autopoiesis. Thus, for example, sport has acquired more and more governing bodies, rule-books and codes of conduct which are distinct from other subsystems. At the same time, the sport subsystem responds in autopoietic style to changes in the environment, as witnessed, for example, in the responses of sport to civil rights campaigns by the introduction of anti-racism or anti-sexism rules or messages. In regard to communication, the basic binary code of sport is win/lose, while its symbolic generalized medium is victory, and positive identity is associated with the winner (Schimank 2005). Sport actions are meaningful vis-à-vis their surrounding subsystem: thus, if the individual is cycling, then she may be racing and race-training (as part of the sport subsystem), but there are other possibilities – for example, she may be seeking to gain fitness (health subsystem), to get to work (economic) or to pay a social call (leisure).

System theory is at its most interesting when we consider complexities and tensions within the social system or subsystems. For example, Tangen (2004, 2010) has argued that, in addition to the win/lose binary, the sport subsystem features the secondary code of improvement/decline or progression/regression – that is, whether the relevant athlete or team has improved or is progressing in performance. Tangen observed that sport fulfilled a wider social function through this secondary code, by demonstrating to other subsystems (such as in education, industry, law and politics) the importance and benefits of examining questions relating to progress and decline.

In addition, subsystems interact and overlap through forms of 'structural coupling'. The sport subsystem, for instance, interacts with political and legal subsystems, such as in the arbitration of sport or in anti-doping policy; with the education and economic subsystems, such as in amateur and elite professional sport; and in regard to health or social integration through national sport models.

On the level of organizations, sport governing bodies play a key role within the subsystem in the self-regulation of sport and in establishing new communication processes and structures (such as coaching courses and public campaigns). In Luhmann's theory of organizations as social systems, decisions form the basic unit of analysis (Luhmann 2000). Organizations develop and reproduce themselves by communicating decisions (cf. Thiel and Meier 2004). To allow for the complexity of these forms, Wagner (2009) has examined hybrid organizations that are able to operate according to different codes of communication; for example, contemporary sport governing bodies feature political, legal, educational and commercial types of communication.

Like any grand theory in social science, system theory has both weaknesses and strengths. First, one opening problem for scholars is the sheer difficulty of reading Luhmann: like that of Parsons, Luhmann's prose and theoretical edifice may confront the reader as obscure and impenetrable. Yet, more positively, system theory may be seen to produce an ambitious, coherent, sophisticated and complex model which may be used by social scientists to examine and investigate human societies. It thus invites critical testing, application and elaboration through sociological research, particularly at middle-range level, where, for example, researchers may explore the functioning of the sport subsystem vis-à-vis its environment. System theory may also be used as a heuristic research framework to explore the extent to which everyday life within the sport subsystem fits with the theoretical model.

Second, in late twentieth-century German sociology, Luhmann and Jürgen Habermas came to appear as binary opponents; unlike Habermas, Luhmann was not interested in critical and normative issues that might explore alternative political arrangements across society. However, it might be possible for us to adjust systems theory in order for it to acquire a critical component. For example, we might examine how one subsystem may be transformed or threatened through particular types of interaction with other subsystems. By way of illustration, we might say that elite sport has been transformed through its relationship to the economic subsystem in liberal-capitalist social systems; for some analysts, such interaction tends to threaten the autonomy (or integrity) of sport and other subsystems through the intrusion of alien codes that focus on profit/loss (cf. Walsh and Giulianotti 2007). Arguably, a more positive response would be to direct the sport subsystem towards greater interaction with the political subsystem, potentially to improve the democratic basis of sport. This type of critical adaptation of Luhmann would enable sociologists to develop and to apply theories of social systems and subsystems while also facilitating adequate engagement with a wider range of normative and political issues.

Goffman and the microsocial order

The third approach which I explore here with reference to Durkheimian themes concerning the social order and social system relates to the work of Erving Goffman. At first glance, Goffman appears to be a peculiar choice for discussion, as his focus was largely on microsociological processes (everyday social interaction), whereas the other perspectives here tend to have a much larger, macrosociological scale of analysis (at societal level). However, Goffman's sociology may be seen as firmly anchored within core Durkheimian themes such as social order and ritualism in social life (see Burns 1992: 361–2; Goffman 1967: 47). Goffman argued that it is not at the systemic level but, instead, at the everyday level that the modern social order is produced and reproduced, through the complex and often fragile techniques of contemporary social interaction. For Goffman (1967: 73), it is the individual person who has become the 'sacred thing' in modern life, and, in support, he notes Durkheim's ([1924] 1974: 37) observation that 'one dare not violate it nor infringe its bounds'.

Goffman emphasized the sacred status of the 'face' of individuals. 'Face' represents the positive respect that is claimed by individuals during social interchanges. The rituals of social interaction are intended to allow individuals to maintain face. Drawing on Durkheim's conception of positive rituals, Goffman (1971: 62–5) explored how individuals support each other's presentation of self and use compliments, greetings and other 'access rituals' to establish and sustain favourable social intercourse (ibid.: 73–91). Negative rites include avoidance rituals, such as minimizing physical contact with strangers, or 'remedial interchanges', such as apologies for bumping into others.

Perhaps most famously, Goffman (1959) developed a comprehensive dramaturgical theory in order to explain the everyday social order. Individuals are seen as social 'actors' who draw on different techniques of 'impression management' in order to persuade different 'audiences' to accept or to believe in these acts. Thus, for Goffman, the social order is maintained so long as the performance is sufficiently successful; to that end, social actors often operate in teams and draw on specific roles, scripts, props and general settings. If the social actors mess up, or if the audience gains discrediting information about the actors, then the act is no longer convincing, and the performance and social order are jeopardized.

Goffman's theories invite application to sport. In sociological studies of UK football, his 'impression management' thesis has helped to explain social interchanges between different supporter groups and the policing of fans (Giulianotti 1991; O'Neill 2003). Ingham (1975) also considered Goffman to be useful for explaining occupational subcultures within sport.

Goffman's theories may be applied further to examine the social dynamics of sport celebrity. The face of the sport star appears as highly sacred; hence interaction with these celebrities is subject to numerous positive and negative rites. Sports interviewers, for example, greet and introduce athletes with effusive compliments and positive affirmations of high status. Negative rites are observed as interviewers or audience members (but rarely athletes) take apologetic responsibilities for any misunderstandings or confusions that disturb interaction. Celebrities, meanwhile, carefully manage impressions, employing appropriate props (trophies or background photographs), dress (specific fashions, branded sportswear) and demeanour (politeness, responsiveness to questions) while protecting against discrediting information.

Susan Birrell (1978, 1981) has provided the most substantive application of Goffman to sport. For Birrell, sports events are ritual contests wherein individuals can aspire to heroic status by showing 'character' through a mixture of courage, gameness, integrity and composure (Birrell 1981: 365–72). Character constitutes the Goffmanesque capacity to 'keep one's entire competitive self in order and under complete control at all times' (ibid.: 372).

Drawing on Goffman's paradigm, the American sociologist Arlie Russell Hochschild (1983) examined the growing social significance of emotional management, particularly in service-sector employment, as part of a wider commercialization of human feelings. These observations may be applied to sport, for example as elite athletes are increasingly required to manage and to manipulate their emotions and feelings before different publics. In part, emotional management involves exercising substantial self-control, such as during media interviews and press conferences that are held just after highly charged sport events. Applying these insights, it might also be claimed that emotional manipulation in sport includes forms of 'deep acting', when the professional athlete induces or cues his or her own feelings in ways that are commercially advantageous – for instance, when athletes seeking new or improved contracts profess strong identification or love for a club and its supporters.

However, notwithstanding its attractive applicability to sport and other areas of social life, the Goffmanesque approach does have some significant explanatory limitations. Notably, as a largely microsociological theory, it has relatively little to say on the structural conditions that underlie power relations between different categories of social actor. In addition, on his dramaturgical theory, we may query the extent to which individuals really are as self-interested, collusive and insincere in their actions, as Goffman might have us assume.

Concluding comments

In this chapter, I have examined a wide range of sociological theories and approaches which derive from or connect to the functionalist tradition in order to explore Durkheimian themes such as social order, solidarity, ritual and system. These perspectives tend to share several crucial weaknesses, some of which were outlined earlier, and may be summarized as follows. First, functionalist and systems theories present an overly deterministic picture of social life; thus, social action tends to appear as an internalized stimulus response to social circumstance rather than as rooted in the critical creativity of social actors. Even in Goffman's work – which is heavily microsociological – social actors appear to be largely fulfilling roles and following scripts rather than creatively exploring different fields of social action. For example, when studying a sport governing body, these theories would enable us to examine the interrelations of different departments, posts and teams of workers with reference to their roles, but they would not be particularly helpful in examining either the different cultures within departments or the different types of decision-making that might be made by individuals in identical roles.

Second, as noted previously, there is an inherent conservatism within these perspectives which is reflected in an emphasis on how social systems maintain their equilibrium rather than how they change or come to an end. While social conflicts and social changes may be discussed by these perspectives, there remains the underlying assumption that such challenges will be accommodated or neutralized, and that the existing social system will remain essentially intact. Such an assumption does not adequately register the long-term and continuing struggles of different social groups – such as women or ethnic minorities – to gain full and equal recognition for their participation in sport. A related problem here is in how functionalist or system theories may leave little room for critical analysis of the social system under study. Thus, if we are studying a long-running, corrupt and despotic sport organization, functionalist approaches will tend to examine how that organization is able to function effectively rather than to explore how it may be fundamentally reformed.

Third, some aspects of functionalist and system theories tend to present a rather idealized view of the systems under discussion rather than examining the dark sides. In the case of Parsons, for example, an unduly positive, somewhat ideological view of post-war American society is presented. Neo-functionalists such as Jeffrey Alexander (1992: 294–5) tend to do the same when discussing in favourable terms the 'cultural codes' of contemporary Western societies rather than critically highlighting the actual lack of 'equality', 'inclusiveness' and democracy within Western states. In the sport context, this weakness may lead social scientists to provide fairly idealized studies of the democratic and inclusive qualities of Western sport governing bodies rather than to probe fully the extent to which these organizations may discriminate against particular social groups.

Fourth, functionalist and systems approaches require more robust, critical theorizations of power relations. Notably, these approaches fail to consider the relatively subtle ways in which power may be exercised by dominant groups, particularly by gaining the consent of weaker groups for policies and practices that serve to maintain existing power inequalities. Thus, for example, these approaches would not enable us to reflect critically on how, in American cities, sport business owners and local politicians are able to win the approval of local people to pay for the building of new sport stadiums, when the construction costs will restrict the provision of such key public services as education, health and policing.

Fifth, the American sociologist C. Wright Mills (1959) famously ridiculed the excessively difficult language of structural-functionalist theory by translating some of Parsons's vast passages into short, simple statements. Notwithstanding the humour here, the forbidding prose of Parsons and also Luhmann is likely to dissuade scholars from seeking to apply these theoretical frameworks.

However, these approaches do have some significant strong points which may be harnessed by sociologists of sport in order to facilitate a qualified engagement and application. First, we may draw heavily on Durkheim's theory and method relating to social facts in order to explore how, across broad populations, deep social structures serve to pattern specific types of social action. These research findings should provide the basis for more effective social policies on sport, for example in identifying where state interventions might be made in order to facilitate sport participation. Second, most importantly, we may draw heavily on functionalist and system perspectives to examine how sports events and institutions serve specific communities, build powerful forms of solidarity and fellow feeling, and facilitate different types of social integration. These studies may elaborate and apply the various theoretical metaphors of Durkheimian and Goffmanesque perspectives to explore sport events as religious ceremonies or as social theatres. Third, at the same time, we should recognize both that sport institutions may have complicated and even dysfunctional relationships to the wider social whole and that many social groups may be excluded from, or have conflicting relationships towards, these sport systems. In this sense, via Merton, we should adopt the open-mindedness of the middle-range researcher to the complexities of the interrelationships between sport and wider society. Fourth, Goffman's focus on the rituals of social interaction and on the potential fragility of the microsocial order may be very fruitfully applied to study specific social groups within sport. I turn to discuss more microsociological issues in sport in the next chapter.

Questions for discussion

1 How do sport teams and sport events promote stronger social bonds and forms of *communitas*? Are there social groups which are excluded or which may not participate?
2 How might we understand sport as a social system or subsystem? How does it relate to other social systems or subsystems – for example, economy, politics and media?
3 What types of 'impression management' are practised by sport celebrities, sport clubs or sport groups (such as fan movements)? How successful are these forms of impression management?
4 To what extent do functionalist and system theories of sport ignore social divisions and conflicts in sport?
5 How might we draw on functionalist and system theories in order to consider new or alternative ways in which sport might be organized or experienced?

2

Weberian and Microsociological Approaches to Sport: Meanings, Identities and Rationalization

A common complaint about modern sports is that they are losing their enchantment. Athletes, it is said, are 'over-coached', teams 'lack heart', stadiums are 'soulless', and play is 'stereotyped' and 'programmed'. The suspicion is that sport may be losing meaning and becoming less 'fun' as it becomes more rationally organized. While certainly having tendencies to romanticize the past, such criticisms do also reflect widespread concerns about the impacts of modernization on sport.

In this chapter, I examine key sociological questions regarding the meanings and the modernization of sport. In doing so, I build largely upon two specific sociological perspectives that are associated with the work of Max Weber.[3] First, there are the microsociological, humanist, *interpretivist* approaches that seek to understand the meanings and motives, the identities and interpretations, of everyday social actors. Second, there are Weberian theories of *rationalization* which highlight the rational organization and bureaucratization of modern society and, in turn, the arising sense of social disenchantment that pervades everyday social life.

The chapter is divided into three main parts. First, I set out the interpretive, microsociological standpoint and its relevance to the study of sport. Second, I address sport's rationalization and bureaucratization, drawing particularly upon the socio-historical insights of Allen Guttmann. Third, I explore Ritzer's McDonaldization thesis and how it may be applied to sport. In doing so, I differentiate between what I term *deep* and *shallow* forms of rationalization.

Interpretive social theories and the meaning of sport

Interpretive social theories encompass a broad family of largely microsociological approaches, including Weberian sociology, social phenomenology, hermeneutics, ethnomethodology, symbolic interactionism and social constructionism. Interpretive sociology explores the interrelations of social action to status, subjectivity, meanings, motives, symbols, context, the self, roles, identities, processes and social change. It eschews positivist thinking – that is, the explanation of human groups with reference to the kinds of causal laws and generalizations that are found in the natural sciences. Instead, Weber ([1922] 1978: 12–13) employed the term *verstehen* to describe, with some appropriate ambiguity, the empathetic understanding that sociologists must exercise in order to explain individuals and their actions in a meaningful way. Thus, interpretive sociology is best pursued through the use of qualitative research methods, involving relatively open-ended interviewing and ethnography among research subjects.

Interpretive microsociological approaches posit that the individual develops meaningful understandings of her subjective motives, the actions of others, and wider social contexts. One such approach, symbolic interactionism, considers how people communicate meanings through spoken language and non-verbal symbols such as gesture or dress. Social interaction is typically structured through sets of roles and identities that accord with the social status of individuals. The self connects individuals to roles and identities and, in turn, leads to different role interpretations and performances. Thus, social identities, actions and interactions are viewed as dynamic, fluid and processual and are influenced by the 'looking-glass self' that allows social actors to imagine how they are seen by others. The social action of individuals is further shaped by the actual or imagined responses of 'significant others' (such as cohabiting partners) or 'generalized others' (such as a team of workmates or community of friends) to specific actions.

Social research that draws on these interpretive insights is best pursued through the use of qualitative methods, as fieldwork and interviews produce the richest data for understanding social interaction. A related method here centres on the 'hermeneutic' approach, which focuses on the interpretation of 'texts'. While hermeneutics initially concentrated on conventional written texts, these 'textual studies' have mushroomed into interpreting and 'decoding' any form of communication system or arrangement of signs, for example in fashion, advertising, and broader television and film. In addition, the phenomenological approach, which is discussed more fully in chapter

7, has been used by social scientists to explore the subjective and intersubjective aspects of sport and leisure, for instance in regard to the sensory aspects of sporting experiences for different social actors.

Interpretive microsociological theories enable sociologists to examine and understand the diverse social meanings, symbols, identities and roles within sport. For example, we may examine how, in team sports, individual players may be allocated different game roles, which are then constantly interpreted and reinterpreted in diverse ways during play. How individuals seek to play during games will be influenced by the anticipated responses of 'significant others' (notably the coach and team captain), as well as 'generalized others' (such as team-mates in general). George Herbert Mead, the founder of symbolic interactionism, argued that game situations and team-based thinking illustrate how children acquire personality and become 'organic members of society'; children learn to take into account the attitude of the other in order to shape how they act 'with reference to a common end' (1934: 159). In addition, we may examine how players and spectators within sport need to learn its distinctive meanings, symbols, roles and identities. To 'make sense' of a baseball game, for instance, these participants need to understand the status and roles of different players, the meaning of different symbols (such as gestures by umpires), and ideally the social and historical identities that connect the club to its fans and wider community. Furthermore, using hermeneutic approaches, we may seek to analyse and to 'decode' how the sport event is presented in the mass media, such as through press reports, radio commentaries, or the televisual framing of specific incidents.

A wide range of sociological and anthropological studies of sport have made substantial use of interpretive approaches. Adler and Adler (1991) employed fieldwork methods to examine the socialization of male athletes within a college basketball team. Using role theory and symbolic interactionism, they revealed how many young student athletes experienced 'role-engulfment' within the college system, as the 'greedy' athletic role came to dominate other roles, including the academic. Yet athletes also came to embrace the 'gloried role', enjoying the addictive intoxication of public adulation through their athletic status. For some, the 'gloried self' became most prominent, despite the athletic role emphasizing self-denial. When college sports careers ended, the athletes adapted with varying success to civilian life; some remained within sports to sustain the gloried self. Upon post-college retirement, many reflected positively that they had been 'touched by fame in a way few experience' (ibid.: 230–1). Yet, the history of college athletes also provided an insight into how many profession-als are engulfed by their specialist roles. Conversely, it seems that 'renaissance' individuals, who have more varied and rounded cultural interests, roles and identities, are increasingly marginal to modern life (ibid.: 228).

A social interactionist perspective was utilized by Donnelly and Young (1988) to study the social construction of identities within sport subcultures. Drawing primarily on research with climbers and rugby players, they advanced a career model for entry into these sports subcultures which ran in four stages:

• first, potential members undergo *presocialization* in terms of gaining diverse information on the subculture from different sources (e.g., media, family and friends);
• second, *selection and recruitment* takes place as individuals become more aware of the subculture and may be invited to join;
• third, *socialization* occurs, as individuals learn and take on the subculture's values and perspectives while developing new forms of self-identity;
• fourth, *acceptance/ostracism* occurs, as the subculture judges whether individuals have sufficient engagement with its key values and practices.

This model is open to much wider application within any type of sport subculture.

The interest of microsociologists in sport subcultures reflects in substantial part the broader concern of many interpretive social scien-tists with the lifeworlds of marginal, deviant and exotic social groups and communities. In sociology, for example, the 'Chicago School' from the 1920s onwards used urban ethnographic methods to study homeless people, dance halls, gangs, 'delinquent' groups, 'slum' neighbourhoods and other such marginal communities. Accordingly, interpretive approaches have been highly influential within the soci-ology of crime and deviance and, thus, also within social scientific studies of deviant sport subcultures – such as in Polsky's (1969) study of pool hustlers or Atkinson's (2000) research with ticket 'scalpers'.

Social anthropologists have close affinities with the core arguments and methods of microsociology, particularly in using deep qualitative research to study and to understand different sport subcultures and communities. For example, Armstrong (1998) used urban anthro-pological methods to undertake long-term ethnographic research with football hooligan groups in England and, in turn, provided the most sustained and convincing account of their meanings, values and identities. Other rich anthropological accounts of sport groups that connect to interpretive traditions include Klein on bodybuilding subcultures and Latino baseball (1991, 1993), Dyck (2012) on North American children's sport, Kelly (2004) on Japanese baseball fans, Carter (2008) on Cuban baseball and identity, and Howe (2001) on pain and injury in Welsh rugby union.

The American anthropologist Clifford Geertz provided arguably the most famous interpretivist study of a sporting culture, the Balinese cockfight. Reflecting this deeply interpretivist standpoint, Geertz (1973: 434) argued that 'the imposition of meaning on life is the major end and primary condition of human existence'. For Geertz, all human behaviour 'signifies', as a kind of symbolic action, and can be interpreted as a text. He interpreted the Balinese cockfight as a form of 'deep play' in which, for the Balinese male cockowner and gambler, personal status (more than money) is at stake. The cockfight 'talks most forcibly' about Balinese status relationships, as 'matters of life and death'; the event allows the Balinese male 'to see a dimension of his own subjectivity . . . In the cockfight, then, the Balinese forms and discovers his temperament and his society's temper at the same time' (ibid.: 451–2). To understand the cockfight, Geertz argued that the researcher must provide 'thick description' of the relevant research groups and also 'read' the event as a cultural text about Bali, although such a reading can only be done 'over the shoulders' of the social actors themselves.

Although they have not been ignored, the most rigorous interpretive approaches have had a relatively restricted impact within the sociology of sport for several reasons. Time-consuming, expensive fieldwork is required for interpretive research to be undertaken fully with different social groups. Theoretically, much of the sociology of sport has tended to favour other approaches – notably varieties of neo-Marxism and poststructuralism – in contrast to interpretive frameworks such as symbolic interactionism. These other approaches enable scholars to probe in greater detail the power relations and structural conditions of contemporary sport. Moreover, many leading figures within the sociology of sport received interdisciplinary training – such as in sport science and kinesiology programmes – which may have featured relatively little discussion or exploration of interpretive theories and methods.

Arguably, in the sociology of sport, the greatest influence of interpretive microsociological approaches has occurred when these have been combined with other perspectives. In this sense, neo-Weberian or neo-interpretivist approaches may be viewed as most prominent. The use of relatively cost-effective hermeneutic methods has been especially evident in Cultural Studies approaches, for example in exploring how the mass media represent women, ethnic minorities and the LGBT community within sport (see Douglas 2005; Messner, Dunbar and Hunt 2000; Sartore-Baldwin 2013). Interpretive field-based methods, when studying sport subcultures, also benefit from the important, structural theorizations of power relations that are afforded by Cultural Studies approaches (see Sugden 1987; Foley 1990). The addition of postmodern or poststructuralist theory may help to combine studies of social interaction with more critical analysis of social practices, discourses and body cultures. For example, drawing on extensive fieldwork, I combined the theories of Michel Foucault with social interactionist standpoints to examine how Scottish football supporters sought to construct and to project particular forms of national identity before different international audiences at the 1990 World Cup finals in Italy (Giulianotti 1991). Overall, interpretive microsociological approaches are most likely to remain relevant within the sociology of sport if they are able to interact creatively and positively with other theoretical approaches in order to explain social phenomena in original ways.

Rationalization and sport

While his interpretive approach emphasized the study of social interrelations, Weber's sociology opened up other fields of inquiry regarding social hierarchies and rationalization. Weber ([1922] 1978: 48–56) explored how power relations and social stratification were underpinned by a mix of economic, cultural and normative factors. Weber associated power in particular with classes, status groups and parties. On social class, Weber differed from Marx in two significant respects: first, he argued that modern classes were more numerous and varied than Marx's division between capitalists and the proletariat, noting instead for example the different positions of ownership, commercial and petty bourgeois classes; second, he defined class in wider terms with reference to life chances, income opportunities in the labour market, and the ownership of property or goods. Weber understood status groups to be 'amorphous communities' – which may include, for instance, ethnic, religious and youth groups – in which honour, esteem and shared lifestyles are often key factors. Parties are more formal, modern organizations – notably in politics but also in social, cultural and economic fields – which pursue specific goals in deliberate and rational ways.

Weber's theories here help us to understand power relations and stratification in sport. For example, in regard to *class*, we may examine how the heavily propertied 'ownership' class and the professional 'commercial' class have interacted in order to dominate elite professional sport in much of Europe and North America. Additionally, many owners of professional sport clubs are motivated by the pursuit of local, national and transnational *status* and honour through association with, and control of, highly prominent institutions within the social and cultural spheres. According to some social psychologists, support for a sport team is often motivated by the pursuit of status: sport fans who publicly support a winning team are claiming association with success in order to develop higher self-esteem, status and honour by 'basking in reflected glory' (BIRG-ing); when the team loses, many fans engage in 'cutting off reflected failure' (CORF-ing), thereby avoiding an associated loss of status (Wann and Branscombe 1990). Finally, in regard to *party*, we may explore how different sport organizations work together to achieve particular goals, such as when sport clubs form leagues in order to establish profitable competitions, or when sport governing bodies combine to lobby government for sport facilities and venues.

I turn next to consider Weber's focus on processes of rationalization and bureaucratization and its influence within the sociology of sport. For Weber, rationalization drives modernity. Modern social life is experienced and structured increasingly along the lines of rational planning, with an emphasis on instrumental and technical know-how rather than reflection on political questions or moral principles. For Weber, bureaucracies dominate modern life, as they have a 'purely technical superiority' to other types of social organization on the basis of their 'precision, despatch, clarity, familiarity with the documents, continuity, discretion, uniformity, rigid subordination, savings in friction and in material and personal costs' (Weber [1922] 1978: 350). Yet, as Weber famously observed, bureaucratization is a deeply disenchanting experience, in terms of creating over-rationalized 'iron cages' that depersonalize and imprison humanity. Hence, sociologists influenced by Weber explore the rational organization of social life and the dehumanizing impacts of these processes for social actors.

Weber's rationalization thesis has been applied to modern sport in several studies. Frisby (1982) developed Weber's approach to examine Canadian voluntary sports organizations, whose efficiency was identified according to nine principles: formalized rules and

procedures, decentralized decision-making, impersonal working relations, professionalism in decision-making, specialization, career sta-
bility, large organizational size, higher proportions of clerical staff,
and an emphasis on science and technology.

Guttmann (1978) provided the most substantive application of the
rationalization thesis in order to explain the modern sportification of
physical culture. He identified seven key aspects of rationalization,
each of which may be illustrated by contrasting modern, rationalized
Western sport with earlier sporting pastimes.

1 *Secularization* Modern sport is independent of religious institutions or belief systems. Conversely, in earlier civilizations and in
pre-modern societies, sporting activities and religious festivities
were intertwined.
2 *Meritocracy* Sport promotes fair competition that is decided according to merit, irrespective of the social standing of participants.
Conversely, pre-modern sport was highly exclusive; among Greeks,
it was largely closed to non-citizens, notably women and slaves.
3 *Specialization* In modern sport, as in industry, there is an increasingly complex division of labour in which individuals must learn
specialized skills and roles; strong illustrations are provided by team
sports such as American football that have many specialist playing
positions. In pre-modern sport, participants had fewer specialist
roles and contributed as they wished towards the collective 'goal'.
4 *Rationalization* Instrumental reason involves identifying the most
efficient means available for achieving the identified end. Modern
sport is characterized by rational preparation, organization and
competition, particularly in the use of sport science, in order to
maximize the athlete's performance and probability of winning.
In pre-modern games, such preparations were far less extensive or
scientific.
5 *Bureaucratization* For Weber, 'the whole pattern of everyday life is
cut to fit' bureaucratic frameworks (quoted in Giddens 1971: 160).
Through the governing bodies, sport is controlled by increasingly
complex apparatuses of governance – notably, vast frameworks
of departments, units, committees and subcommittees – that are
layered into local, national, continental and global levels. Sport
events themselves are controlled by referees and umpires who
should be appointed on the grounds of competence, not connections. Conversely, pre-modern games did not have governing
bodies, while sports contests tended to be organized and judged
on an informal basis.

6 *Quantification* Modern sport, through its use of statistical data to measure and compare sports performances, is increasingly positivist; for example, in North American baseball, 'sabermetrics' is used to measure all aspects of player performance, and such data often provides the basis for decisions on player recruitment.[4] Pre-modern games rarely produced such statistical records: nobody recorded losing streaks in the chariot races of ancient Rome.

7 *The pursuit of records* The modern Olympic motto *citius, altius, fortius* (faster, higher, stronger) captures the athletic compulsion to win tournaments and break records. Pre-modern games lacked modern time-keeping technology and so athletes concentrated essentially on winning contests.

Guttmann's typology represents a concise and thoughtful elaboration of Weber's approach and offers scholars of sport a very useful seven-point heuristic against which they may assess the extent to which rationalization has occurred in specific sporting disciplines.

We might subject Guttmann's typology to some critical scrutiny on three main points. First, in regard to theory, his model provides an incomplete application of Weber's approach: rationalization in sport is viewed in a relatively positive way, so that Weber's pessimism on the modern iron cage is overlooked. Alternatively, the model would be improved if we considered the extent to which the rationalization of sport has led to alienating or disenchanting experiences. For example, the focus on measurable performance levels and results may have served to degrade participant enjoyment and experimental play. Moreover, the systematic doping of athletes in order to maximize performance levels represents an extreme application of instrumental logic to both sport performance and the broader dehumanizing of sport participants (Hoberman 2001).

Second, Guttmann might also note the limitations of the rationalization thesis in terms of what it fails to explain within sport. For example, the rationalization thesis rather ignores such social goods and qualities within sport as its aesthetic aspects, moral education and community-building capacities (Loland 2000; Lasch 1979; Walsh and Giulianotti 2001). Indeed, we might argue that, like the performing arts, the improvised and creative quality of sport 'pulls against the rationalised and the bureaucratised view of aesthetics' (Blake 1995: 201).

Third, Guttmann's thesis may contain empirical weaknesses by overplaying the extent to which rationalization actually takes hold within sport. For example, on secularization, we may note that religious practices are still evident in much of sport, such as in athlete pre-match prayers, charms and superstitions. On meritocracy, we also find that deeper structural factors still largely determine sporting access and success: after all, Olympic medal tables are dominated by nations that are able to direct large economic resources into sport facilities and training, and expensive sports such as yachting are dominated by participants from the higher social classes.

In addition, we might note how sport's modern features may be rejected or remoulded by counter-cultural movements. For example, 'extreme sports' may prioritize the corporeal pleasures of sports participation over modern ethics such as record-setting and specialization. Some educational philosophies promote a fully inclusive, sport-for-all approach in opposition to modern sport rationalization, which would otherwise prioritize the participation and performances of the best athletes.

Finally, in critical response to negative experiences of rationalization, some participants may seek to 're-enchant' their sport. Numerato (2009) identified this process in Czech sailing clubs, which sought to challenge a disenchanting decline in volunteers and a greater focus on legal rather than sporting issues through such re-enchantment strategies as staging more social regattas, drawing on the collective memories of sailing communities, and making greater use of new social media. Thus, overall, bureaucratization, rationalization and disenchantment are not absolute and irreversible processes; there is substantial scope for sport organizations and actors to explore alternative processes and possibilities.

Contemporary rationalization: Ritzer's McDonaldization thesis

Weber's rationalization thesis has been updated and reapplied by the American sociologist George Ritzer (1993) through his theory of 'McDonaldization'. For Ritzer, the rationalized basis of modern society is encapsulated in the organizational logic of McDonald's, the American fast-food business chain. McDonaldization is based on four organizing principles.

1 *Efficiency* Speed and ease of service are optimized in 'the search for the best means to the end' (Ritzer 1996: 443). For example, highly rationalized divisions of labour and 'drive-through' windows facilitate rapid sales to passing motorists.

2 *Predictability* 'A world with no surprises' minimizes risk. McDonald's consumers safely assume they will receive the same products, services and sensory experiences in any franchise throughout the world.
3 *Quantity over quality* The product's (large) size is emphasized over its gastronomic value, complexity or distinction.
4 *Automation* Wherever possible, human labour is replaced by non-human production, making the organization more efficient and reliable. At McDonald's, cooking is highly automated and requires minimal employee training.

The results are obvious: the rationalized production and retail of fast food is enormously successful, establishing a paradigm that is copied by competing companies. The organizing principles of McDonaldization pervade numerous other areas of modern life, from financial services to higher education. In Weberian mode, Ritzer (1993: 121) added that rational systems such as McDonald's have disenchanting, alienating and irrational consequences: 'they serve to deny the basic humanity, the human reason, of the people who work within them or are served by them'. McDonald's dehumanizes the dining experience while deculturalizing the gastronomic arts.

Ritzer noted that some organizations seek to implement 'de-McDonaldization' – that is, strategies that head off disenchantment through forms of re-enchantment. However, usually de-McDonaldization involves surface derationalization, which in itself represents a highly rationalized attempt to retain consumers. Examples for McDonald's *per se* might include the colourful decor of fast-food restaurants or the cheap toys given away with meals. There are parallels here with the arguments of Cohen and Taylor (1976) on how some modern individuals seek to re-enchant their lives by escaping from a disenchanting 'paramount reality' of fixed roles and routines. However, sport, gambling, sex, violence, drug use, tourism and fantasy all fail to deliver a satisfactory escape from paramount reality; instead, they become part of the carefully organized modern world, as routine leisure experiences on offer to consumers (ibid.: 222).

Ritzer's McDonaldization thesis is certainly helpful in explaining the organizational structures of modern sport. For example, consider the organization of American football teams: on *efficiency*, players are allocated specific team positions and roles; on *predictability*, players are expected to fulfil these roles reliably; on *quantity over quality*, players are assessed according to statistical measures, with a focus on consistent performances; and *automation* is apparent in the use of scientific equipment to train players and, more subtly, in the emphasis on set team formations and moves that are intended to function like clockwork during games. 'De-McDonaldization', or re-enchantment, is suggested by, for instance, team marketing and media focus on top athletes with unpredictable styles. Yet even these seemingly 'unique' talents are integrated within sport's complex divisions of labour; their value is still measured in terms of efficient production of predictable results.

Despite its effective description of rationalization processes, Ritzer's model has significant limitations. To begin, Ritzer's reference to both 'McDonaldization' *and* 'de-McDonaldization' makes his arguments untestable and unfalsifiable: he cannot be proved wrong, but then he cannot be proved correct.

Moreover, Ritzer overemphasizes the cultural aspects of McDonaldization while underplaying its political economic features. Most importantly, the rational organization of fast-food production depends less on a culture of rationalization and more on the economic aim of maximizing profit. In sport, some institutions have the economic resources to implement McDonaldization more concertedly than their rivals. To reiterate my earlier point on Guttmann and rationalization: huge inequalities in sport performance exist because the wealthiest clubs, nations and social groups can afford the most scientifically advanced facilities and personnel. Ritzer might also make more of the wider nefarious consequences of McDonaldization, such as environmental devastation, reduction in food qualities, and serious dietary and health problems across entire populations. To major corporations, these 'irrational' outcomes are secondary to the goals of profit, growth and shareholder reward. In sport, McDonaldization contains similar costs – notably athlete injury, environmental devastation, and the social exclusion of poorer communities – but these are considered secondary to producing good results and increasing the market value and profitability of the relevant sport organizations.

A subsequent weakness arises in how Ritzer suggests we might challenge McDonaldization through individual acts of avoidance and evasion. In sport, this approach would entail avoiding automated ticket-lines; taking pre-game meals and drinks at intimate hostelries rather than at fast-food outlets; and celebrating spontaneous, risky types of play while criticizing predictable techniques. Laudable though these may be at the everyday level, such examples of individualistic, savvy consumerism lack the strength of collective critical responses and organized opposition that might otherwise challenge the rationalization of sport.

Finally, it is worthwhile comparing the different Weberian approaches that are favoured by Ritzer and Guttmann. In short, following Ritzer would lead us to identify a *deep rationalization* occurring across sports, whereas Guttmann leads us to a far more plausible argument that finds *shallow rationalization* taking hold. For Ritzer, rationalization entails a modern cultural homogenization that can be offset only superficially by de-McDonaldization. Guttmann's perspective is more cautious; indeed, elsewhere he recognized that different societies may interpret, organize and play sport in radically diverse ways (1994: 186). For example, in nations such as Brazil, rationalization and modernization come into a complex, dialectical relationship with specific traditional values and established power structures. The result is a sport culture that is distinctive and hybrid: on the one hand, it harbours modern rationalized principles centred on rules, merit, performance and measurement; on the other hand, 'traditional' values are influential, centred on privilege, patronage and personal connections. Brazilian football and society are shaped by the interplay of these two cultural codes (DaMatta 1991: 154–5; Gaffney 2013). Thus, shallow (diversified) rather than deep (uniform) types of rationalization appear to be more significant.

Concluding comments

Weberian approaches make some highly insightful contributions to the sociological understanding of sport, though I have noted also some significant limitations. Interpretive standpoints help to explain athlete socialization and the stages of identity construction when participating in sport subcultures. They also enable the sociology of sport to engage with valuable anthropological perspectives, notably through ethnographic research. The focus on rationalization processes helps to clarify sport's disenchanting dimensions. Guttmann provides a thoughtful and elaborate sports application of Weber's rationalization thesis, albeit with specific weaknesses. Ritzer's McDonaldization thesis identifies a deep rationalization process within modern routines of production and consumption that invites application to sport. A sociological focus on processes of shallow rather than deep rationalization is more plausible for research in the field of sport.

We might also bear in mind that the relationships between rationalization and processes of enchantment or disenchantment are rather more complex than some of these theories might allow. Indeed, a good deal of the enchantment of contemporary elite sport is rooted in rationalization. For example, quantification is a key aspect of the rationalization of sport, but it also serves to make sport meaningful and emotionally engaging. World sport audiences are riveted by record-breaking performances such as Usain Bolt's various world records in the men's 100 and 200 metres. They also depend significantly upon statistics to make sense of sport events and to experience fully the potential tension within play – for example, when cricket teams are chasing runs or wickets to win, or when high-average pitchers and batters face each other in baseball games. Thus, we should recognize that aspects of rationalization may enhance the enchantment of the sporting experience.

Weberian approaches help to explain socio-cultural meanings and rational forms of modernization within sport, but they are less effective in examining how power relationships underpin social identities, practices and processes. Thus, for example, Weberian approaches here might enable us to recognize the relevance of 'generalized others' in shaping actions and identities but do not draw us into examining systematically who these 'others' may be, which ones are most influential, and how exactly they are able to position themselves in such powerful ways. Similarly, Weberian approaches register the dehumanizing and 'irrational' costs of rationalization but do not necessarily demand that we should study which social groups benefit most from implementing these alienating processes. Moreover, as I noted in relation to Ritzer's thesis, the Weberian approach does not in itself encourage us to consider collective, resistant responses to the negative aspects of rationalization. These criticisms of the Weberian approach are rooted in the recognition of relations of domination and subjugation within sport, and such issues are considered rather more fully in the next chapter.

Questions for discussion

1 How do sport activities become meaningful for participants and spectators? How are people socialized into sports? How do sports serve to create and to shape social identities?
2 In what ways have sports undergone rationalization? What are the advantages and disadvantages of rationalization in sport?
3 How might sport participants and spectators challenge processes of rationalization?

3
Marxist and Neo-Marxist Theories of Sport: Capitalism, Alienation and Class Conflict

The commercial development and economic scale of sport appear to have become increasingly significant over the past few decades. One study in the late 2000s valued the 'global sport market' at up to €450 billion.[5] In world football, Europe's twenty largest clubs generated a combined annual revenue of over €5 billion during the 2012/13 season. Much of the vast revenues in sport are derived from contracts with television companies. Thus, for example, in 2011, the NFL signed a new nine-year $27 billion deal with US television networks, while the NCAA began a men's basketball contract with CBS/Turner worth almost $11 billion over fourteen years.

Marxist and neo-Marxist perspectives are particularly important when we turn to examine the commercial aspects of sport. Marxist approaches engage directly and fully with the central components of Marx's theories, particularly on class conflict. Neo-Marxist approaches draw also on other theorists and theoretical frameworks, such as Freudian psychology and Weberian sociology. In this chapter I discuss these various contributions to the sociology of sport in five main parts. First, I outline Marx's social theory and his reading of capitalism. Second, I turn to examine briefly Marxist and neo-Marxist positions on sport and mass culture. Third, I explore neo-Marxist contributions to the sociology of sport. Fourth, I consider the specific perspectives of the neo-Marxist Frankfurt School on sport. Fifth, I examine how a neo-Marxist perspective contributes to our understanding of the commodification of sport. Overall, I argue that, while Marxist and neo-Marxist positions illuminate the commercialization of sport, greater consideration might be given to the creative agency and critical reflexivity of social actors.

Marx and the critique of capitalism

Most of Marx's writing was undertaken in the latter half of the nineteenth century in England, as he witnessed at first hand the intensification and spread of industrial capitalism. Marx understood capitalism as an advanced, market-based system in which capital is employed to fund commodity production. The relations of production within capitalist society feature two main classes whose respective interests are in direct conflict: on one side, the ruling capitalist class, the bourgeoisie, own and control the means of production (such as land or industrial machinery); on the other, the working class, or proletariat, has only its labour power to sell. The capitalist buys the labour of the proletariat and owns the product that is produced; the capitalist also derives 'surplus value' from the difference between the value of the product and the capital that is expended in its production (including, in particular, the wages of workers). Thus, as a social system, capitalism is based on the class exploitation of workers by capitalists, particularly as the latter have an explicit interest in holding down wages and raising productivity in order to maximize profits. Capitalism also engenders human 'alienation' particularly among workers, who come to experience their productive labour, fellow men and women, and human potential as alien to them.

According to Marx's theory of historical materialism, the class which controls the means of production will dominate all other spheres of society. Under capitalism, the bourgeoisie constitutes such a ruling class. Thus, the state becomes merely 'a committee for managing the common affairs of the whole bourgeoisie' – in effect, a bourgeois tool through which to dominate the proletariat (Marx and Engels [1848] 1998: 44). The ruling class also shapes the dominant sets of ideas (or 'ideologies') within society.[6] Accordingly, the bourgeoisie promote a pro-capitalist 'false consciousness' among the proletariat, who are thereby unable to understand the true conditions of their exploitation or to envision the possibility of revolutionary change. Capitalism further produces a false 'commodity fetishism', wherein human qualities are projected onto objects, which has the ideological effect of hiding the oppressive social relations that actually lie behind the creation of these market goods. Lukács ([1923] 1967) added the concept of 'reification' to explain how, under capitalism, exploitative social relations were presented falsely as thing-like entities.

Marx's perspective was rooted in a revolutionary commitment to change the world rather than simply interpret it (McDonald 2009:

33–4). He anticipated that the capitalist system would ultimately collapse due to its inherent flaws and contradictions: competition between capitalists would reduce them to a tiny number; the ever expanding proletariat would experience lower wages, unemployment and ever more hardship, thus reducing the capacity of workers to buy products; in turn, business slumps would become longer and deeper; ultimately, the proletariat would start to shake off bourgeois ideologies, become a class that is conscious 'for itself', and pursue the revolutionary overthrow of capitalism. Marx ([1875] 1938) envisaged that, when capitalism was overthrown, a socialist 'revolutionary dictatorship of the proletariat' would initially seize the state; then, under communism, the state and bourgeois ideology would disappear, and a new society would be established, founded on the maxim 'From each according to his ability, to each according to his needs.'

As we shall see in this and the next chapter, Marx's theory has undergone diverse and substantial reinterpretation. Its most powerful political application occurred with the creation of the Soviet Union, whose socialist state, led initially by Lenin, adhered to the ideology of Marxism-Leninism. Lenin ([1902] 1998, [1916] 1997) argued that capitalism was an imperial system in which the greatest revolutionary potential was located in the poorest nations and that the class struggle should be driven by the Communist Party, which had legitimacy to act in workers' interest. Lenin's successor, Stalin, subsequently remoulded 'Marxism-Leninism' in order to legitimize the totalitarian powers of the Soviet state and to mask the mass atrocities that were enacted in his and its name.

Marx is most commonly criticized on account of his unfulfilled predictions (global communism never occurred); his oversimplification of the class system (capitalist societies are more complex than his two-class model); and his 'economism', which viewed the economic base as determining all other 'superstructures' (cultural activities, for example, are not always determined by economic interests or pressures).

Certainly, the type of communist system that was envisioned and advocated by Marx has yet to appear. However, these criticisms oversimplify his range of thinking and writing. In his other historical studies, Marx advanced acute analyses of complex stratification and variable power struggles. For example, in his account of Louis Bonaparte's seizure of power in France in 1848, Marx ([1852] 1934) explored the relations between different class fractions, such as large landholders, industrial capitalists, finance capitalists, proletariat and peasantry. In theoretical terms, he also evaded the charge of 'economism' by placing both human structures *and* social agency at the core of his philosophy, for instance through his famous maxim 'Men make their own history, but they do not make it just as they please; they do not make it under circumstances chosen by themselves, but under circumstances directly encountered, given, and transmitted from the past' (ibid.: 10). This statement captures the crucial balance or tension that sociologists continue to identify between structural context and social action. For Marx, it also pointed to how the political, juridical and cultural superstructures of society are not dependent simply upon their economic or material base (Hall 1977: 60). Difficulties arise with later Marxist theories when these points on human agency and the 'relative autonomy' of different superstructures are forgotten.

Marxists and neo-Marxists on sport and mass culture

How would Marx and Lenin have viewed sport? The Marx of *Capital* ([1867] 1999) would see sport as rooted in the economic context, such that only communist revolution would negate its commodification and alienation. Marx recognized that capitalism functioned more efficiently if rest and recreation replenished workers' energies; at the same time, in their leisure, workers could feel 'at home' (Marx [1844] 1973). Nevertheless, class societies are understood as stunting human development and progress; hence bourgeois-controlled sport must be interpreted as a regressive and ideological force. For Marx, only under communism would recreation be freely chosen and undertaken.

Unlike Marx, Lenin was a keen sportsman, mainly in skating, cycling and mountaineering, and extolled the developmental benefits of gymnastic exercise. Following the Russian revolution, Lenin recognized more fully sport's state-supporting aspects in boosting military and industrial power (Riordan 1976). Soviet sport was controlled by the Communist Party and interwoven with Marxist-Leninist ideology. It was viewed as an important mechanism for advancing the struggle of the international proletariat, challenging bourgeois norms and meeting communist aspirations in healthcare, military training, female emancipation and political education (Rigauer 2001: 37). Subsequently, under Stalin, 'mass sport' became integral to nation-building programmes, while spectator sports were subjected to regular (if comparatively small) levels of state intervention (Edelman 1993: 124). Yet, in effect, Soviet spectator sports were relatively weak instruments for mobilizing citizen support for state or party (ibid.: 245). In the post-war era, elite international sport became a corporeal theatre for Cold War politics, pitting the Soviet Union and Eastern bloc countries against different liberal-democratic nations in the West. The Soviet bloc was particularly successful in Olympic competition and football, largely on account of state-driven sport development programmes that often included the systematic doping of athletes.

Outside the communist bloc, sport was an uneven forum for working-class organization and political mobilization. In the run-up to the Second World War, Europe's working-class sports movements expanded to counteract fascist formations. The US Communist Party sponsored the Chicago Counter-Olympics in 1932, challenging the Los Angeles Olympics; though generating little attention or noteworthy athletic performances, the event's anti-racist policies were particularly commendable. In 1936, the People's Olympics were scheduled for Barcelona as a festival of peace, emancipation and anti-fascism but were cancelled when the Spanish Civil War erupted (Baker 1992). After the Second World War, left-wing political and industrial movements developed more substantial workers' sports movements in different European nations, such as the Unione Italiana Sport per Tutti (UISP) in Italy, which were in turn harbingers of mass 'sport-for-all' policies that were adopted by many European governments from the 1970s onwards. Yet these social and participatory models for sport were increasingly marginal to elite professional and commercial forms, which have tended to be the main subject of neo-Marxist critiques of sport.

Neo-Marxist sociologies of sport

A diverse range of social commentators and scholars, deploying very varied levels of theoretical sophistication, have analysed sport, particularly elite sport, from neo-Marxist standpoints. According to the most straightforward contributions, sport is another arena of capitalist domination and class control. Professional sport is a capitalist industry wherein 'the athlete is the producer, the spectators the consumers' (Rigauer 1981: 68–9). Athletes are thus no different to other alienated workers who must give up their labour power: even the champion athlete 'is totally governed by his trainer, a veritable foreman, whose sole aim is to increase the productivity of his athletes' (Brohm 1978: 105). As with capitalist factory production, elite sport is interested not in creative and expressive play but in performances that deliver results, as specialized divisions of labour and fixed productive systems force sports workers to execute designated moves with intense repetition rather than to play creatively and experimentally (Vinnai 1973: 38). Meanwhile, the alienation and degradation of athletes are completed when commodification transforms their bodies into advertising 'sandwich-boards' for major corporations. The professional athlete may feel thankful for having escaped other, less rewarding forms of work, but there is no industrial autonomy to be found on the sport field: 'in the illusory belief that he [*sic*] is free, the athlete locks the door of his cell' (Guttmann 1988: 183).

Aronowitz (1973: 410–11) pointed to the diversionary ideological power of spectator sports in capitalist society, as they 'retain the alienated character of labour, but create the aura of participation for the observer'. So long as worker spectators lose themselves in sports gambling or in disputes over teams and players, 'the system has a few years left'. Aronowitz argued for a return to earlier forms of working-class leisure, notably bar-rooms, where political discussions and local gossip can combine with the reassertion of a fraternity that is otherwise denied in work.

The French social scientist Jean-Marie Brohm advanced a similar diagnosis in polemical style, asserting that the Olympic Games are 'opiates' that keep the masses in stupefied happiness in order to secure 'class collaboration at every level' (1978: 108). Sport tournaments enable televised 'brainwashing' that 'aids the process of reducing the population to a servile mass' (ibid.: 114). Sport's talk of neutral refereeing, impartiality and cross-team sportsmanship is pure ideology, promoting the pro-capitalist myth of an effective 'partnership between capital and labour' which keeps the system ticking. Brohm insisted that the Olympics are exploited to promote a pro-capitalist national unity that is even backed by the French Communist Party. Meanwhile, there are fascistic undertones to the mass worshipping of the Olympic athlete, the 'superman-champion', while behind-the-scenes training regimes create drug-fed athletic 'monsters' and 'cybernetic robots' who are 'imprisoned, indoctrinated, regimented and repressed' (ibid.: 112). This line of argument has been taken up directly by another French intellectual, Marc Perelman (2012), who associated sport with brain-dead consumption by the hysterical and politically befuddled masses.

What solutions are proposed? The American Marxist Paul Hoch reckoned that we face a stark choice between 'socialism or fascism, global human liberation or barbarism' (1972: 212). The far more

theoretically sophisticated work of Beamish (1993: 205–7) recognized the complexities of class relations in sport. He noted,
for example, that Canadian sport remains strongly influenced by
old amateurist principles rather than employer–employee relations.
Athletes lack basic industrial rights and should turn to the courts
to gain collective bargaining status, a minimum wage, overtime and
holiday pay. Rigauer (1981: 103–5) proposed the most speculative
neo-Marxist solutions to sport. He recommended:

1 the removal of sport's work-like structures, repressive rationalization and achievement obsession;
2 the dissolution of conformism and the promotion of democracy;
3 the overt politicization of sports, against the old fallacy that sport
   is 'free' of politics;
4 the removal of ideologies to promote sport's liberal and educational aspects.

In later work, Rigauer (2001: 45) focused on how Marxist sport
sociology might 'open and widen' its paradigm to engage with other
sociological perspectives.

The Frankfurt School

The sharply critical arguments of Brohm, Rigauer and Vinnai on
sport were particularly indebted to the Frankfurt School of social
philosophy that emerged in Germany in the 1920s, with Horkheimer,
Adorno, Marcuse and Fromm among its prominent members.
In establishing 'critical theory', the Frankfurt School combined
Marxism with other intellectual disciplines, notably psychoanalysis
and Weberian theories of rationalization and modern disenchantment, and was broadly committed to the Enlightenment principles of critical reason, intellectual and aesthetic progress, scientific
advancement, and human emancipation. Frankfurt School theorists
understood modern capitalist industrial society as negating these
principles, for example through the alienating rise of scientific rationalization and 'instrumental reason' (note the Weberian influences
here) and the debasement of modern high culture into commercial products (Adorno and Horkheimer [1944] 1979; Poster 1990:
34–5). In broader terms, the work of the Frankfurt School helped to
shift the focus of neo-Marxist thinkers away from the economy and
on to the role of cultural, social and political spheres within modern

industrial capitalism from the mid-twentieth century onwards. The 'culture industries' (such as in film, television, music, popular media and sport) were identified as playing a powerful ideological role in diverting 'the masses' away from political dissent and emancipation and into a dreamscape of frivolous consumption that sustained modern capitalism.

Many of the Frankfurt School arguments were crystallized in Adorno's (1982, 2001) analysis of modern sports as being a field of both alienating work and ideological containment. Sports, he argued, may 'seek to restore to the body some of the functions of which the machine has deprived it. But they do so only in order to train men all the more inexorably to serve the machine.' The physical exertion of manual labour is replicated in sport, which its alienated practitioners must 'learn to enjoy' (Adorno 2001: 194–5). Sport is 'pseudo-praxis', with rules that resemble the brutal competitiveness of the capitalist market. Sport events are a 'model for totalitarian mass rallies', offering no emancipation for the 'powerless' spectators, the 'applauding hooligans', the 'howling devotees of the stadium' (ibid.: 91; Morgan 1988: 818). Like Hollywood celebrities, many 'star' athletes obediently perform routine functions while being marketed to the distracted masses as having pseudo-individualistic properties, such as an unusual haircut or a new romantic interest.

In a broader context, the Frankfurt School viewed sport as a component of the culture industry, which otherwise 'impedes the development of autonomous, independent individuals who judge and decide consciously for themselves' (Adorno 2001: 106). Popular cultural products, in film, music and sport, lack the critical and transcendent qualities of high culture, such as great literature or music; instead, they are instrumentally standardized and packaged as commodities, with a 'pseudo-individualization' that distracts the masses from a state of 'unfreedom'. For Marcuse (1964), advanced industrialism creates a 'one-dimensional' humanity; 'false needs' (such as in consumer culture) generate 'euphoria in unhappiness', distracting the masses from critical reflection and emancipation.[7]

These critical themes were taken up by later analysts of mass consumer culture. Jameson (1979, 1981), a neo-Marxist literary theorist, argued that mass culture is intrinsically ideological; it provokes genuine emotions and desires that cannot be properly met under capitalism's oppressive relations.[8] In the global context, Sklair (2001: 149–50) observed that Western transnational corporations have imposed a 'culture-ideology of consumerism' across developing regions, inspiring what he termed 'induced wants' (rather than 'false needs') that function to direct individuals and social groups into the pursuit of consumer products. Modern, professional, commercial sport – as an aspect of mass culture in itself (with its emotional demands and distractions from critical politics), and also through its extensive interpenetration by capitalist interests (such as corporate sponsors and merchandise companies) – may thus be seen as functioning to induce and spread these false needs and induced wants at a transnational level.

The Frankfurt School thesis partly paralleled the highly elitist, English cultural theory of Arnold, Eliot and Leavis, who condemned the unedifying mass culture of the working classes, bemoaned postwar Americanization, and lamented England's cultural entropy. From this moralizing standpoint, sport's ambiguous identity and status may be viewed as determined largely by class associations: such 'plebian' pastimes as wrestling might be dismissed with disgust as inherently anti-intellectual, while such elitist sports as cricket may be venerated for their intellectual and aesthetic refinement.[9]

While the Frankfurt School in many ways advanced a sweeping condemnation of mass culture – as Hoberman (1984: 244) puts it, they seemed 'literally unable to imagine sport as something other than a complex of pathological attitudes and instincts' – we do need to recognize some important underlying historical and theoretical nuances in their position. Unlike later neo-Marxists such as Brohm and Rigauer, Adorno and Horkheimer did not have the advantage of writing at a time when more subtle sociological methods or perspectives, such as hermeneutic or semiotic theories, would have been available, and which would otherwise have enabled a more patient decoding of popular culture (Poster 1990: 34–5). Moreover, Adorno (2001: 195–6) did soften his position on consumerism, noting that people consume products and discourses 'with a kind of reservation' such that the latter are 'not quite believed in'.[10] The public were also interpreted as having a 'double-consciousness' on sport, which combined enjoyment of rationalized fun along with explicit misgivings. According to the sympathetic and insightful interpretation by Morgan (1988), Adorno understood sport as a form of *regression*: at an individual level, sport features spontaneous, childlike play, while at the societal level it represents a return to when nature dominated humanity. Children's play may seem infantile and silly, but for Adorno its very 'uselessness' and freedom from instrumental reason must be preserved. According to this reading, sport should be an end in itself, defined by standards of excellence that 'contribute to our self-understanding and self-mastery' (Morgan 1988: 831–2).

Like the arts, 'the usefulness of work' and 'the uselessness of play' in sport should be harmoniously and freely interwoven (ibid.: 833). This reading of Adorno represents a relatively positive argument on the possibilities of sport that goes beyond his polemics on sport under modern industrial capitalism. The claims here on the beneficial psychological and sociological aspects of play have a deeper resonance when we consider how many sporting publics celebrate 'folk heroes' who *play* with a child-like absorption with comparatively stronger self-expression and enjoyment of the occasion. In everyday public discourses on sport, these participants are often positively contrasted with more instrumental athletes and teams, who may be well drilled and efficient, but who produce inherently dull spectacles.

Neo-Marxism and the commodification of sport

The commodification of sport represents one field of inquiry in which neo-Marxist approaches appear to have substantial explanatory impact and value. The commercial development of sport is, of course, a long-standing process that predates modern capitalism: indeed, the word *athlete* in ancient Greek referred to someone that 'competes for a prize', while Roman sport arenas often included better viewing areas that could be purchased by wealthier patrons (Miller 2006: 11). In the late nineteenth and early twentieth centuries, as modern capitalism took hold in most industrializing societies, so processes of professionalization and commercialization became more embedded in elite male sport. To maximize revenues, many team sports were organized into league competitions by club owners and controllers, while sport stadiums were erected to accommodate more paying spectators. Professional athletes were soon endorsing products and contributing articles in popular media. In some sports, the struggle against amateur rules by athletes and cultural entrepreneurs lasted a long time, such as for most Olympic disciplines (finally professionalized in 1988) or tennis (with the professional 'Open Era' running from 1968); once successful, however, these professional athletes and their wider sports were more fully integrated into the general culture industries.

In broad terms, elite sports have undergone more exaggerated forms of commodification since the early 1960s, especially since the late 1980s with the growth of international pay-TV networks. In the UK, for example, elite professional football became focused more on its 'entertainment' value and the off-field activities of celebrity players (such as in association with the fashion, film and music indus-tries) from the early 1960s onwards (Taylor 1971). From the late 1980s onwards, the hypercommodification of football took hold in the UK and much of Western Europe through the influx of massive revenues from merchandise outlets and advertisers, the sale of club equity on stock markets and, in particular, the exponential growth of pay-TV revenues (Walsh and Giulianotti 2001, 2007). Thus, English football's top division saw its annual primary television contracts rise from £2.6 million in 1984 to £1.7 billion in 2016. In North America, television has also been the main driver of sport's hypercommodifica-tion. In 'amateur' college sports, the television value of the NCAA's basketball tournament ballooned from around $40 million in 1985 to over $770 million in 2011 (Sperber 2000: 36, 216; *USA Today*, 22 April 2010). In line with economistic strands of Marxism, these pro-cesses of hypercommodification indicate that corporate interests (led specifically by major television companies) will come to dominate the politics and culture of sports. If some structures within the sport are not to their liking, these powerful corporations are able to leverage their influence to press for changes that will maximize profitability. For instance, rugby league in England and Australia is effectively owned and controlled by leading media corporations; league compe-titions were radically reorganized in the late 1990s and early 2000s, and many clubs closed or were forcibly merged, while new ones were opened, in order to satisfy commercial television interests and to facilitate the pursuit of new consumers/viewers in 'target markets' in major cities. In some team sports – such as in the major American and Australian leagues – we also find that governing bodies have established a highly profitable cartel business model: in effect their leagues are open only to invited members who are granted 'franchise' positions. Meanwhile, sport's most commercial elite leagues and tournaments have become heavily branded; thus, we find that the NBA, NFL, and Formula 1 are transformed through commodifica-tion from sporting competitions into global 'commodity-signs', to sit alongside other corporate brands such as Disney, Microsoft and Nike (Andrews 1997).

Processes of hypercommodification mean that leading sports clubs are no longer 'local firms' with a 'single product line, in a single geo-graphic area' (Hardy 1986: 22–3). Rather, clubs such as the New York Yankees, the Dallas Cowboys, Real Madrid and Manchester United operate more like transnational corporations, with elite employees (athletes) who are hired from across the world, and with the international marketing and sales of diverse product ranges in clothing and textiles, insurance, perishable foods and tourism (Giulianotti and Robertson 2004, 2009). Elite sport club ownership is increasingly dominated by cartels of billionaires – in North American sport, there were forty-seven such billionaire controllers in 2013 – who favour leagues that prevent relegation, thus permanently guaranteeing lucrative membership (*Forbes*, 3 June 2013). Although some owners are attracted largely by the pursuit of status and enjoyment of control, others own or have key shareholdings in several clubs across different sports, notably the Fenway Sport Group, led by John Henry (the Boston Red Sox and Liverpool), the Glazer family, formerly headed by the late Malcolm Glazer (Manchester United and the Tampa Bay Buccaneers), and the Red Bull group, founded by Dietrich Mateschitz (with sport team ownership in football, ice-hockey and motorsport).

Many elite sport team owners run these organizations with a principal focus on business models of profit or the growth of asset value. In the MLB in the late 2000s, even poor-performing teams such as the Florida Marlins and Pittsburgh Pirates had their budgets squeezed in order to secure profits (*New York Times*, 23 August 2010). In English football, the move towards owners seeking financial gain from elite clubs rose to a new level in the mid-2000s, when American businessmen used the 'leveraged buyout' model to acquire separate ownership of Liverpool and Manchester United. According to this model, most of the money to buy the clubs was actually borrowed by these new owners from financial institutions, with the debt then loaded back onto the clubs, to be paid out of club revenue streams such as television money, ticket sales and player transfers (*The Guardian*, 22 February 2012; *The Telegraph*, 9 October 2010).

Drawing on a normative neo-Marxist standpoint, it might be argued that processes of commodification undermine the integrity of sports, which are transformed into mere television entertainment (see Lasch 1979: 106–7). For example, American sports are constantly punctuated by unnecessary play-breaks purely to accommodate television adverts. In football, the European Cup tournament was altered and rebranded in the early 1990s as the 'Champions League', in large part to offer greater revenues to the biggest clubs in Europe's largest and richest television markets. In cricket, there has been a long-term move away from the classic model of matches that are contested over several days and towards the staging of shorter fixtures which appeal to big-money television stations and sponsors: first, 'one-day' games were introduced in the early 1960s and then, from 2003 onwards, there was a rapid rise of '20Twenty' matches that are played over three to four hours. From a Frankfurt School perspective, it might be argued that, as a result, many of cricket's complex aesthetics, strategies and skills are lost, particularly the subtle contests that develop over time between batsmen and bowlers.

A further threat to the integrity of sport that follows from commercial pressures and influences concerns the corrupt fixing of sport events. Such practices include match-fixing (fixing the full result), spot-fixing (fixing passages of play) and point-shaving (restricting scoring within a specific range). Fixing has always been a part of sport: in athletic contests in the ancient world; in early modern sports such as cricket, horse-racing and pugilism/boxing since at least the nineteenth century; and through notorious cases in professional modern sport, such as baseball's 1919 'Black Sox' World Series baseball scandal and numerous fixing cases in both Italian football and world cricket. In recent years, substantial attention has been paid to the role of national and transnational cartels in fixing sport events, notably in European football, cricket and American college sports (football and basketball) (Hill 2010; Sport Accord 2011). The aim of such fixing is financial gain from secured bets placed in legal or illegal gambling markets. The background economics for this activity are vast: one major report estimated that global gambling markets were worth €200 to €500 billion annually, with more than 80 per cent of this involving illegal gambling, particularly through Asian markets (ICSS/Sorbonne 2014).

More broadly, the top-level management and governance of sport has been continually beset by many cases and allegations of corruption. The leadership of football's world governing body, FIFA, was deeply implicated in one $100 million bribery scandal during the 1990s and in highly detailed reports of widespread corruption surrounding the awarding of the 2022 World Cup finals to Qatar (*The Guardian*, 30 April 2013; *The Sunday Times*, 1 June 2014). Opposition political parties in Russia claimed that $25 to $30 billion of the projected $50 billion budget for the 2014 Sochi Winter Olympics had been stolen by oligarchs and their political allies (*The Telegraph*, 30 May 2013). In India, ten leading sports officials, including the head of the organizing committee, were charged with corruption following the 2010 Commonwealth Games in Delhi (*Wall Street Journal*, 4 February 2013). Following a neo-Marxist position here, we might observe that these instances of increasingly transnational corruption and other financial crime highlight the extent to which sport has been transformed from a field of cultural practice into a commodity with expanding exchange values.

Finally, in line with Marxist expectations, we might note the occasions in which conflicts arise in class terms or, more broadly, in opposition to the intensified commodification of sport. Three types of conflict may be considered here.

First, direct labour disputes have occurred as professional sport 'workers'/athletes have fought to win better wages and conditions from their employers, although rarely does this extend to taking full control over the sport. For example, in the MLB, eight strikes and lockouts occurred between 1972 and 1995, including the dispute which prematurely ended the 1994 season; and, in the NHL, four lockouts occurred between 1992 and 2013, including the cancelled 2004/5 season. In professional tennis, the men's ATP tour was established in 1990 after many leading players organized to gain more control over the annual tournament circuit. In American college sports – which claim to be 'amateur' despite constituting a multibillion-dollar industry – American football players at Northwestern University won the legal right to form a union, in effect gaining recognition as professional athletes (*New York Times*, 26 March 2014).

Second, disputes have arisen since the early 1990s over the use of sweatshop labour by sport merchandise companies such as Nike and Adidas, particularly in South-East Asia. Campaigning groups against these practices have included the Clean Clothes Campaign, the United Students against Sweatshops, and War on Want (cf. Giulianotti et al. 2014b).

Third, fans and local communities have campaigned against the commodification of sports, such as on how 'supporters' are reclassified as 'consumers' by club marketing people, how some club owners have sought to maximize profits from sports involvement, and also how owners of North American 'major league' clubs gain from pressing public authorities to pay for new stadiums and tax breaks (Giulianotti 2005; DeMause and Cagan 2008).

These different conflicts point to the major social divisions and fractures that underlie the commodification of sport. Moreover, in the second and third categories, these conflicting economic interests are not confined to the relations of production (involving athletes and other sports workers) but also encompass relations of consumption (involving sport spectators and local communities). Overall, it is when exploring the commodification and hypercommodification of sport that the influence of Marxist and neo-Marxist perspectives upon the sociology of sport is perhaps at its most persuasive.

Concluding comments

Sociologists influenced heavily by Marx argue that, through modern capitalism, sport is dominated by commercial interests and has become suffused with alienation, ruling-class ideologies and commodification. For some groups of neo-Marxist sociologists, modern capitalist sport is also shaped by instrumental reason, plays a key role in the ideological control of the masses, and thus needs to be reinvented as a field of free play and non-work. To develop further these arguments, we might agree that, from the mid-1980s onwards, elite professional sport entered a phase of hypercommodification which is categorically distinct from earlier periods of commercialization. Class conflicts have also broken out in relations of production (such as through athlete strikes) and in relations of consumption (such as those involving spectators and local communities). Overall, the diverse arguments of various Marxist and neo-Marxist theories contribute substantially towards a theoretically sophisticated, empirically grounded and critical sociology of sport, pointing to alternative, more socially just ways in which sport might be organized.

Marxist and neo-Marxist approaches have specific weaknesses and flaws in their analyses. A first potential criticism, for Marxists, relates to Marx's misdirected expectation that capitalism would collapse under the weight of its internal contradictions. However, this specific criticism has been effectively addressed by most Marxists and neo-Marxists, who seek to explore how capitalist societies have managed to survive since the late nineteenth century. Several crucial historical processes have played key roles in this regard. For example, European capitalist societies staved off economic crises by enriching themselves through imperial expansion in the late nineteenth and twentieth centuries; the diffusion of sport was a significant component of that process, and it might be argued that sport systems in Europe and North America have latterly continued to enrich themselves through a neo-imperialist importation of top athletes from poorer developing countries. Socialist revolution did not occur in the West for a mixture of reasons, including the ideological hold of consumerism and mass media; the uneven impact of labour movements in improving industrial conditions and establishing different levels of welfare provision; and the state's use of effective repressive and other security measures, particularly during periods of political crisis. In sport, these features have been evidenced through the omnipresence of commercial advertising in elite sport; industrial and legal struggles that have brought higher earnings for elite athletes in the wealthiest sport systems; the public provision of sport facilities, especially in Northern Europe, where socialist and other left-of-centre political movements have been most influential; and the use of extensive policing and advanced security technologies to control sport crowds. Additionally, nation-states and intergovernmental organizations (such as the EU, UN, World Bank and IMF) have played crucial interventionist roles in protecting and advancing capitalist interests, particularly during moments of crisis; for example, during the world economic downturn from 2007 onwards, these governments and organizations pumped hundreds of billions of dollars into the world economic system while also taking over or refinancing deeply indebted private financial institutions. In the sport context, such interventions serve to safeguard the market environment for commercial leagues. In broader terms, public authorities provide major support to privately owned sport clubs, such as through the development of stadiums, the construction of key infrastructure (such as new transport systems), security provisions (notably policing) and the education of club employees. All of these broad factors may be understood as contributing significantly to the post-Marx survival and spread of industrial capitalism, and thus to the diffusion and development of modern commercial sport.

A second and substantial criticism directed at some neo-Marxist sociologists of sport relates to their 'left functionalism' (Hargreaves 1994: 17; Gruneau 1999: 140n). The problem here is the direct opposite of the first criticism and arises when neo-Marxists assume that the capitalist system is always effective in sustaining itself. For example, Hoch and Brohm appear to assume that all social structures (including sport-related ones) 'function' in order to preserve capitalism. A key problem here is that exponents of this argument are effectively claiming to have a privileged epistemological vantage point: that is, they claim to tower intellectually over all other social groups and to see social processes that these others cannot glimpse. For example, the Frankfurt School members assume that only they can peer through the ideological fog to view the true nature of capitalist exploitation. This kind of intellectual dichotomy is difficult to defend, particularly as it underplays the critical agency of individuals and social groups who are otherwise presented as 'brain-dead' consumers. Certainly, we may agree that there are powerful, indeed dominant ideologies that are operationalized across modern capitalist societies, including the realm of sport. Yet, as noted in this chapter and in the next, sport and other cultural spheres are often the sites of conflict, resistance and opposition, as initiated by weak or subordinate groups towards powerful and dominant forces. As the Marxist political historian Ralph Miliband (1977: 52–3) pointed out, we should not assume that support for a sports team is incompatible with development of a class consciousness. More broadly, as Oriard (1993) has indicated, the neo-Marxist 'containment model' of sport fails to recognize how, at times, sport generates (rather than dissipates) aggressive emotions, which may be expressed in unpredictable and disorderly ways, and which are thus more dysfunctional than functional for the smooth running of modern capitalism. Consider, for example, spectacular outbreaks of spectator disorder and violence, such as involving 'militant' or 'hooligan' football fan subcultures across the world, or the urban riots that have occurred after major finals in North American sport in baseball (Detroit 1984), basketball (Los Angeles in 2000, 2009, 2010), American football (Denver 1998) and ice-hockey (Montreal 1993, Vancouver 2011).

A third point here is that some Marxist approaches have been justifiably criticized for adopting a position of 'economic determinism', wherein economic factors are held to determine other social structures, notably in culture and politics. In contrast, we might draw on neo-Marxist, neo-Weberian and neo-Parsonian arguments to recognize the growing differentiation of social structures in modern societies. Thus, cultural structures (including sport) should be viewed as at least partly separate and distinct from, rather than simply dependent upon, the economic 'base'. In making this point, we are not ignoring the impact of hypercommodification but recognizing the many other, non-commercial aspects of sport structures, cultures and practices. For example, sport has many diverse subcultures among athletes and fans which generate distinctive identities and practices that are not simply dependent on the commercial aspects of sport. The specific aesthetics of sport – forms of play that are interpreted and admired as skilful, graceful and beautiful – surely cannot be reduced in meaning to the dominant ideologies of industrial capitalism. Moreover, sport has many innocent attractions, formats and logics that sit outside of industrial capitalist life – for instance, while unnecessary obstacles are avoided or removed in ordinary life, sport is full of contrived impediments such as rules that prohibit ball-handling, or the holding of opponents, or the forward passing of the ball that make for enjoyable play and spectating (Morgan 1993: 44–5).

Thus, overall, the most plausible neo-Marxist perspectives on sport must account for the critical faculties and interpretive capacities of social actors within the realm of commercialized sport. One way ahead here is in reclaiming the more politically interpretivist strand of Marx's work and legacy, which had, for example, sought to account for the complexities of French Bonapartism. To that end, the Cultural Studies approach, which is discussed in the next chapter, is significantly more successful.

Questions for discussion

1 To what extent is elite sport a form of alienating work for athletes?
2 How might we argue that sport promotes ideologies that support modern capitalism?
3 What processes of hypercommodification have occurred in sport?
4 From a neo-Marxist perspective, what are the key social conflicts that occur in sport?
5 Drawing on Marxist or neo-Marxist approaches, in what ways might we radically reorganize or reform modern sport?

4
Cultural Studies Approaches to Sport: Domination, Resistance and Transgression

Interdisciplinary Cultural Studies is the most influential theoretical and research paradigm within sport studies. Cultural Studies was born out of social scientific endeavours to explain the major cultural struggles of the post-war period, such as those pursued through civil rights movements in North America, internationalist feminist movements, youth counter-cultures and subcultures, environmental movements, and France's political uprisings in May 1968. Cultural Studies approaches have reworked Marxist and neo-Marxist theories in order to understand the growing significance of 'cultural politics' among marginalized and subordinate social groups that were stratified according to class, youth, gender and ethnicity/race.

The Cultural Studies tradition emerged in particular from the work of Richard Hoggart (1958) and E. P. Thompson (1963) on British working-class culture, Raymond Williams (1961, 1975, 1977, 1981) on modern cultural history, and the research undertaken by the Centre for Contemporary Cultural Studies (CCCS) at the University of Birmingham under the stewardship of Stuart Hall. Continental theories were heavily influential – notably, from France, Louis Althusser's structural Marxism and Roland Barthes's semiotic theory and, from Italy, belatedly, the visionary analyses of Antonio Gramsci.

Cultural Studies has mushroomed into a vast and diverse field of academic research and inquiry, encompassing sociology, political science, history, geography, literary criticism, linguistics and semiotics, media and communication. Its influence has been pivotal to the creation and development of various 'studies' fields in academe in regard to gender, sexuality, race and ethnicity, which have grown enormously, particularly in North America, since the 1970s. The sociology of sport, and sport studies in general, have also been deeply influenced by this transdisciplinary diffusion of Cultural Studies.

In this chapter, I address the core themes and issues of Cultural Studies in relation to sport; in later chapters, I consider these wider influences in substantive study areas such as on gender, ethnicity and the body. The discussion has five parts. First, I set out the emergence of Cultural Studies and some of its key research themes. Second, I examine the critical contribution of Gramsci's hegemony theory and its relevance to the analysis of sport. Third, I assess the key Cultural Studies themes of 'resistance' and 'transgression' and the associated theme of the 'carnivalesque'. The final two parts then discuss two different paths that may be taken to develop a Cultural Studies analysis of sport. Fourth, I explore how a distinctive normative approach, in the tradition of German critical theory, may be constructed, notably by drawing on the work of Jürgen Habermas. Alternatively, and fifth, I consider briefly how Cultural Studies has been adapted in recent years by one group of social scientists of sport to produce what they have termed 'Physical Cultural Studies' (PCS). I conclude with some critical reflections on the Cultural Studies contribution to research and analysis in the field of sport.

Cultural Studies: origins and key themes

Cultural Studies focuses on the cultural struggles that arise between dominant groups, which produce official culture, and dominated or subordinate groups, which are associated with the creation of popular culture, including much of popular sport culture. Drawing on a neo-Marxist standpoint, popular culture is understood as being essentially contradictory and paradoxical in character: on the one hand, it is made by dominated groups out of the material and symbolic resources that facilitate their domination; on the other, popular culture may also serve to challenge and to express opposition towards dominant groups and the prevailing social order. For example, the popular cultural practices of sport spectators involve paying admission fees to watch their teams and buying sport merchandise; but, within the stadium, fans may also challenge or undermine more powerful groups in sport, such as by booing or mocking sport authorities, developing their own styles of support (e.g., raucous songs, boisterous or 'excessive' behaviour), or using blogs and other social media to protest against the management of the club or the sport. Thus, unlike some neo-Marxist perspectives (such as those of the Frankfurt

School), which tend to present social agents as relatively passive consumers of popular culture, Cultural Studies analyses draw on Marx to conceive of subordinate groups as active agents in shaping and reshaping their identities and practices within particular historical contexts or 'conjunctures'. Paraphrasing Marx, Grossberg (1988: 22) explained that, for Cultural Studies analysts, 'if people make history but in conditions not of their own making, cultural studies explores the ways this is enacted within cultural practices and the place of these practices within specific historical formations'.

Crucial early contributions to Cultural Studies were advanced by the Marxist literary theorist Raymond Williams (1958, 1977). Williams insisted that culture is not elite (as in 'high culture', such as modern literature or the performing arts) but 'ordinary', in terms of being made by people at the everyday level. For early Cultural Studies scholars, it is this 'common culture', particularly in working-class communities, that requires academic investigation. For Williams (1977: 132–3), a common culture emerges from the 'deep community' and strong 'structure of feeling' which bind the members of working-class locales. Unlike ideologies, this structure of feeling is neither formal nor systematic but, instead, comprises the community members' shared beliefs, assumptions, styles of expression, manners of speech and behaviour, and senses of belonging (Williams 1961: 62–7).

Sporting rituals and practices in working-class communities are often imbued with potent structures of feeling. Hoggart (1958: 85) noted how, for example, rugby league teams were 'an important element in the group life' of working-class districts. Robson (2000) examined the intense structure of feeling surrounding the Millwall football club within working-class south-east London, which plays a critical role at matches in developing powerful forms of belonging and solidarity. The concepts of 'deep community' and 'structure of feeling' may be applied to many other sport clubs that have strong forms of community identity, particularly among working-class fans.

Williams (1977) provided a valuable model for examining the politics of culture, indicating that at any historical juncture various 'dominant', 'residual' and 'emergent' forces are at play. Dominant forces establish the most conventional forms of social relations and practices within society; residual and emergent trends respectively comprise past and future forces. The residual also differs from the 'archaic': the archaic comes from the past and is knowingly 'revived'; the residual emerges from the past but remains significantly involved within present culture (ibid.: 122–3). Similarly, the emergent is 'substantially alternative or oppositional' to dominant forces, whereas the 'novel' merely extends the dominant culture. Changes within the class structure serve to reshape these political relations historically.

The modern Olympics help to illustrate Williams's model. The modern Olympic movement was founded in the late nineteenth century in part as an attempt to revive the 'archaic' athletic contests of ancient Greece. Today, the dominant cultures within the modern Olympics are male, bourgeois and Western and tend to celebrate ideologies of nationalism and internationalism, professionalism and measurable competitive success, and capitalism and consumerism (notably through sponsors). Residual Olympic culture reflects some older values and political influences, notably surrounding amateurism (as backed particularly by upper- and upper-middle-class social forces) and old links between Olympic officialdom and fascist movements. Novel aspects in Olympism are found, for example, in technical innovations such as athlete drug-testing or in the support of some members of the governing body, the International Olympic Committee (IOC), for the recognition of new sports, such as 'extreme' sports. The emergent is found in new social forces that point to significant changes such as the addition of 'the environment' as a 'pillar' of Olympism in 1994 and the continuing pressure from non-governmental organizations and social movements for the Olympics to adopt 'human rights'.[11]

Williams (1961) also enables us to examine critically how commodification processes change our social identities and relationships. He argued that individuals and social groups could hold three distinctive relationships to cultural institutions. 'Members' consider that non-economic reciprocity and mutual duties exist between the individual and the institution. 'Customers' are more utilitarian, remaining loyal to the institution but expecting it to meet particular wants. 'Consumers' have a purely instrumental, market-focused relationship to the cultural institution and its products; hence, consumers simply shop around cultural markets in order to get what they want.

Critcher (1979: 170–1) applied these classifications to explain changes in the identities of spectators and players in English football. He identified a strong rise in 'customer' and 'consumer' identities, which in turn weakened (and rendered 'residual') the membership-based structure of feeling within working-class clubs. It might be argued that these processes have intensified in elite professional sport in Europe and North America, particularly as players regularly move teams throughout their careers, as armchair sport fans are understood to switch allegiances to winning sides rather than pursue rituals of local team identification, and as club marketing officials promote the consumption side of game-day attendance and team identification (e.g., through buying merchandise) (cf. Alt 1983: 100).

Perhaps the most extensive and influential application of Cultural Studies theory to the study of popular culture was provided by the CCCS at the University of Birmingham. The CCCS examined in particular how young people within dominated groups (such as the working class or ethnic minorities) create spectacular youth subcultures by appropriating and restyling everyday elements of modern material culture (Hall and Jefferson 1976). At the same time, these young people face personal and collective problems in regard both to these structural relations of domination and to their own 'parent culture', which features older generations of dominated groups whom they will soon join. Thus, Cultural Studies analysts interpret youth subcultures both as the 'authentic' expressions of the lived experiences of these dominated young groups and as the 'magical', temporary solutions that are produced by young groups to the structural problems they face. For Hebdige (1979, 1988), youth subcultures engage in semiotic conflicts or sign warfare with dominant groups and their norms and social conventions. For example, punk fashion accessories (such as bin liners and safety pins) and raucous music served to symbolize youth solidarity in temporarily escaping the boredom of modern education, routine industrial labour and pre-packaged leisure and to challenge dominant cultural codes regarding dress, music and 'civil' forms of behaviour.

Obviously, rebellious subcultures and other challenging cultural movements and practices do not overthrow the social order. The French Marxist Guy Debord (1984) had argued in the 1960s that there occur processes of 'recuperation' whereby radical or subversive practices are 'made safe' and commercialized by the mass media and then drawn back into the cultural system. Similarly, Cultural Studies scholars note how youth subcultural styles undergo processes of 'defusion' (to remove the radical or 'offensive' content) and 'diffusion' (to be sold on to mass audiences) (Clarke 1976: 185–9). Thus, while punk began as a nihilistic underground subculture, many of its major bands and fashions were toned down by the music and fashion industries and then sold on to mass markets. Yet, at the same time, many committed participants continued to object to, or to resist, the 'selling out' of 'their' subculture.

This broad model for explaining youth subcultures might be applied to explain subcultures within sport. For example, surfing and snowboarding subcultures initially suggested a youthful resistance to mainstream sport cultures. In turn, significant aspects of these subcultures, including their resistant stances, were commodified and institutionalized by major corporations and sport governing bodies.[12] Early snowboarders, for example, resembled punk in promoting senses of 'freedom and self-expression' and in opposing the commercialization of their subculture. They were viewed negatively, as countercultural 'misfits' and 'subversive nomads', by many ski organizations and corporations and were banned from many ski parks (Humphreys 2003: 407–8). However, in turn, despite the ongoing opposition of many committed snowboarders, the individualism and radicalism of snowboarding were softened and commercially repackaged by winter sport and leisurewear companies and sold on to mass consumer markets, which were often located many thousands of miles from ski slopes. Similar conflicts arose over political control of snowboarding: the influence of the International Snowboarding Federation (ISF), which had represented early snowboarders, was greatly threatened by the mainstream Fédération Internationale de Ski (FIS), which decided to include snowboarding in the 2002 Olympic Games (indeed, the ISF lost influence and finance and came to an end in 2002). For the FIS, this move would serve to put snowboarding 'at the next level', for new audiences and participants. For many snowboarders, this represented a political and economic grab by the FIS to 'sell out' snowboarding, with the organization interested merely in colonizing and extending its commercial and political power. Indicatively, the world-leading snowboarder, the Norwegian Terje Haakonsen, refused to participate in the Winter Olympics, arguing that snowboarding was 'not about nationalism and politics and money'; in response, he founded a new tournament, the Arctic Challenge, committed to athlete interests, the environment and outdoor life (Humphreys 2003: 421; Thorpe 2012: 88–9). The resistance put up by Haakonsen and others against the perceived 'selling out' or 'takeover' of snowboarding culture highlights the general extent to which subcultural movements may continue to oppose powerful political and economic interests within sport.

Similar processes of commodification and resistance have been at play in surfing. Major corporations such as Quiksilver, Rip Curl, Billabong, Nike and Hollister have turned surfing into a multi-billion-dollar industry, where the vast majority of revenue is generated many miles from beaches, through selling fashion items in shopping malls to non-surfing consumers. Much of this commercial success has been based on associating these brands with authentic surfing subcultures – for example, by recruiting world-leading surfers to endorse these products; by associating products with surfing subcultural identities (especially the ultra-laid-back 'soul surfer' who connects with Eastern cultures and the environment); or, in the case of Hollister, by inventing a completely fictitious company history that tries to build links with early surf culture. (At the same time, of course, in direct contradiction of their professed enlightened spirituality, these surfing corporations make full, highly profitable use of non-unionized, low-wage, low-skill workforces in South and South-East Asia in the mass production of commodities.) Thus, surfing corporations package the illusion of rebelliousness for mass markets, although many committed surfers would never consider wearing their apparel (Laderman 2014: 150).

The cases of snowboarding and surfing throw substantial light on relations of domination and opposition in the cultural politics of sporting subcultures. These themes are played out more fully within hegemony theory, which has been widely drawn upon by Cultural Studies scholars, and to which I now turn.

Hegemony theory

The concept of hegemony, initially advanced by Antonio Gramsci, is a crucial component of Cultural Studies. Hegemony describes the fluid power relationships, methods and techniques by which dominant groups secure their position, by obtaining the ideological consent, rather than the physical coercion, of dominated groups. Hegemony functions most smoothly when dominated groups are persuaded that the exploitative social order is 'natural' or 'common sense' and thus come to accept their position and to 'live their subordination' as an everyday fact of life. Dominant groups establish a 'hegemonic bloc', which also seeks to head off opposition by strategically accommodating key elements of subordinate social groups. However, hegemony is always open to contestation, and thus resistant counter-hegemonic formations may emerge. Hegemonic relations are established and contested within diverse societal fields (in politics, business and industry, and cultural arenas such as sport) by different social classes or class fractions. Where it is employed flexibly with a strong focus on contextual diversity and empirical detail, hegemony theory is highly effective in explaining power relationships at the everyday level. It also encourages social scientists to capture cultural traditions, practices and relations 'as they are', in social relationships, leisure, art and entertainment (Williams 1977: 110–11).

State and civil society relationships help to shape and to establish hegemony.[13] In advanced states, civil society is a highly complex 'superstructure' comprising many social associations and institutions that are not economically pre-determined (Gramsci 1971: 235). States promote consent for the status quo across civil society, but hegemony is always redefined and contested. The 'national-popular' represents one key battleground, as different classes seek to establish hegemony through successfully representing their ideologies as being in the national and general interest (ibid.: 421). Gramsci recognized that all people were intellectuals but argued that only a particular category – 'organic intellectuals' – could advance the revolutionary interests of the subordinate classes; for Stuart Hall, Cultural Studies should be practised by such intellectuals who are committed to movements of social emancipation (Bennett 1998: 31).

Hegemony theory clearly departs from other Marxist tendencies towards economic determinism and has been developed in a variety of ways. For example, Laclau and Mouffe (1985) extended Gramscian theory to advocate the foundation of a 'radical democracy' which would be premised upon 'difference' in terms of the full recognition and empowerment of diverse political and cultural identities.

Gramsci's work also has significant parallels with the later theories of the French structural Marxist Louis Althusser, who provided a further influence upon Cultural Studies. Althusser argued that repressive and ideological state apparatuses function to secure social domination (cf. Gramsci 1971: 12); ideological state apparatuses include the educational system or mass media and would appear to have gained greater significance within advanced capitalist societies since the mid-twentieth century. Althusser (1971: 174) used the concept of 'interpellation' to explain how ideology works; through interpellation, people are 'hailed' as particular kinds of subject in ways that serve to construct particular kinds of ideological subjectivity and personal identity. For example, televised sports are filled with advertising messages and images that 'hail' the viewers as 'consumers' and thus serve to promote subjective identities that are centred on consumption. More broadly, media sports commentaries interpellate other subjectivities and social identities that are rooted in specific divisions within capitalist society and thereby serve to reproduce these identities: viewers, for instance, are hailed according to certain forms of gender, national and racial identity.

A second key aspect of Althusser's work centres on his evasion of the charge of 'economism'. Althusser borrowed a Gramscian phrase to argue that the political and ideological (or 'cultural') superstructures of society are 'relatively autonomous' from their economic base. Thus, economic power does not predetermine the outcome of hegemonic struggles inside sport or in other social fields. However, somewhat paradoxically, Althusser (1971: 136) also stated that the economic structure *is* still determinant 'in the last instance'.

Hegemony theory may be widely applied to explain relationships of domination, opposition and struggle within sport. Historically, it may be argued, the emergence of British sport culture in the late nineteenth and early twentieth centuries was driven by different hegemonic blocs, notably featuring fluid power balances between the upper classes (who tended to have a greater focus on amateurism, particularly in southern England) and the entrepreneurial middle classes (who in northern England tended to be more supportive of commerce and professionalism in organizing sport competition) (cf. Hargreaves 1986: 206). Hegemonic 'leadership' was exercised by these classes, such as through the heads of new sport clubs and governing bodies and through school headmasters who, acting as 'intellectuals', promoted games as part of the 'normal' and 'common-sense' civilizing virtues of British imperialism (Mangan 1986: 22). Sport was a key tool in the hegemonic strategies of the British ruling classes in the colonies. Through sports, 'muscular Christian' ideologies were imposed and inculcated, often in direct contravention of local cultural values and belief systems – for example, Indian Brahmins avoided strenuous exercise and contact with leather but were nevertheless driven into 'manly' ball games (ibid.: 182–6). Sports have also served to promote the hegemonic interests of dominant groups through appeals to the 'national-popular', as when, at international sport competitions, hegemonic groups attach themselves to successful and popular national athletes, or when specific 'national values' are identified and celebrated by the national media, politicians and sport officials. The opening ceremonies of Olympic Games provide important case studies of particular and shifting visions of the national-popular: at the London 2012 Olympics, the ceremony was planned by the director Danny Boyle and included an extended celebration of the state-funded National Health Service, thereby representing a strong symbolic rejection of neoliberal or 'free-market' policies on healthcare.

In terms of individual sports, hegemony theory might be used to explain cricket's historical development. Throughout the late nineteenth and early twentieth centuries, this quintessential English sport was spread across the empire to act as an 'innocuous outlet for mass frustrations', while facilitating

> the transmission of values like respect for authority, especially that of Whites, deferred gratification, and team spirit; the inculcation of norms such as unquestioned acceptance of the decisions of authority figures, in particular Whites (this was embodied in the term, 'it's not cricket'), the use of myths such as the inherent superiority of the colonizer and inferiority of the colonized, and the utilization of the bat as a symbol of authority – this explains why Whites were expected to be batsmen. (St Pierre [1995] 2008: 79)

Local elite social groups – such as high-caste Indians – were often drawn into this cultural hegemony through membership of cricket clubs, while, in the West Indies, cricket clubs were strongly stratified along race lines, with black players excluded from the national team captaincy.

Crucially, however, as Gramsci's theory recognizes, counter-hegemonic forces spring up and oppositional organic intellectuals emerge. In the case of West Indian cricket, subordinate and subaltern non-white populations – backed by organic intellectuals such as the West Indian Marxist historian and cricket-lover C. L. R. James (1963) – challenged their domination within sport and in the wider civil society. The majority black population embraced cricket to create an alternative and more empowering 'collective national-popular will', as conveyed through distinctive subcultures on and off the field of play, which contrasted with, and often consciously resisted, the hegemonic white, English conventions within the game. For example, in sharp departure from white bourgeois norms of peaceful and polite spectatorship, West Indian cricket crowds became renowned for their carnival atmosphere (including music, heavy drinking and ribald humour) and the derision of whites and authority figures (Manning 1981). When the all-black West Indian team twice annihilated England 5–0 in test match series (1984 and 1985–6), fans celebrated these victories as 'blackwashes' over their old colonial masters (Beckles and Stoddart 1995).

Yet the interrelations between hegemonic and counter-hegemonic forces are fluid and often display substantial overlaps between the two categories. In cricket, England's establishment and media frequently disparaged West Indian cricket culture – by banning from English grounds particular styles of support associated with Caribbean fans or by suggesting that the West Indies' use of four fast bowlers betrayed the ethos of cricket (Williams 2001: 131–4). Ironically, in some parts of the West Indies (notably Barbados), post-colonial authorities retained some British political codes and cultural values, so that many English playing ethics in cricket were deliberately retained (Sandiford and Stoddart 1995: 56–8).

Indian cricket provides an interesting and more recent site for the application of hegemony theory to sport. According to Appadurai, cricket in India underwent extensive 'Indianization', as locals 'hijacked the game from its English habitus' to produce new playing styles, supporter cultures and popular meanings (Appadurai 1995: 46). India has since grown to become the hegemonic national force within world cricket, both in political terms (within the global governing body, the ICC) and in economic terms (through the lucrative Indian Premier League [IPL] tournament). On the one hand, this aspect of 'post-Westernization' points to a new political hegemony, as a postcolonial nation comes to dominate a global sport. On the other hand, familiar hegemonic forces remain at work here, as the IPL is a hugely commodified exercise which appeals to the growing Indian middle classes, while the Indian cricket team has often featured a majority of elite-caste Brahmin players (cf. Rumford 2007).

Overall, hegemony theory helps us to examine the cultural politics of sport involving dominant and subordinate groups. I turn now to explore the concepts of resistance, transgression and the carnivalesque, which further facilitate this form of critical inquiry.

Resistance, transgression and the carnivalesque

Resistance

A key concept within Cultural Studies, 'resistance' registers how subordinate groups engage in particular cultural practices to resist their domination by hegemonic groups. Cultural Studies analysts identify resistance in overt and deliberate forms of opposition and protest, as well as in more latent and unconscious practices that run counter to the norms and conventions of dominant groups (Hall and Jefferson 1976; Fiske 1993; Grossberg 1992; McRobbie 2005).

In sport, we have witnessed many striking instances of conscious resistance and protest by athletes in regard to their subordinate or subaltern position: on 'race', perhaps the strongest example is provided by the 'black power' salutes of African-American athletes at the 1968 Mexico City Olympics; other incidents have involved black athletes (such as Viv Richards in cricket, Nicky Winmar in Australian Rules football, and Marco Zoro and many others in football) publicly objecting to racial abuse from fellow athletes or crowds. At the everyday level, less spectacular forms of resistance tend to be confined to cultural politics within sport (cf. Wren-Lewis and Clarke 1983), such as community opposition to new stadium plans or spectator protests against the perceived mismanagement of sports clubs.

One problem arises, however, when some analysts in the neo-Marxist or Cultural Studies traditions interpret the actions of individuals or social groups as being motivated by a form of covert, latent or unconscious resistance towards their social marginalization or domination. When these sorts of interpretation are put forward by Cultural Studies scholars, it becomes possible to claim that acts of resistance are 'virtually *everywhere*' in popular culture, despite the lack of persuasive data, such as supporting comments from the social actors *per se* (Gruneau, quoted in Donnelly 1993: 141). Conversely, if we conduct empirical research with different subcultures, we tend to find that their members attach a wide range of motives and meanings to their actions, which may say little about 'resistance' and much more about other aspects of subcultural identity, such as internal status contests or the aesthetic and pleasurable aspects of subcultural activity (see Rojek 1995: 23–4).

By way of illustration, we might consider sociological studies of football hooliganism in England. One early analysis interpreted football hooliganism as a form of inarticulate 'resistance' by young supporters towards the commercialization of their sport (Taylor 1970, 1971). Subsequent research revealed that 'football hooligans' are not motivated in this way; rather, alongside their enjoyment of participation in violent exchanges, they are engaged mainly in pursuing status within their own subculture (see Armstrong 1998; Giulianotti and Armstrong 2002).

Transgression and the carnivalesque

The anthropological concept of 'transgression' provides a more useful alternative to resistance for explaining practices that apparently undermine the social order but lack explicit intentional or conscious forms of opposition (Bale 2000: 154). Transgression involves boundary crossing, particularly breaching moral parameters or hierarchical codes. While resistance implies *intentional* social opposition, transgression focuses instead on the *consequences* of actions. Thus, for example, while football hooligans are not motivated by their latent resistance towards the commercialization of sport, their violence does involve a transgression of the social codes, conventions and norms which predominate within modern, professional, commercial football.

Transgressions may be commonly found in 'carnivalesque' practices and activities which occur at folk or popular events such as public carnivals and street parties. In broad terms, unlike routine periods of ordinary life, carnivalesque activities tend to celebrate the 'lower body' (as sensual, playful, expressive and, in extreme cases, grotesque) over the 'upper body' (intellect or mind). Thus, historically, carnivalesque activities have tended to transgress bourgeois or 'respectable' behavioural codes and conventions, for example when partying includes an excess of game-playing, laughter, drinking, carousing, sexual activity and gambling. Moreover, the carnivalesque may also involve the symbolic transgression or upsetting of social hierarchies; medieval carnivals sometimes included the election of boys as local bishops for the day or the mocking of local elites in popular songs and parades (cf. Brophy 1997).[14]

It is possible to identify elements of the carnivalesque within modern sport events. Historically, many modern sports – horse-racing, cricket, wrestling, boxing and football – are derived in large part from folk games that were played during popular festivals. These sports retain significant aspects of this folk culture, for example among spectators in regard to heavy drinking, gambling, raucous songs, the mocking of powerful figures within the sport and, more broadly, the celebration of popular sports participants (or 'folk heroes') who have reputations for 'excessive' behaviour (Giulianotti 1991, 1995; Pearson 2013).

In sport, the cultural politics of transgression and the carnivalesque tend to involve underlying struggles between dominant social forces, which seek to commodify 'folk' events and to constrain transgressive behaviours, and dominated groups, which wish to party more freely. At elite-level sport events, stadium and club officials will seek to 'recuperate' the match-day carnival, in part by manufacturing pseudo-carnival entertainment and atmosphere among spectators, perhaps through leading songs via the public address systems; meanwhile, event spectators are closely monitored by security officials for signs of offensive or excessive behaviour. Leading sport merchandise corporations look to colonize and to commercialize the carnivalesque energies and identities of sport subcultures in order to lend their products the appearance of a sport-based authenticity – for instance, through advertisements that are filled with images of colourful, celebrating sport crowds and with messages on how the company is obsessed or passionate about sport. In contrast, spectator subcultures, such as 'fan scenes' in European football, which are usually male but feature significant female participation, seek to produce their own carnivalesque practices in and around stadiums, such as through informal and raucous association among supporters, elaborate pyrotechnic displays, the unfurling of critical and humorous messages on the politics of sport, and adopting a critical stance towards attempts to regulate or to commodify their practices and identities. In turn, tensions may arise between these 'top-down' (club- or corporate-led) and 'bottom-up' (supporter-led) forms of the carnivalesque, such as when clubs or sport authorities seek to prohibit certain supporter-based activities.

Thus, overall, while the concept of resistance registers conscious protests and opposition, other terms such as transgression and the carnivalesque enable Cultural Studies to examine and to explain, in more anthropological and historical ways, those social actions and cultural practices that breach or discomfort dominant social conventions without always making claims about the explicit intentions of social actors. In the final two sections, I turn to consider two particular paths that may be taken by Cultural Studies scholars in the critical study of sport.

A normative focus in Cultural Studies

One relatively small but important strand within the broad Cultural Studies field builds on neo-Marxist and critical theory to develop a normative analysis of sport. The most significant contribution is advanced by Morgan (1993, 2002, 2004) – one of the world's leading philosophers of sport – and is particularly underpinned by the work of the German critical theorist Jürgen Habermas. To explain this approach, it is necessary to set out Habermas's position in a little detail.

As a student Habermas studied under Adorno and Horkheimer, and he has been the most influential figure associated with the Frankfurt School since the 1970s. His social theory is premised on the defence of modernity as an unfinished historical project; thus, he has been a leading advocate of reason, progress, science, enlightenment and human emancipation and a powerful critic of postmodernist and poststructuralist social theory (Habermas 1987a). Habermas (1989) has argued for the foundation of a truly democratic 'public sphere': an open, inclusive and status-blind domain wherein citizens freely discuss and debate social issues and decide on political action. Relatedly, he has sought also to protect and to strengthen the everyday 'lifeworlds' in which people explore and develop their identities, practices, norms and common understandings.

Habermas has criticized processes which countermand the creation of a modern, genuinely democratic and ethical society, particularly the influence of instrumental reason, which by definition lacks normative components (Habermas 1970). He has been concerned that democratic communication and debate within the public sphere are distorted or corrupted, notably through media misrepresentations of public issues, and that everyday 'lifeworlds' are devalued and 'colonized' by top-down, instrumental 'systems', such as large bureaucracies, corporations or political machines, that flex their power through money, status and votes (Habermas 1987b). However, he has also reasoned that the 'project of modernity' remains capable of rationally challenging these processes in order to establish what he terms a 'distortion-free' public sphere, devoid of sectional interests and ideologies, wherein communication is free and arguments are judged according to rational debate and reflection rather than the speaker's status or wealth.

Morgan demonstrated the relevance of these critical normative arguments for examining the current condition and future development of modern sport. Sport has been badly served by the domination of instrumental reason over normative reflection and action, as evidenced, for example, by athlete and spectator violence, corruption among sports officials, and the systematic promotion of doping in some sports (Morgan 2004). More generally, the governance of sport is dominated by the instrumental media of money, departmental bargaining, and the manipulation of debates through public relations; thus, the politics of sport are severely lacking in democratic communication, popular participation, critical debate and moral reflection. The lifeworlds of sport communities are further threatened by rationalized and corporate forces. For instance, the everyday making and remaking of collective supporter identities at the community level is shaped or colonized by instrumental sport advertising and marketing with the aim of securing more consumers and sales. Modern social media provide a further, contemporary illustration: in sport, Facebook and Twitter may have facilitated a lively social 'lifeworld' and public sphere for different fans and communities, but much of this space has been crowded and colonized by the public relations and marketing departments of sport-related corporations (McLean and Wainwright 2009).

To resolve these sorts of problems in sport, Morgan (1993: 234–7) advanced the Habermasian model of an enlightened, democratic 'practice-community'. In line with Raymond Williams and the American philosopher Michael Walzer, Morgan argued that community itself is an 'internal good' of sport which should be shared by members of the 'practice-community'. Morgan has tended to restrict membership of this practice-community in sport to athletes, although, in line with Habermas's inclusive principle for the public sphere, it should also include non-athletes, particularly supporters, employees and officials (Walsh and Giulianotti 2001, 2007). The practice-community should constitute a highly mature public sphere wherein debaters 'come into the athletic forum armed only with their arguments, leaving behind all titles, goods, and vantage points that derive from their standing in other spheres' (Morgan 1993: 242). However, Morgan does appreciate that 'rational authorities on the game', who hold a master–apprentice relationship with relative novices in sport, will have some greater discursive and political powers within the practice-community. In addition, such critical dialogue and reflection may help to inspire new possibilities, such as the development of alternative sports that move beyond existing masculine codes and conventions (Morgan 2015).

Overall, Morgan's Habermasian model establishes important and valuable normative principles for the democratic reform of sport. At the everyday level, it also points towards the democratic, community-based control of sport and sporting institutions. There are strains of a Habermasian political vision in the arguments of some community and social movements which advocate the mutual or member ownership model for sport, wherein elite-level clubs are owned and controlled not by rich clusters of individuals or corporations but by the inclusive community of fans. Illustrations are provided by some Spanish and German clubs in football, the Green Bay Packers in the NFL, and some clubs in the AFL and NRL in Australia. These forms of ownership do not in themselves remove forms of distorted communication or corruption from club politics – witness, for example, the notoriously corrupt practices at some member-owned football clubs in South America – but such arrangements may be seen as establishing the essential foundations for genuinely democratic debate and governance within sporting institutions.

Physical Cultural Studies

A further significant development in the sport field of Cultural Studies has been the emergence of 'Physical Cultural Studies'

(PCS). Calls for the pursuit of a physical cultural studies had earlier been made by several leading sport scholars, notably Ingham (1997) and Hargreaves and Vertinsky (2007), but its formal inauguration has been driven by a later cluster of academics, primarily in North America, and led by the work of David Andrews (2008; Andrews and Silk 2011, 2015). Andrews (2008: 55) has forwarded the following definition for this approach:

> Physical Cultural Studies advances the critical and theoretical analysis of physical culture, in all its myriad forms . . . PCS is dedicated to the contextually based understanding of the corporeal practices, discourses, and subjectivities through which active bodies become organized, represented, and experienced in relation to the operations of social power. PCS thus identifies the role played by physical culture in reproducing, and sometimes challenging, particular class, ethnic, gender, ability, generational, national, racial, and/or sexual norms and differences. Through the development and strategic dissemination of potentially empowering forms of knowledge and understanding, PCS seeks to illuminate, and intervene into, sites of physical cultural injustice and inequity.

Advocates of PCS argue that their approach has several key drivers, including, as they see it, the need to move analysis beyond a focus on organized sport and to examine also dance, exercise, leisure and recreation, and rehabilitation activities; to go beyond the confines of traditional sociology in order to produce transdisciplinary and transtheoretical work; and to respond fully to what they see as the 'physical turn' within the sociology of sport and to the growing interest in physical culture from scholars working in other disciplines (especially in the cultural, gender and ethnic studies fields). These advocates further contend that PCS constitutes a collective, democratic and diverse community of scholars, engaged in dialogue and learning, and a complementary field rather than a rival to the sociology of sport (Andrews & Silk 2015). They aim for PCS to have substantial social impacts, 'to intervene into the broader social world and *make a difference*' (Andrews 2008: 56, original emphasis).

PCS's development hitherto has been centred largely on North America, which is reflected in part in the distinctive interpretive techniques and discursive tropes of its proponents. Some PCS advocates have made strong claims regarding its prospective influence and impact and have sought to advance the approach strategically within the academy, nurturing powerful senses of collective identification and also founding eponymous research centres and groups in marked differentiation to the broader sociology of sport.

An ambitious field of inquiry still in infancy, PCS will require a decade or more of further research and publications in order for firm conclusions to be drawn on its significance and merits. In the meantime, four main questions may be raised on its constitution and development.

First, the extent to which PCS does or should represent a categorical break from other disciplines, including the sociology of sport, is highly debatable. To begin, we might note that the most prominent research issues, techniques of analysis, and styles of writing within PCS were being utilized long before this approach was formally announced or branded (see, for example, the outstanding earlier work of Andrews). At this stage, rather than representing a meta-discipline that encompasses the best aspects of these paradigms, PCS appears as one recent brand of one broad and highly influential approach (Cultural Studies) within the sociology of sport. In addition, many of the critical themes of inquiry identified by PCS – such as investigating power relations and social divisions, nurturing constructive dialogue across diverse groups of scholars, promoting the 'sociological imagination', adopting an anti-relativist position in research, and pursuing the empowerment of subordinate social groups and progressive social change – have long been central to much of the sociology of sport and indeed sociology *per se*. In contrast to the statements of some PCS scholars, contemporary sociology is an increasingly diverse discipline in terms of theoretical influences, methodologies, and engagement with other collaborations and inter-relationships with other disciplines, and many of these theoretical paradigms have yet to be mined sufficiently and fruitfully by sociologists of sport. More broadly, the challenge for sociologists of sport is to engage more effectively with mainstream sociology rather than to move further away.

Second, the actual title of PCS with regard to 'the physical' is not fully convincing. One issue here is that the 'physical' is not hugely prominent in many research areas for PCS or the sociology of sport – see, for example, studies of media discourses on sport, the staging of sport mega-events, the commodification of sport, or the globalization of sport. Additionally, the extent to which a 'physical turn' has occurred across the social sciences and humanities may be queried: it has certainly not had anything like the same influence as other claimed intellectual 'turns' (such as on the postmodern, global, risk, mobility, and so on); at the same time, PCS does not encompass all physical research, as many sociologists and anthropologists of the body within sport continue to work outside of this approach. Finally, and reflecting the continuing relevance of sociology for studies of 'the physical', we might note that many of the world's founding and leading figures in the social scientific study of the body – such as Bryan Turner, Mike Featherstone, Chris Shilling and Mike Hepworth – did not create a new PCS-like identity for themselves; rather, they continued to define themselves as sociologists while also working fully with a vast range of other disciplines.

Third, I commend the commitment of PCS scholars to 'get their hands dirty' by conducting substantial empirical research with diverse social groups with the aim of having real social and political impacts. To achieve those ends, we might expect that future PCS research will be founded upon extensive data collection, most obviously through qualitative methods (such as ethnography, participant observation, interviews, use of video diaries, and so on). Despite some stated hostility to scientific positivism, there are no obvious reasons why quantitative methods cannot be fully utilized; indeed, there are many critical social scientists who utilize these methods to make similar arguments to PCS regarding relations of power and progressive social change. Additionally, if PCS research is serious about pursuing significant social and political impacts, we would anticipate that there will be proportionately less focus on dissemination of findings within the academy and much greater focus both on participatory action research (such as community-level engagement and advocacy work with subordinate groups) and on broader policy and advocacy work across the public sphere.

Fourth, the commitment of PCS scholars to intellectual diversity is also to be commended. The pursuit of methodological and analytical diversity is a prerequisite for the healthy development of any theoretical paradigm. For PCS, this diversity might be facilitated in three ways: by ensuring that different scholars, particularly junior ones, are encouraged fully to develop their own distinctive voices, styles of writing, methods, theoretical frameworks, and general research contributions; by maximizing the scope for 'glocal' varieties of PCS to emerge, so that PCS (as a transnational approach) may be substantially adapted and transformed by scholars from different national and regional contexts; and by developing forms of hybrid or 'neo-PCS' which engage fully with other theoretical paradigms to generate new research questions, concepts, analytical frameworks and methodologies. The creation of such a poly-vocal, glocal and hybrid PCS would certainly enhance the influence of this approach; it would also provide us with more standpoints from which to conduct the critical sociological investigation of sport.

Concluding comments

The Cultural Studies approach represents the most influential and diverse research paradigm within the sociology of sport. Providing a clear advance on Marxist and neo-Marxist perspectives, Cultural Studies serves to highlight the critical significance of popular culture (including sport) and the subtleties of power relations and conflicts between dominant and dominated groups. To facilitate investigation and analysis, the Cultural Studies approach harnesses a range of highly useful concepts, such as community, structure of feeling, hegemony, the national-popular, resistance, transgression and the carnivalesque. Two subsequent developments in Cultural Studies were identified – PCS and Habermasian critical theory on sport – both of which (and particularly in the latter instance) extend the normative analysis of sport, pointing towards its radical transformation.

There are aspects of the Cultural Studies approach which require some critical reflection and development, and here I consider four such areas.

First, Cultural Studies theorizations of community have substantial power in capturing the forms of solidarity and *communitas* that may emerge among dominated social groups over time. However, the concept of community requires critical reflection, updating and reapplication. To begin with, many communities are not as socially inclusive, tight-knit or homogeneous as the Cultural Studies approach often implies. The 'dark side' of community might involve minority or 'deviant' groups being harassed, victimized or pressurized into conforming. Since the 1980s, many old industrial working-class communities have also been impoverished and have experienced fragmentation in the wake of neoliberal policies and the loss of heavy industries. Moreover, contemporary 'communities' are increasingly fluid in membership and socially diverse, particularly in ethnic composition.

In sport, we find illustrations of these processes occurring when gay or lesbian athletes or fans are marginalized within sport clubs; when sport clubs in poor de-industrializing areas lose members and players and are unable to pay for facilities; and in the short lifespan of some sport clubs in global cities such as London or New York as a result of constant changes in the local population. Moreover, as Dyck's (2012) superb ethnographic study of children's sport demonstrates, much community-level sport has uneven benefits: in positive terms, this may include exercise, socialization and skill development, but in negative terms it also features parental pressures, excessive competitiveness and exclusivity because of cost.

Second, and following from this, older Cultural Studies approaches need to be updated to account more fully for the long-term impact of globalization processes, and in particular the 'deterritorialization' or 'disembedding' of cultural identities, practices and communities (cf. Giddens 1990; Tomlinson 1999). The hugely influential concept of 'imagined community' points to the ways in which strong senses of collective identity and solidarity are shared by people across the world, without any prospect of actually encountering all 'community' members (Anderson 1983). Similarly, we might update the Gramscian concept of 'collective national-popular will' to study the production of 'collective transnational-popular will' in sport and other popular cultural contexts. For example, the 'imagined communities' of many elite sport clubs are increasingly transnational, with supporters often spread across the world. Meanwhile, sport governing bodies such as the IOC and FIFA are increasingly engaged in developing a particular 'collective transnational-popular will' which is centred on combining close ties to transnational capitalism with universalist messages on tolerance, development and peace.

Third, I criticized earlier the Cultural Studies tendency to use the concept of 'resistance' in a rather blunt fashion to explain all kinds of diverse practices among individuals, groups and subcultures. The concepts of transgression and the carnivalesque help to explain practices which cross social boundaries without necessarily assuming that conscious resistance or opposition is always in play. Additionally, some theories of resistance may exaggerate the extent to which subcultures are purely oppositional, as some may be open to commodification or entry into the hegemonic bloc within that field of popular culture. For example, the 'Barmy Army' subculture of England cricket fans emerged in the 1990s, producing a raucous, exuberant carnivalesque atmosphere at matches, in deliberate contrast and opposition to the quiet, sedate and genteel spectator culture that otherwise dominated English cricket grounds. The Barmy Army also developed into a professional business organization, as its founding members established a tour agency and merchandising machine under its trademarked name and attracted corporate sponsorships. Thus, the concept of resistance might be used in rather more nuanced ways in relation to sport subcultures.

Fourth, in regard to broad theory and method, the Cultural Studies approach may be positively developed through the extension of a strong normative focus that draws heavily on contemporary critical theory, particularly from the Habermasian legacy. Moreover, one prior weakness in some Cultural Studies research was a tendency to over-interpret social actions or, perhaps worse, to 'decode' cultural 'texts' such as media reports without sufficient empirical detail or rigour in the collection and analysis of data. In order to advance persuasive analyses of contemporary sport, Cultural Studies researchers might look to recapture some of the methods of the old CCCS, featuring substantial, detailed qualitative research that is conducted with diverse, subordinate research groups.

These adjustments would help to advance further the capacity of Cultural Studies to lead scholars in the provision of a critical sociology of sport. There is no doubting the continuing influence of Cultural Studies perspectives within the sociology of sport, and that hold is reflected in the core 'cultural politics' fields of 'race'/ethnicity and gender/sexuality, to which I turn in the next chapters.

Questions for discussion

1 In what ways does sport reflect the 'way of life' of working-class communities?
2 What subcultures are to be found in sport? How do they resist the influence or control of corporations and sport governing bodies?
3 How useful is the concept of 'hegemony' for describing how different social groups seek to exercise control, or to challenge control, within sport?
4 What examples of transgression or the carnivalesque may be identified in modern sport?
5 Considering the idea of a 'practice-community', how might the governance of sports undergo reform in order to become more democratic?

5

'Race' and Ethnicity in Sport: Competing against Racism and Intolerance

Sport, like other domains of social life, has always been characterized by racist social relations. Historically, the word 'race' has carried different meanings (Banton 1988: 16–23). Racism in modern times is widely understood as being focused on differences in skin colour, leading to claims and assumptions on the physiological differences between peoples. Forms of 'race logic' extend back at least as far as European colonial times, when much of the planet was invaded and the indigenous peoples were subjected to systematic subjugation and annihilation. The modern 'post-colonial' world continues to be largely shaped by the consequences, notably in how vast inequalities remain between different peoples in life chances and quality of life. Yet modern history is also substantially defined by the struggles of these racially subjugated peoples for social equality and recognition. Overall, colonialism and post-colonialism, 'racial' stratification, and resistant identities and struggles are core themes that are addressed in the academic field of 'race and ethnic studies', and sport is an important and often crucial setting in which they are played out.

In this chapter I build upon the critical insights of the opening four chapters, and in particular the discussion of Cultural Studies, to examine five broad areas concerning racism and ethnic intolerance within sport. First, I provide a sociological critique of the historical and physiological arguments which surround sports performance and 'race'. Second, I outline international histories of sport and racism within four key contexts: the United States, Africa (particularly South Africa), Australia and Britain; these sections may be read in conjunction with earlier discussions of cricket in the Caribbean in chapter 4. Third, I examine the relationship of race and sport to social stratification. Fourth, I consider cultural, ideological and aesthetic issues surrounding race. Fifth, I widen the discussion to explore how a broadened definition of racism, beyond 'colour-coding', might be applied to examine the mistreatment of different ethnic minorities within sport.

'Race', athleticism and sport performance

For much of the nineteenth and twentieth centuries, theories of 'scientific racism' were substantially influential in the West. These theories utilized pseudo-scientific 'evidence' – now entirely discredited – in order to classify different population groups into 'race' categories or hierarchies. In the 1850s, the French Count Arthur de Gobineau advocated an influential thesis that depicted white 'races' as physically and intellectually superior to 'American savages', 'Negroes' and others who are 'infinitely less able to bear fatigue' (quoted in Miller 1998: 126; Carrington 2010). Soon afterwards, Charles Darwin sought to explain the evolution of species through theories of natural selection and the 'survival of the fittest'. These theories of the natural world were seized upon by some 'Social Darwinists' and misapplied to human societies in order to argue that Western nations and peoples were technically, morally and culturally more advanced – and thus racially more advanced – than peoples on other continents. Such racist ideologies were marshalled to legitimize Western imperialist and militarist policies, particularly in the colonization of 'inferior' non-white peoples, and to warn against the dangers of racial interbreeding for the future of Western civilization (Hawkins 1997). 'Scientific racism' often extended to the negative classification of some white minorities, such as the portrayal of the Irish or Jews as beneath Anglo-Saxons or 'Anglo-Teutonics' in the racial hierarchy.

For Western European colonists, sport played a key role in the endeavour to establish and reproduce their 'racial' power (Carrington 2010). For the British in particular, sport was understood as advancing their 'racial' development and demonstrating their physical and moral superiority. Non-whites were initially excluded, in part because of the perceived racial lack of moral fibre and mental agility. When non-whites did win struggles to participate, and subsequently excelled in sports – notably in athletic or boxing contests in the early twentieth century – the 'race logic' of dominant white groups was adapted to explain away these awkward outcomes, creating a pseudo-scientific, inverse relationship between physique and intellect. Thus, for example, Anglo-Saxons defined themselves as more advanced in mind and morality than in physical prowess; the converse was deemed to be true for social groups of African extraction. In other words, while non-white athletes may run faster, jump higher and punch harder, they are unable to understand the strategic subtleties and moral education within sport. Such 'race logic' has lingered in the organization and culture of many modern sports and in wider societies.

Racist 'explanations' of the athletic capabilities of non-whites have continued to be premised upon crude myths and absurd simplifications of Darwinian theory. One American basketball coach claimed blacks outran whites because, back in Africa, 'the lions and tigers had caught all the slow ones' (Roberts and Olsen 1989: 45). The 'Middle Passage' myth claimed that only the toughest Africans survived capture, transportation and enslavement and then went on to mate and to spawn a micro-race of super-slaves and super-athletes (Hoberman 1997: 78, 194–5; Miller 1998: 135). Of course, such myths lack supporting historical evidence, ignore the many social reasons (such as early selection, specialization and elite coaching) for black athletic success, and conveniently fail to be applied to whites, who, after centuries of deadly wars, pandemics and climactic disasters, might otherwise have been expected to produce their own super-race of Anglo-Saxon survivors.

Sailes (1998: 190–6) outlines some other false assumptions regarding African-American athleticism, including the following.

- *Matriarchal theory* 'Absent fathers' in black families mean sports become outlets for male children's hostility and frustration; the sports coach becomes a surrogate father. Counter-research confirms young athletes are suspicious of coaches and often hail from two-parent families.
- *Mandingo theory* According to one sport journalist, blacks are physically advanced on account of careful breeding by slave owners (Wiggins 1989: 179). Counter-evidence demonstrates that most slaves chose their own mates, that slave-owners commonly raped or otherwise sexually engaged slave women, and that any possible gene pool in slave breeding would have been lost by the early twentieth century.
- *Psychological theory* African Americans lack the leadership qualities of intelligence and emotional self-control. Yet this myth creates a self-fulfilling prophecy: African Americans are excluded from leadership roles *because* the myth influences the recruitment policies of white sports officials.

- *Dumb Jock theory* African Americans enter further or higher education as athletes and cannot match non-athletes academically. Conversely, research indicates athletes marginally outperform non-athletes academically; lower grades among some African-American athletes are primarily a result of lack of resources during earlier education.

A further argument, known as the *Bell Curve* thesis, claimed that high African-American fertility rates (possibly linked to larger genitals) were depressing US intelligence levels and that African Americans should turn to athletics to compensate for their genetically weak intellects and to increase clan 'self-esteem' (Herrnstein and Murray 1994). This theory has been justifiably criticized for combining poor evidence with neo-conservative, racist assumptions (Hoberman 1997: 3–4).

Genetic theories of 'race'-specific sport performance have been advanced by the television journalist Jon Entine (2000), who argued that specific population groups ('races') possess distinctive genetic features which produce physiological advantages in specific sports. Hence, Entine observed, those of West African background (including African Americans and Afro-Caribbeans) dominate sprinting, East and North Africans dominate distance running, Eurasian whites excel in field and strength sports, and East Asians prioritize gymnastics.

In the interests of genuinely interdisciplinary research, it would be wrong simply to dismiss this type of analysis on the grounds of perceived 'racism' (Wiggins 1989: 185). Nevertheless, genetic arguments are not persuasive when subjected to close scrutiny. Genetics would otherwise require African Americans to have implausibly high physical advantages over Caucasians; in basketball this would measure 27 to 1. Moreover, sports such as basketball, sprinting, baseball (notably pitching), tennis and volleyball all require similar 'bioenergetics', yet African Americans predominate only in the first two. Hence, social rather than physical explanations are more persuasive when accounting for different sport performances across ethnicities and nationalities (Hunter 1998: 97–8). Genetics arguments underplay the roles played by sport coaches, scientists and institutions in identifying, training and maximizing the performance outcomes of elite athletes. Greater variations in athletic capability exist *within* each ethnicity than between elite athletes of different skin colour (Harpalani 1998: 118). Elite athletes are themselves already exceptional performers; hence it is not valid to use them as the basis for generalizations about large population groups (Koppett 1981: 205).

To elaborate our understanding of 'race' and ethnicity within sport, I turn now to examine specific histories of racism, ethnic intolerance and cultural struggle through brief national and regional case studies. These histories are underpinned by intersecting social divisions, notably in relation to gender and the marginalization and exclusion of women.

Racism and sport: outlining international histories

The United States

Racist oppression of African Americans within sport began during slavery, for example as plantation owners promoted boxing among slaves with heavy wagers placed on fights. After the Civil War, slavery was abolished, but 'Jim Crow' laws, particularly in the Southern states, served to institutionalize racial divisions or segregation at everyday level, so that African Americans were often segregated in recreational parks, sports stadiums and sport competitions, such as the 'Negro Leagues' in baseball.

In sport and other social fields, African Americans fought to compete on fair terms and for social equality and political emancipation. In 1908, the world heavyweight championship victory of Jack Johnson over Jim Jeffries (the 'Great White Hope') undermined white supremacist ideologies and sparked riots across America against African Americans (Harris 1998: 5–6). During the 1930s, Joe Louis (boxing) and Jesse Owens (athletics) became the first African-American national sports heroes for whites; unlike Johnson, who enjoyed conspicuous consumption and dalliances with white women, both athletes 'knew their place' in white eyes and successfully represented the United States in competition. Owens dominated the 1936 Berlin Olympics, enhancing his popularity by defeating the representatives of Hitler's 'master race', but the athlete's life afterwards involved numerous financial struggles.

In team sports, African-American athletes struggled to break segregation. The 'color line' was most symbolically challenged in 1947 when Jackie Robinson joined baseball's Brooklyn Dodgers; though he was not the best African-American baseball player, it was hoped (wrongly) that Robinson's military and college career would appease racist whites. Later desegregation was often slow: the Boston Red Sox were the last major baseball team to recruit an African American, in 1959; American football's Washington Redskins held out until 1962;

and, in basketball, artificial restrictions on team composition were introduced so that all-white teams still reached the NCAA finals until 1966 (Reiss 1991: 121; Roberts and Olsen 1989: 39–45). At desegregated clubs, African-American athletes received inferior contracts and accommodation and often endured abusive testing by coaches, allegedly in preparation for mistreatment by opposing players.

The African-American civil rights movement exploded into sport at the 1968 Mexico Olympics when champion sprinters Jon Carlos and Tommie Smith gave the famous 'Unity' salute on the medal podium. Prior to the Games, the Olympic Project for Human Rights, led by the sociologist (and, in Gramscian terms, organic intellectual) Harry Edwards, had publicized the exploitation of black athletes and advocated boycotting the event (Edwards 1969; Spivey 1985).

Sport retains a highly ambiguous meaning for African-American communities. African-American predominance in some sports since the 1970s has inspired community pride and defiance (Boyd 1997: 132–3). Yet African Americans still experience significant occupational segregation in sport, in being underrepresented in key decision-making roles such as assistant coach in college sport (Cunningham 2012). Meanwhile, celebrity athletes such as Michael Jordan and Tiger Woods are typically constructed as having transcended their African-American backgrounds and are in effect 'whitened' to reach white consumer audiences, who in turn avoid facing issues of wider societal racism (Andrews 2001; Carrington 2010; Cashmore 2008; Leonard and King 2011).

The sport–racism nexus snares other ethnic minorities in North America. European civilization entailed the systematic annihilation and the annexation of the homelands of Native Americans. Despite contributing the stickball games that became modern lacrosse and embracing ice-hockey in good numbers, Native Americans in Canada have endured institutionalized racism that still undermines full sports participation. In the United States, major league sports teams such as the Washington Redskins, Atlanta Braves and Cleveland Indians have utilized 'pseudo-Indian' mascots and symbols, thereby demeaning and disempowering Native American culture and reinforcing the subaltern position of indigenous peoples within American society (Staurowsky 2000).

Africa

In colonial Africa, sports were integral to the British imperial mission, which sought to mould a particular model of racialized male identity

– that is, as 'a universal Tom Brown: loyal, brave, truthful, a gentleman and, if at all possible, a Christian' (Mangan 1998: 18).

Before colonization, many African societies had developed extensive physical or movement cultures. In what became colonial Kenya, early British settlers were astonished by the jumping feats of Watussi peoples and distance running by the Maasai. Yet these forms of physical culture were forcibly replaced by modern sports that were rationalized (measuring time, distance, performance), bureaucratized (managed by sports officials and pedagogues) and 'civilizing' (in manliness, obedience and rule-following), while also diverting local people away from 'lascivious' customs and political unrest (Bale and Sang 1996).

White elites in British colonies tended to embrace sports (especially rugby and cricket) with even greater fervour than their counterparts in Britain. Conversely, among African schoolboys, academic rather than sporting pursuits were seen as better avenues to social mobility and political autonomy (Mangan 1987: 164–5). Nevertheless, in African townships, more accessible and 'culture-neutral' sports such as boxing and football were most popular; football teams also enhanced local identity and independence from church and state (Martin 1995; Ranger 1987; Giulianotti 1999: 7–8; Alegi 2010).

Sport represented an important cultural space in anti-colonial and pro-independence struggles, most obviously in South Africa. Formally established by white elites in 1948, Apartheid in South Africa was rooted in the systematic segregation and subjugation of different 'races'. Sport competition was integral to white South African identity, hence the anti-Apartheid movements exerted strong pressure to exclude South African teams from all international sport, particularly during the 1970s and 1980s (Guelke 1993: 152–3). In response, the Apartheid regime organized 'rebel' cricket and rugby tours featuring foreign 'mercenary' players, but opposition groups mounted increasingly effective campaigns of disruption (Booth 1998). Meanwhile, for Nelson Mandela and many other nationalist leaders imprisoned by the Apartheid regime, football was organized and played with great commitment as a source of personal respite and a focus for collective resistance (Korr and Close 2009).

The Apartheid system collapsed in 1994, when free elections were won by the African National Congress and Mandela was sworn in as president. Upon its re-entry to the international community, sport came to provide some powerful symbolic moments of a post-Apartheid South Africa, notably when Nelson Mandela donned a South African rugby shirt (previously worn only by whites) to celebrate victory in the 1995 World Cup finals, 'non-white' athletes (such as Ashwell Prince, Hashim Amla and Chester Williams) starred in South African teams, and global mega-events in football, rugby and cricket were successfully hosted. Yet, despite a growing black middle class, very deep racialized divisions remain: in 2011, black households earned only 16 per cent of white household income, and over 40 per cent of South Africans (almost all are black) lived below the poverty line (Hofmeyer 2012). In sport, whites still dominate resources at the everyday level as well as the places in many national sport teams. Moreover, the hosting of mega-events has promoted neoliberal urban development policies which benefit whites and the growing black middle classes, while having negative impacts, such as mass evictions and loss of spending on basic social services, on poor black communities (Merrett 1994: 115; Cornelissen 2011).

In the broader post-colonial context, many African nations have endured exceptional difficulties and hardships. Sub-Saharan African nations fill the lowest places in the United Nations *Human Development Index* (United Nations 2014). Many African nations have suffered the mass traumas of war and famine; dependency relationships with Global North nations, corporations and institutions; crippling debts, largely because of high borrowing, political corruption and instability, and ill-advised 'development' strategies; and greater social inequalities following the imposition of free-market policies by the IMF and World Bank.

African sport is inevitably shaped by these powerful political and economic processes and crises (Armstrong and Giulianotti 2004). African elite professional sport is deeply embedded within the global sport system, feeding wealthier regions with a 'brawn drain' of cheap African talent – for example, low-cost football players hired by French, Belgian and other European clubs and Kenyan runners recruited cheaply to represent American colleges or to change nationality (such as to Qatar or Bahrain) to compete for these new nations (Bale 1991b; *The Economist*, 28 August 2003; Giulianotti and Robertson 2009). Elite African football clubs struggle to continue, typically relying on foreign transfers and personal philanthropy to survive financially, while local fans are drawn to television coverage of English and other European leagues.

In response to Africa's deep structural problems and humanitarian disasters, international governmental organizations (such as the United Nations and Commonwealth Secretariat), national governments and non-governmental organizations (NGOs) have undertaken development and peace-building programmes across the continent.

As I discuss in chapter 12, sport has played a significant role here as a tool of social intervention, for example to facilitate normal social contact in divided societies, the involvement of children in education, and better health practices among young people to safeguard against HIV/AIDS. The long-term impact of such initiatives is uncertain. What is clear is that any real solution must go far beyond sport, to address the fundamental issues behind the continuing disempowerment and exploitation of African populations.

Australia

The making of modern Australian society has been underpinned by the racist annihilation and colonization of indigenous Australians (Aboriginals). British colonial settlers mounted extermination campaigns against Aboriginals and then placed remaining indigenous peoples under 'protective' control in segregated 'reserves'. Some Aboriginals were introduced to sport, with occasional, exceptional results: for example, an Aboriginal cricket team was established and toured England in 1868 and the Aborigine Charlie Samuels was Australia's leading all-round athlete in the nineteenth century. Between the world wars, to enter sport, Aborigines were required either to disguise themselves (as Maoris or West Indians) or to endure highly prejudicial and patronizing treatment by white Australians: the brilliant Aboriginal cricketer Eddie Gilbert was denied competitive openings and required a chaperone to travel in white society (Booth and Tatz 2000: 131–2). Australian state control over Aboriginals extended to 'stolen generations' of children being removed systematically from their parents to be placed with white guardians. Prominent Aboriginal athletes endured racist exclusion, although some entered athletics, rugby league, boxing and Australian Rules football. During the 1960s, some Aboriginal athletes (notably football's Charles Perkins) drew public attention to their racist experiences in sport, thereby connecting their personal troubles to deep political issues.

The political and structural barriers to sporting equality have remained daunting. In the run-up to hosting the 1982 Commonwealth Games, the Queensland state government passed draconian legislation that prevented Aboriginals from protesting against racial discrimination (Booth and Tatz 1994). Planned civil rights protests by Aboriginal groups at the 2000 Sydney Olympics were subjected to divide-and-rule criticism and pressure from Australian media and sports institutions (Lenskyj 2000: 77). Anti-racism campaigns made advances in domestic sport, notably in Australian Rules football, which led the AFL to appoint a 'racial and religious vilification' officer. Yet some media commentators dismissed such campaigning as misunderstanding on-field 'gamesmanship' by white players, while also mocking politically vocal Aboriginal players (Nadel 1998: 241–5). At the everyday level, the distribution of resources continued to be still stratified by 'race', with 'sports facilities' in Aboriginal communities often consisting of little more than an unmarked dusty paddock in which to practise football or cricket (Booth and Tatz 2000: 202–3).

Britain

In Britain, the participation of non-European individuals in sport has a lengthy history. In the 1880s, Arthur Wharton was a champion sprinter and England's first black professional football player, while high-caste South Asian cricketers have long represented the English national team, notably Prince Kumar Shri Ranjitsinhji ('Ranji') in the 1890s. In tandem with the decline of Britain's empire, Afro-Caribbean and Asian migration to the UK began in earnest in the 1950s. In sport, Afro-Caribbean athletes became increasingly prominent in British elite football, cricket, boxing, and track and field disciplines, particularly from the 1970s onwards, while players of South Asian extraction also figured strongly in cricket (Back, Crabbe and Solomos 2001; Malcolm 2013).

Inevitably, racism has permeated Afro-Caribbean and Asian sporting experiences. Sport spectators, notably through the 1980s, routinely directed racist insults at elite black athletes such as football's John Barnes (in England) and Mark Walters (in Scotland). Anti-racism campaigns gained traction when black players expressed collective disgust at such treatment. While such racism is now formally outlawed, it is still experienced at the everyday level, and deep-seated forms of institutionalized racism and structural exclusion remain. In sports such as football, few non-whites hold leading decision-making roles as team coaches or chief executives (Bradbury 2013). Underlying racist stereotyping in education continues to lead teachers and coaches into channelling particular ethnic minorities into or (in the case of Asians and football) out of particular sports (Burdsey 2011). For a mix of economic and socio-cultural reasons (such as high admission prices and persistently unwelcoming environments), ethnic minorities in poor communities have relatively low levels of attendance at elite football and cricket fixtures.

The cultural politics of 'race' have been particularly apparent in English cricket. In a particularly notorious episode, the England cricket selectors bowed to pressure from the Apartheid regime by initially omitting the brilliant non-white cricketer Basil D'Oliveira from a touring party for South Africa; only after one player dropped out was D'Oliveira selected, whereupon the South Africans objected, and the tour was cancelled. English cricket counties such as Yorkshire, which had long hosted large ethnic minority populations, were often slow to recruit local players of South Asian extraction. In the 1990s, the leading Conservative politician Norman (later Lord) Tebbit stoked racist sentiments by recommending a 'cricket test' for incoming immigrants (in effect, non-whites from old British colonies): those cheering for their nation of origin, and not for England, should not be permitted to stay (Marqusee 1994: 137–41). And yet those cricketers with Asian or Caribbean backgrounds who do play for England have been accused of lacking patriotism and effort (Henderson 1995). Such inherently racist arguments grossly misunderstand the complex, multi-layered and fluid nature of ethnic and cultural identities (cf. Burdsey 2006; Finn 1999). For example, the British-Pakistani boxer Amir Khan and his supporters display a mix of Bolton (his home town), English, British, Pakistani and Muslim symbols and identities (Burdsey 2006). In recent years, issues of 'Islamophobia' in the UK have been highlighted by social scientists, notably regarding the impacts on British Muslim players in cricket (Burdsey 2010).

* * *

These brief historical portraits, when read alongside the discussion of cricket in chapter 4, highlight the utility of the Cultural Studies approach for examining the cultural politics of sport. On one side, institutionalized racism in sport has played significant roles in the broader cultural domination of white populations over other weaker populations, such as through the eradication of indigenous physical or movement cultures, exclusion from sport facilities, or the reproduction and intensification of social inequalities. Yet, for subordinate ethnic groups, sport has also constituted a popular space for pleasurable physical recreation and public participation and for forms of counter-hegemonic resistance, in terms of pursuing social recognition and inclusion and for the exploration and expression of collective identities. I turn now to consider these dual processes – 'racial' domination and empowerment in sport – in more detail with reference to the key sociological issues of social stratification and cultural meaning.

Sport, 'race' and social stratification

Analysis of social stratification enables us to explore in more detail some of the ways in which institutionalized racism emerges and is experienced within sport.

First, we may examine how sport connects to broader social stratification and opportunities for social mobility. In North America, the 'social facts' are that professional sport offers few mobility openings: for example, despite high representation in the NBA, young African-American males have only a 135,800 to 1 chance of making the grade (LaFeber 2002: 92). In poor communities, the chasing of sport careers may reflect very limited everyday evidence of labour market mobility elsewhere and also the everyday direction of African-American school pupils into sports rather than academic pursuits (Cashmore 1982: 98–109).

Second, ethnic differences in sports participation reflect the deep structural intersections of 'race' with class and gender (Carrington 2010; Crenshaw 1989; McCall 2005). In North America, the leading sociologist William Julius Wilson (1978, 2009) has argued that class rather than 'race' has greater impact on the life chances and experiences of African Americans, particularly those in poverty. In sport, class and 'race' intersections are demonstrated most extremely in how elite sports such as sailing, golf or Olympic equestrian disciplines have produced few if any leading black competitors and in how working-class African-American involvement in baseball has declined, partly through the sport's move from free-to-air to subscription television and the restricted spaces in poor neighbourhoods for playing and practising.

The intersection of gender and 'race' is registered in how women from ethnic minorities experience a dual oppression in sport and other social fields. Patriarchal ideological pressures serve to discourage girls and women from ethnic minorities from participating in sport. Social class also intersects with gender and 'race' to underpin these forms of social exclusion in sport. In the Global North, at the everyday level, black women have disproportionately low access to sport resources and, in the context of neoliberalism, have been badly affected by the closure or commercialization of public sport facilities. In the North American education system, legal measures to counteract gender discrimination and inequalities in sport have largely helped whites rather than ethnic minorities; thus, African-American girls and women have low participation rates in school sport and remain hugely underrepresented in almost all intercollegiate sport

(*New York Times*, 10 June 2012). In the Global South, notably in Africa, material and ideological divisions along the lines of gender, 'race' and class are often more extreme and are strongly manifested through sport (cf. Shehu 2010); thus, in response, a significant volume of sport-related work to promote development in the Global South is focused on the empowerment of women (Hayhurst 2013). In some regions, particularly some Islamic societies in the Middle East or South Asia, women's freedom to participate in sport may be legally proscribed, strongly restricted or controlled by patriarchal structures and influences, or undertaken in closely regulated ways (Zaman 1997). At the elite level, in the Global North, successful black female athletes tend to receive lower levels of public acclaim or commercial reward. Where racist prejudices appear to be challenged, other forms of symbolic domination are intensified: for example, the sexualization in media coverage of the late American athlete Florence Griffith-Joyner expanded as her ethnic identity became less apparent (Vertinsky and Captain 1998: 552–3).

Third, we may consider the representation and stratification of ethnic groups within specific sports. Notably, in major sports, ethnic minorities are hugely underrepresented in decision-making positions as head coaches, chief executives and general managers. In European football, less than 1 per cent of executives and white-collar officials are drawn from ethnic minorities, even in locations with high cultural diversity. There is little overt racism, but underlying racial stereotypes on leadership requirements and 'cultural incompatibility' serve to 'filter out' minorities from these roles (Bradbury 2013). In North American sports, annual 'report cards' on the hiring practices of major league and college sports highlight the continuing underrepresentation of ethnic minorities (particularly African Americans) in key roles.[15]

One research focus has been on how 'stacking' represents a significant form of institutionalized racism in elite team sports. Stacking involves the allocation of athletes into playing positions on the basis of 'racial' stereotyping. Where it occurs, white athletes are typically stacked into central positions associated with intelligence, decision-making, leadership, calmness and dependability and non-whites into more peripheral positions requiring explosive physical powers (especially speed), unpredictability and irregular participation. Sociological research has demonstrated at least the prior prevalence of stacking in sport. Loy and McElvogue's (1970) pioneering US study found African-American athletes were overrepresented in positions that emphasize athleticism, such as baseball's outfield and American football's defence and offence backfield. Similarly, Aboriginals in rugby league and Australian Rules football have been stacked into non-central positions, while, in New Zealand rugby, Polynesians are deemed to lack mental coolness, inevitably affecting their positional allocation (Hallinan 1991; Miller 1998: 138). In English football, black players were underrepresented in central midfield and featured more obviously as attacking wingers, to exploit their pace and unpredictability (Maguire 1991). In Brazil, when the national football team lost the final match in the 1950 World Cup finals, the unfortunate black goalkeeper, Moacir Barbosa, shouldered most of the blame; Brazil did not field another black player in this central position for a World Cup match for more than fifty years (Goldblatt 2014).

While stacking in sport appears to correlate with racist ideologies, other structural factors may be at play. For example, the 'unequal skill development' theory indicates that young people from ethnic minorities, particularly from lower-class backgrounds, lack access to the crucial resources required to develop key skills associated with 'intelligent' positions such as catcher or pitcher in baseball. These resources include good-quality sport facilities, specialist equipment, professional coaching and well-organized sport competitions (Sack, Singh and Thiel 2005: 313–14).

Uneven progress has been made in confronting some of these issues. In American football, the 'Rooney Rule' was introduced in 2003 and requires all NFL teams to interview candidates from minority backgrounds when head coach and senior management posts become available (Duru 2011). However, the rule has had insufficient impact, with many interviewees from minority backgrounds considering that they are treated merely as 'paper candidates' for posts. Moreover, the rule should be extended to encompass other positions, such as assistant coach on NFL teams or head coach in college teams, which are crucial for gaining experience before taking top positions with NFL teams.

Cultural, ideological and aesthetic issues

The contemporary cultural, ideological and aesthetic aspects of 'race' in sport are complex and form a strong site for critical Cultural Studies methods of investigation and analysis. Here, I explore overt and more subtle forms of racism, together with the complex issues of domination and resistance surrounding minority identities and aesthetics in sport.

Overt and other forms of racism

Despite significant advances, minority elite athletes continue to be subjected to racist representation, interpretation or treatment. First, while overt expressions of racism within sport have declined significantly, they are far from disappearing. In more explicit cases, the public and media, and often corporate sponsors and sport authorities, tend to be far more critical than would have been the case in the 1980s or earlier. In golf, when Tiger Woods won the 1997 US Masters with a record score, the leading American golfer, Fuzzy Zoeller, made a racist comment about African-American food habits; Zoeller later apologized but lost several of his sponsors. In April 2014, Donald Sterling, owner of the NBA's Los Angeles Clippers team, was exposed making highly racist remarks to a girlfriend; following widespread political, public, media and sponsor criticism, Sterling was banned for life from the sport.

In European football in recent years, notably in Southern and Eastern Europe, black players have been booed and jeered systematically by spectators. In Italy, AC Milan's black players Kevin-Prince Boateng and Kevin Constant walked off the pitch during different games in 2013 in protest at their racist treatment by supporters. In 2012, the largest supporters' group at the leading Russian side, Zenit St Petersburg, called for the recruitment of only white, heterosexual players. In English football, the Chelsea and England captain, John Terry, was fined and suspended for four games for 'using abusive language' (specifically the phrase 'fucking black cunt') towards an opponent in 2012, and the Liverpool striker Luis Suarez was fined and suspended for eight games for racially abusing an opponent in 2012. Subsequently, the European football governing body, UEFA, announced minimum ten-match bans for players and officials found guilty of racism.

The rise of social media – notably through Twitter, Facebook, messaging services and blogs – has provided a relatively new and instant outlet for the expression of racist comments (sometimes referred to as 'twacism'), particularly from sport fans. For example, in 2012, when the black NHL player Joel Ward scored a play-off winner for the Washington Capitals against the Boston Bruins, he was subjected to a large volume of racist abuse on Twitter. Elite football, rugby and cricket have all witnessed individual cases in which athletes have been similarly abused.

Second, more subtle forms of racism – known as 'enlightened racism' – may be evident with respect to the seemingly positive receptions of non-white star athletes and other such celebrities by white audiences. Despite such adulation, 'enlightened racism' occurs on occasions when these non-white athletes appear to 'fail' in sport or in other contexts, and the response of white audiences is to interpret or to explain these results with reference to particular 'race logics', notably racist stereotypes (cf. Jhally and Lewis 1992). For example, English football coaches and former players tended to discuss ethnic minority players such as Patrick Vieira and Theo Walcott, in racialized terms, as 'rather impulsive' or as not having a 'footballing brain' for making the correct on-field decisions (Rosbrook-Thompson 2013: 12).

Third, we may also consider the ways in which 'whiteness' is constructed in sport. Whiteness refers to 'the powerful processes that privilege white voices, images, or imagined communities' (Hylton 2008: 90). One focus here may be on how sport officials and media commentators refer to the ethnicity of non-white athletes but not the white identity of other athletes; in effect, the 'whiteness' of the latter is 'silent', taken for granted, and thus presented as 'the norm' in elite sport (Long and Hylton 2002). Moreover, in sports such as skiing or swimming there is a 'hegemony of whiteness' which, through a mix of economic and cultural factors, serves to segregate participation along 'racial' lines (Harrison 2013). In broad terms, the focus on 'whiteness' and enlightened racism represents two ways in which 'critical race theory' may contribute to the sociological study of institutionalized racism in sport.

Fourth, we should recognize that the public meaning of elite athletes is not fixed and singular but, instead, polysemous – that is, these athletes may be interpreted in different ways by diverse individuals and social groups. For example, depending on the audience, the African-American boxer Muhammad Ali might be said to have had many different public identities, including brilliant boxer, foolishly brave fighter, civil rights campaigner, Muslim convert, brash self-publicist, business dupe, sexual patriarch, humanitarian and tragic physical figure. Certainly, athletes such as Ali have been subjected to dominant forms of racist interpretation. Yet, if we accept that the public identities of elite athletes are polysemous, then we have the basis on which to challenge and to contest these negative or racialized representations, including with reference to issues of 'enlightened racism' and 'whiteness'.

'Race' ideologies and sport aesthetics

A further issue for sociological consideration concerns aesthetics within sport in relation to 'race'. Here we need recall Cultural Studies' definition of popular culture as being fashioned by disadvantaged and oppressed peoples from the materials and symbols that mark their domination. Thus, as a form of empowerment, minority groups construct distinctive aesthetic practices, traditions and codes within sport, often as symbolic challenges to dominant cultural meanings and customs. For example, in North American baseball, and in marked contrast to leading white teams, the 'Negro Leagues' during the period of segregation were renowned for spectacular and visually entertaining play. African Americans transformed elite-level basketball from the 1950s onwards, through urban or 'street basketball' playing styles that are fast, skilful and expressive and which came to dominate the NBA and NCAA tournaments. In football, through most of the twentieth century, South American players and teams developed techniques, skills and styles that differed markedly from European methods. Brazil provides a particularly powerful illustration, as Brazilian players (particularly non-white artists such as Pele, Rivaldo, Ronaldinho and Neymar) are associated in global football with 'the beautiful game' (*jogo bonito*). Indeed, the Brazilian sociologist, public intellectual and politician Gilberto Freyre (1964, 1967) had argued positively that Brazil was developing a 'mixed-race', 'Lusotropical civilization'; one cultural manifestation was provided in football, through the particular technical skills and forms of artistry that were being created by working-class 'mulatto' players.

In contradistinction, a more structuralist type of Cultural Studies approach would remind us that, in the cultural politics of sport, the materials, symbols and ideologies of dominant groups will tend to hold the upper hand. Thus, when reading the aesthetic aspects of sport, the 'race hierarchy' may continue to be a dominant force, even when forms of minority empowerment appear to be emerging. For example, white elites own and control top-level North American basketball, while whites dominate attendances; by contrast, we might interpret African-American players as being hired to perform like 'magical minstrels' before these audiences (Gems 1995). Similar arguments might be made about North American baseball and about European football clubs which hire Latin American players. In addition, there may be occasions when non-white athletes internalize dominant racial stereotypes as forms of self-identity and self-knowledge in order to explain their 'natural' sporting styles, attributes or limitations.

Viewed in this way, what appears as cultural self-expression may be underpinned by subtle forms of ethnic or racial stereotyping.

The theoretical tensions – between domination and empowerment in the construction of sport-related aesthetics – may be succinctly demonstrated in the double-edged meaning of 'cool pose'. For Majors (1990), 'cool pose' represents the celebration and corporeal display of black masculinity: as part of an 'expressive lifestyle', cool pose 'transforms the mundane into the sublime and makes the routine spectacular' and connects to the particular styles of play by black males in sport (ibid.: 111). Yet cool pose is also culturally problematic: it may undermine the pursuit of a strong education and positive relationships with women; moreover, its meaning appears to be anchored in the dominant discourses that racially construct African-American male identity with particular forms of athleticism and corporeality. Thus, despite its creative expressivity, 'cool pose' is never quite dislocated from the cultural assumptions that are held and inculcated by white-dominated institutions and structures with regard to African Americans. In this way, a specific type of cultural and aesthetic identity represents both a form of personal and collective empowerment and a further confirmation of social relations of domination.

Racism and ethnicity: cultural prejudices and intolerance

Discussion of race and sport should not be restricted to 'colour-coded' racist treatment of non-whites. Indeed, forms of 'race logic' have been directed towards many ethno-national groups or ethnic communities. For example, one extensive study of international media discourses on sport indicated that particular 'race logics' were applied to many regions and nationalities. Media discourses tended to present Scandinavian athletes as 'cool', rational whites *par excellence*; Southern Europeans and 'Celtic races' as more fiery, temperamental and often physically courageous; Latin Americans as possessing a natural flamboyance; and Africans as having an 'unscientific, irrational' nature – hence references were made to their 'spontaneous', even 'magical' types of play (O'Donnell 1994).

Thus, in broad terms, we need to extend the critical analysis of 'race' to encompass forms of discrimination, prejudice, bigotry and intolerance that are directed towards many diverse communities along ethno-religious, ethno-linguistic and ethno-national lines. In such cases, as with minorities of African descent, sport may also provide a popular cultural venue both for the exploration and expression of collective identities and for the contestation of marginalization or oppression.

We might look for example at the case of Irish Catholics in the UK. In Northern Ireland, the maltreatment of Irish Catholics' sporting institutions (especially football clubs) reflected more deeply entrenched forms of ethno-religious discrimination. In Scotland, the ethno-religious antagonism between the Glasgow clubs of Rangers (associated with the Protestant, British Unionist majority) and Celtic (with origins in the large Irish-Catholic community) is routinely described as 'sectarianism', though for some the term camouflages rather than exposes anti-Irish racism (Finn 1990: 5–6). Sport, notably football, has been one domain through which Irish Catholics have pursued competitive relations with the majority (Protestant, British) community, while also exploring 'dual identities' as Scots and Irish Catholics. For some analysts, anti-Irish songs and abuse by Rangers fans are archaic rituals of rivalry in a society with no paramilitary presence and low measurements of religious discrimination (Bruce 2000). Others argue that anti-Irish discourses disclose continuing, unrecognized problems in Scottish society (Finn 1994b; 2000). In recent years, sectarianism and bigotry have been major policy areas for the Scottish government through legislation and public campaigns, with the focus on tackling abuse or maltreatment on the grounds of any ethnic, religious or national identity.

In North America, while sports have been viewed as functional for the acculturation and Americanization of white immigrants, media and public discourses have at different times expressed substantial intolerance towards Irish Catholics, Italians, Jews, Poles and others. In American football, at Notre Dame college in the 1920s, Knute Rockne assembled a highly talented, multi-ethnic team of American footballers that was regularly disparaged by such insulting nicknames as 'Fighting Irish', 'Horrible Hibernians' and 'Dumb Micks'. Sports journalists mocked the striking surnames of Polish players, although many great coaches insisted Poles were the very best American footballers (Oriard 2001: 261–7). Jewish and Italian athletes were subjected to explicit racist stereotyping, but their successes directly challenged such characterizations. Jewish-American newspapers argued that American footballers such as Benny Friedman and Sammy Behr refuted racist depictions of 'weak, cowardly Jews'. Jewish athletes during the interwar years were viewed by fellow Jews as symbols of anti-racist resistance; for the Jewish writer Meyer Liben, 'These heroes were fighting for us – each hook, pass, basket was a kind of blow against oppression' (quoted in Levine 1992: 272). Thus, overall, as these brief illustrations indicate, racism in sport – and the cultural contestation of racist treatment – needs to be understood in its broadest sense, as directed at many white as well as non-white groups.

Concluding comments

In this chapter, I have provided a critical sociological analysis of 'race' and racism within sport. The aim here has been to build on the previous chapter to advance a form of Cultural Studies analysis on domination and contestation with respect to 'race' and ethnic minorities within sport. In exploring the modern history of racist ideologies, I have argued that, while 'scientific racism' may be discredited, we continue to live with its underlying influences. Short cultural histories of specific national and regional locations highlight the ethnocentric, imperialistic and racist roots of sport's diverse inculcation across the globe. Sport's cultural politics are reflected by anti-racism initiatives and the advances of ethnically marginalized communities within sporting institutions. Yet 'racialized' forms of social stratification and cultural practice continue to survive in relatively covert ways, such as through 'stacking' in sports teams, in the 'enlightened racism' of popular culture audiences, and in the reified 'whiteness' of many sports. Even black sports aesthetics harbour some problematic bases through some self-racializing practices and identities.

The sociological reading of racism within sport should broaden its geographical and epistemological remits. Much sport sociology on 'race' retraces the Atlantic triangle that has connected the UK, the Caribbean and the United States since the earliest days of modern slavery – all the while, of course, largely omitting the continent that actually supplied slaves in the first instance. The vast geographical and social expanses of Africa (excepting South Africa), Latin America, and both Southern and Eastern Europe are insufficiently examined. Furthermore, substantial research needs to be undertaken into the ways in which Arab and Muslim populations are portrayed in the context of global sport.

Additionally, we should reflect more deeply upon the ontological roots of racism to explore how the core features of modern racism are not 'colour-coded' and culturally exclusive but isolate other collectives for prejudicial treatment. Indeed, the systematically negative treatment of some lower-class whites in the Global North

– caricatured as 'white trash' in North America or as 'chavs' in the UK – has substantial racist undertones (cf. Wray and Newitz 1997).

Since the 1980s, sport has been a focus for more and more anti-racism campaigns and educational initiatives that are often inspired by non-governmental organizations and key figures from ethnic minorities. Social scientists have opportunities to contribute to these activities, as well as to make calls for the transformation of the governance and structure of sport in order to challenge racism and intolerance. Moreover, deeper empirical and theoretical analyses of 'race' can have the greater benefit of tackling more concertedly the social roots of racism. Such approaches move us beyond seeking merely technical, incremental solutions to racism, such as arresting abusive sports fans or increasing the proportion of non-whites in 'central' playing positions. If the nature of race logic *per se* is confronted, then social scientists will be in a much stronger position to develop a robust, normative redefinition of sport as a cultural field that is free of racism, prejudice and ethnic intolerance.

Questions for discussion

1 What different racist myths have surrounded the treatment of non-white groups in sport?
2 How have non-white and other minority ethnic groups struggled to gain greater recognition and better rights within sport?
3 What forms of racist 'stacking' or social exclusion continue to occur within sport?
4 How does racism in sport impact upon some minority white groups?
5 How might sport be transformed in order to challenge and ultimately to remove racism and ethnic intolerance?

6

Gender and Sexuality in Sport: Playing against Patriarchy

Modern sport has always been a crucial cultural domain for the construction and reproduction of dominant, heterosexual masculine identities. Sports institutions at elite and grassroots levels still harbour formal and informal restrictions on the full participation of women and sexual minorities. Yet critical social scientific studies of sport highlight the capacity of these social groups to contest such marginalization.

To explore these issues, this chapter is organized into four main parts. First, I outline the historical gendering of modern sport. Second, I advance a detailed social history and critical sociology of women's experiences and potentialities within sport. Third, I examine the position of sexual minorities within sport. Fourth, I address sociological issues relating to masculinity within sport.

The making of sexist sport

Historically, modern sport has been a key social space for the production and reproduction of different kinds of patriarchal social relations and identities, in which power is held by men and women are confined to subordinate roles and positions. Early modern sporting activities were often part of a raucous male subculture: for example, up to the late nineteenth century in Britain, North America and Australasia, many blood sports such as 'ratting' and crude pugilism contests featured male subcultures of heavy gambling, camaraderie, and varying levels of violence (Brailsford 1985: 126; Cashman 1995: 206; Gorn and Goldstein 1993: 70–5). The rise of the British 'games cult' from the second half of the nineteenth century provided the basis for the cultivation of a new masculine ideal – the 'muscular Christian gentleman' – which embodied the dominant bourgeois, patriarchal and imperialist ideologies within the British Empire. Sport played a crucial role in promoting muscular Christianity: on the fields of play, boys and young men were required to display 'stoicism, hardiness and endurance' and to subordinate themselves to the team cause (Mangan 1986: 147). Those who shirked sport were presented in highly negative terms, as having a weak moral compass, degenerate physique and effeminate character.

'Muscular Christianity' was deeply inculcated across Britain's colonies and dominions and spread to other parts among the Anglophile elites, particularly in Europe and the Americas. In turn, these patriarchal sport-based ideologies were 'glocalized', in being adapted by local males to suit their needs and interests. For example, in Australian Rules football, true men were deemed to display 'courage', while critics of the game's violent aspects were disparaged as 'cowards' or 'old women' (Booth and Tatz 2000: 68). In rugby, the white Afrikaners of South Africa cultivated a distinctive masculine, nationalist identity that emphasized 'ruggedness, endurance, forcefulness and determination' (Grundlingh 1994: 186–7). In American football, leading college teams (Yale, Princeton and Harvard) presented the violent game as a crucial pedagogical instrument for young men intent on pursuing professional leadership roles (Sammons 1997: 384). Also in the United States, baseball served to shape working-class masculine identities centred on myths of female and non-white inferiority, political democracy and class mobility (Kimmel 1990: 64–5). In France, the founder of the modern Olympics, Baron Pierre de Coubertin, returned from his sojourns in England, convinced that sports would reinvigorate the nation's 'effete' upper-class schoolboys (Mangan 1981). Perhaps most strikingly, other religions and cultures adopted and adapted the muscular Christian credo, thereby giving rise for example to 'muscular Judaism' (Presner 2007).

Patriarchal ideologies at this time largely insisted that women should be excluded from sport participation. De Coubertin, for instance, believed that sport would breach women's 'fixed destiny' as mothers and male companions. 'Respectable' women exercised in such private surroundings as secluded tennis courts; noticeable female exertion was strongly discouraged, in part due to association with sexual deviance. Thus, during the *belle époque*, Frenchmen viewed female cyclists according to the 'madonna/mistress' syndrome: as asexual spinsters or 'half-naked, voluptuous and sexually available' (Holt 1991: 125). Overall, then, the foundation and spread of modern sports have been deeply influenced by these patriarchal ideologies and assumptions.

Women and modern sport

Origins to 1945

Women have engaged in a long and still incomplete struggle to engage fully with modern sport. Class divisions and ideologies have played critical intersecting roles in shaping women's relationship to sport. In Victorian Britain, the moderate, notable increase of women in sport 'was limited almost entirely to the middle class' (Tranter 1998: 80). In North America and Australia, light sports such as croquet and archery were adopted before middle- and upper-class women played tennis and golf (Vamplew 1994: 15). If teachers permitted, schoolgirls had opportunities to play such sports as hockey, which facilitated the 'unladylike' pleasures of getting dirty, playing rough and competing strenuously (Hall 2002: 34–5; C. Smith 1997: 67). Conversely, lower-class women's sports involvement was curtailed by low finance, social influence and energy (due to the daily grind of labour) and by the wealthier classes' broader regulation of the bodies and sexualities of lower-class populations.

The physical activity of women through the nineteenth century and beyond was subjected to extensive medical guidance according to prevailing gender ideologies. For example, Victorian middle-class women were constructed as 'delicate females', with medics advising only 'gentle exercises, remedial gymnastics, and massage', in part to safeguard reproductive organs (Hargreaves 2002: 56–7). Gymnastic drill became the major regime of exercise pedagogy for young women across Northern Europe and the Anglophone world, such as through the *Turnvereine* (gymnastic clubs) in Germany or the 'Swedish system' of calisthenics in Britain. The political tensions within these activities were neatly embodied by the leader of calisthenics, Madame Martina Bergman-Osterberg, who aimed to improve 'the race' by cultivating women who were 'strong, healthy, pure, and true', but who was, at the same time, a 'committed feminist who laboured throughout her life to remove barriers to women's progress' (Hargreaves 1994: 77; McCrone 1988: 109).

Women's involvement in popular team sports tended to be closely controlled by men in accordance with patriarchal norms. Thus, for example, specific 'feminine/diminutive' rules for basketball, which restricted movement, were introduced for women, although often ignored by players (Dean 2002). At the elite level of sport, significant numbers of women attended major events; in some sports, such as Australian Rules football, grounds were gender segregated to safeguard gentle women from expressive masculine behaviours, while women also contributed substantially to administrative roles in running sport clubs (Hess 1998: 102–4).

Women's greater participation in more strenuous physical activity occurred alongside wider legal, political and civil struggles. 'First-wave feminism', which began as early as 1850 and lasted until the 1930s, helped gain women political suffrage, educational and employment opportunities, and resistance to sexual subordination (Walby 1997: 149–52). Some early female athletes were inevitably connected to these struggles, but most were pragmatic in seeking to play games as they wanted.

In the early and mid-twentieth century, substantial numbers of women, particularly in urban industrialized societies, enjoyed significant empowerment, reflecting their crucial wartime roles, wider political emancipation, growth in employment, and position within the expanding mass consumer culture. Separate women's sports clubs and associations were established, notably in the UK and North America, dominated mainly by the middle classes and inculcating bourgeois norms of female respectability among working-class members (Hargreaves 1993: 138–9). At the elite international level in sport, having allowed female participants since 1900, the IOC grudgingly recognized women's events in 1924. Female Olympians doubled numerically during the 1920s, reaching almost 10 per cent of all competitors in 1928, but distance running, equestrianism and hockey remained prohibited. Successful female athletes were still expected to conform to conventional gender norms within the public domain; thus the multi-sport champion Babe Didrikson was subjected to constant 'tomboy' or 'muscled moll' jibes, whereas 'feminine' athletes such as the tennis champion Helen Wills were depicted more favourably (Guttmann 1991: 144–52).

Cultural continuities and differences in the gender–sport relationship were highlighted by social systems outside the realm of Western liberal capitalism. Socialist societies promoted women's sport alongside official policies of militarized nation-building and female industrial equality. In China, the communist-inspired Red Sport Movement was founded in 1932 and sought to produce more active identities, 'iron bodies', and fresh duties and responsibilities for women (Hong 1997). The Soviet state valorized those female athletes who displayed 'courage, grace, skill, even strength, in the sporting area, winning prestige for club, factory, farm region, ethnic group and republic' (Riordan 1991: 199). In paradoxical contrast, fascist regimes pursued social policies that relegated women to domestic drudgery yet also exploited the rational nationalism of sporting successes for both genders. Notably, Nazi Germany promoted female exercise to assist reproduction and racial health and fielded a large team of women athletes at the 1936 Olympics to buttress state propaganda (Pfister 2002: 169–70).[16]

Women and post-war sport

In the West from the early 1960s onwards, 'second-wave' feminism was particularly influential in challenging gender inequalities as well as in advancing women's interests and rights with regard to the workplace, education, the private sphere, and the growing politics of the body.

At the same time, these pursuits of civil rights and equality were reflected in part in sport through women's steady increase in participation, albeit mainly in amateur disciplines. Women's Olympic participation grew gradually, from 12 per cent of all competitors in 1956, to 20 per cent in 1976, around 29 per cent in 1992, 38 per cent in 2000, 42 per cent in 2008, and almost 45 per cent at London 2012; the range of disciplines for women's participation also expanded consistently. In North America, legal and political advances have been important preludes to notable progress for women's sport. In the United States, the landmark 'Title IX' federal law was passed in June 1972, prohibiting gender discrimination within sports at colleges and high schools. In the same year, six female competitors at the New York marathon staged a successful protest against the barring of women from starting alongside men. In 1974, the Little League permitted girls to play baseball and softball. In turn, numerous other 'firsts' were achieved, such as having a woman first compete in the Indianapolis 500 motor race (1977), or becoming NCAA president (1991), or competing on the men's American golf tour (2003).

Yet these regulative advances require strong structural and cultural changes to take root within sport in order to have impact. Title IX, however, is a controversial piece of legislation. Men continue significantly to outnumber women in college sport participation, while colleges still spend lavishly on big-time male sports, mainly American football and basketball. To counterbalance the gender divide and conform to Title IX, colleges spend heavily to attract women into sports; doing so often necessitates reduced spending on popular men's sports. Political conservatives insist that Title IX must be repealed to meet demand for sport, while liberals advocate its wholehearted enforcement to destabilize long-term gender inequalities (Eitzen 1999: 164; Gavora 2002). Yet legislation such as Title IX needs wider support in order to succeed: in education, for example, college presidents should divert less funding into big-time men's sports, while women's sports must be nurtured assiduously from childhood. Overall, then, the historical record highlights how women's struggles for greater sport participation have had gradually productive if uneven results. In the remaining sections here, I consider both how contemporary gender identities are constructed in sport and the broader political strategies which women may pursue with regard to sport participation.

Women, sport and the construction of gender identities

Women's sport participation has long been shaped by the diverse and shifting patriarchal ideologies surrounding the body, femininity and sexuality. Most obviously, the musculature of the body is built up through the physical exertion that is part and parcel of most sports; yet such physical development may run counter to dominant modern gender codes which have otherwise associated muscularity with 'masculinization' rather than 'natural femininity'.

There have been significant challenges to these traditional gender ideologies. At the everyday level, in most Western societies, muscular female physiques are far more evident than was the case in the 1970s or 1980s; as Hargreaves (2000: 151) notes, in broad terms, such 'muscularity in the female body is valued and admired, appropriated by women as physical capital'. Women's exercise regimes have significantly stretched the boundaries of 'permissible' muscularity and female body 'hardness'. The strongest effects are perhaps experienced at the youngest ages: some research suggests that the pursuit of 'hard', gender-challenging athletic styles is more apparent in childhood (Mennesson 2000).

However, there are ways in which dominant political economic and cultural forces seek to recuperate or otherwise appropriate women's advances within sport. Women's sport continues to be heavily commodified through integration within multi-billion-dollar consumer culture and fitness industries, which have largely reproduced hegemonic patriarchal norms regarding the idealized female body shape. Thus, women's aerobics has tended to market the 'firm but shapely, fit but sexy, strong but thin' female body (Markula 1995). Those women who develop greater musculature are also expected to affirm their heterosexuality, to head off old stereotypes regarding significant exercise and lesbianism (Hargreaves 2000).

Moreover, women's everyday sport participation still encounters patriarchal forms of social closure. Some elite sport organizations, such as high-status golf clubs, are open only to men or discourage female involvement. For example, the Augusta National Golf Club in Georgia, which hosts the Masters tournament, admitted its first two women members only in 2012; in Scotland, a private male-only club continues to control the Muirfield golf course, which regularly hosts the Open championship. Within many local sports clubs, we also find that, rather than playing, it is the 'voluntary' domestic tasks – such as preparing food, cleaning, and washing sport kit – that still fall to women (Thompson 1999).

On television, sports news and highlights programmes under-report the significant growth of women's sport over the past few decades, assuming that viewers are heterosexual males; hence, actual coverage of women's sport tends to trivialize events or to sexualize the competitors (Duncan and Brummet 1989; Messner, Duncan and Cooky 2003). Women athletes who are deemed attractive receive disproportionately large coverage, particularly in print media. Sport's commodification packages female athletes via off-court endorsements of perfume and underwear that satisfy in particular the heterosexual male gaze. Sexual metaphors and promises imbue sports packaging: for example, since the 1920s, men's golf vacations have been presented as opportunities to 'score' on and off the course. At sports events, voyeuristic camera crews pursue 'honey shots' of female spectators and athletes. Women sport television journalists tend to fall into the young and visually attractive categories and are typically confined to presentation rather than analysis roles. The American *Sports Illustrated* magazine contin-ues to run an annual 'swimsuit issue' for the male gaze; yet, aside from this issue, women athletes very rarely appear on the magazine front cover (Davis 1997; Weber and Carini 2013). Avowed soft-porn media such as *Playboy* pay heavily for photo-shoots with celebrity athletes, while some female athletes (such as the Australian women's football team the Matildas) have posed nude to publicize their sport. These exercises in self-sexualization reproduce the patriarchal objectifica-tion of women's bodies and represent a desperate attempt to generate mass-media interest and corporate backing.

Women's objectification within sport extends to the institutionali-zation of sex subcultures, involving 'completely asymmetrical' relationships between male athletes and female followers (Gmelch and San Antonio 1998). At the edges of this subculture of sexual entitlement are high-profile rape and sexual assault cases involving male athletes: for example, in 2013, the Steubenville High School case in Ohio saw two young footballers imprisoned for the rape of a minor; and, in football, the Sheffield United and Wales striker Ched Evans was convicted of rape and jailed for five years. There is no reason to presume that sport is different to other social contexts, in which women who are raped or sexually assaulted tend either not to report these crimes or to find that perpetrators evade justice (Westmarland and Gangoli 2011). Hence, such incidents point to a potentially large, submerged subculture of sexual abuse and exploitation among elite athletes towards women (Benedict 1998).

In recent years we have also witnessed the mass-media construction of particular identities for the WAGs (wives and girlfriends) of leading male athletes. WAGs tend to have two media identities. First, there are the conforming WAGs who are portrayed as performing essentially conservative gender roles, as subordinate, decorative, wifely partners given to conspicuous consumption. Media representations of these WAGs occur, for example, at golf's Ryder Cup contest between Europe and the United States, men's major tennis tournaments, and football's key fixtures. A second media identity is markedly more negative, and portrays the WAG as 'lover' of the male athlete, as a sexualized *femme fatale* who threatens the athlete's performance (Vaczi 2014). Neither media construction provides a particularly positive, empowered identity for women in sport.

In terms of the gender politics of sport participation, some further advances have been made at elite and everyday levels. Strongly conservative, patriarchal societies have come under pressure to increase women's role within sport and wider society. For example, in 2012 and 2013, female athletes from Saudi Arabia – where women are still banned from driving and require male guardians to open bank accounts, marry and travel abroad – were sent to the Olympics for the first time, were allowed to do sport in private schools, and were permitted to establish state-regulated sport clubs.

At the elite level, more international sport tournaments offer equal prize money for male and female competitors: in tennis, the US Open was the first major event to do so, in 1973, and the other three majors eventually followed (Australian in 2001, French and Wimbledon in 2007), while sports such as football and American football have allowed some women to officiate at top-level fixtures. In some nations, overt sexism by sport media commentators now draws strong critical responses: in the UK, when the BBC commentator John Inverdale criticized the physical appearance of the 2013 Wimbledon tennis champion, Marion Bartoli, the corporation received over 700 complaints and many rebukes from politicians, journalists and sports people; and, in 2011, two football presenters left Sky television after their off-air comments were released to the wider public.

Instances of resistance, transgression or critical ambivalence are evident in how women respond to their positioning within sport and physical culture. Ethnographic research reveals how women comment on the absurdity of the idealized female body in consumer culture while enjoying the expressive, emancipatory aspects of meeting and exercising (Markula 1995; Real 1999). Some communities of women also adopt an agency-orientated approach towards sports eroticism (cf. Guttmann 1991, 1996). For example, the thriving lesbian carnival around some LPGA golf tournaments suggests that eroticism and consumerism in sport can move beyond patriarchal social relations and ideologies, and enable diverse and largely subordinate communities to transgress or to challenge the 'heteronormativity' (normalizing of heterosexuality) that otherwise envelops sport events.

These latter practices and cultures connect strongly with the rise of 'third-wave' feminism since the early 1990s. Moving beyond the basic equality focus of second-wave feminism, the third wave celebrates the diversity of women, such as in terms of ethnicity and sexuality, and challenges deep-seated assumptions about gender and sexual norms, roles and identities. Third-wave feminism has been substantially influenced by poststructuralist and postmodernist theories, with one significant offshoot being 'queer theory', which I discuss later. Key issues have centred on the politics of the body, notably around gender-based violence, reproduction, and norms regarding body shapes and sizes.

Third-wave feminist approaches may be identified as underpinning the critical analysis of 'gender verification tests' or 'sex testing' in sport. In many single-sex sports, athletes may be medically tested to 'confirm' their sex according to particular criteria; historically, the focus has tended to be on X and Y chromosomes. Tests have almost always been concerned with seeking to identify possible 'male' athletes participating in women's sports. Prominent tests in recent years have involved the track athletes Caster Semenya (South Africa) and Pinki Pramanik (India). Such tests have been criticized by scientists for being discriminatory and potentially inaccurate (Simpson et al. 2000). From a third-wave feminist perspective, these tests reinforce deep-seated patriarchal sex categories and discriminate particularly against 'intersex' people (cf. Vannini and Fornssler 2007). Thus, sex-testing represents an important everyday political issue in which feminists may contest the continuation of oppressive gender ideologies and practices.

Feminist political strategies within sport

I turn now from specific political issues to explore the different political strategies that women might pursue in order to advance their position within sport. In a classic analysis, Hargreaves (1993) sets out three potential strategies. First, the *co-option* strategy, advocated by 'liberal feminists', involves women 'catching up with men', notably by pursuing more equal representation in sport, such as a fairer share of roles and positions, and equal access to facilities and rewards. The progress of this strategy may be measured quantitatively, such as in the numerical balance between male and female athletes and events at the Olympics. Co-option rejects conservative claims that biological differences or traditional gender values undermine women's sports participation. However, by reducing the political advancement of women to the issue of equality, co-option cannot challenge underlying masculine sport cultures which, for example, promote violent play and discursive sexism. In effect, co-option may also force women to engage with men on male ground and thus join male sporting rituals, in which they will continue to 'seem out of place' (see Novak [1976] 1993: 208–12).

Second, the *separatism* strategy, advocated by 'radical feminists', involves 'self-realization' for women through women-only sports tournaments or associations. Separatism would enhance women's sports participation and enable the exploration of emotional intimacies in sport which masculine values would otherwise suppress. Politicizing everyday life, separatism empowers women to explore alternative sport values, aesthetics, bodily techniques and organizational frameworks. However, separatism may harbour regressive or reactionary aspects – for example, by slipping into essentialism when theorizing gender in terms of innate norms and inclinations, rather than socialization and cultural difference.

Third, the *co-operation* strategy, advocated by 'socialist feminists', establishes new sporting models that negate gender differences. Co-operation recognizes the diversity of struggles within contemporary capitalist societies (including 'race' and sexuality, for example) and is geared towards liberation. Co-operation engages with men (unlike separatism) and is more extensive than co-option: rather than seeking equality, it pursues policies of *equity*, which restructure the sport system to ensure sport experiences are qualitatively similar for women and men (cf. Hall 2002: 203–4). Co-operation posits that men are not inherently oppressive but are socialized into reproducing oppressive roles and practices which ultimately damage both sexes; it requires feminists to explore sport's possible experiences and meanings for women before developing a radically reformed sporting model.

Overall, the co-option model, with its focus on greater equality, has been most evident in boosting women's sporting presence and participation, such as through Title IX, higher financial rewards and more Olympic competitors (Simon 2005). Arguably, co-option is associated with the legal and institutional focus of 'second-wave' feminism in pressing for these forms of equal representation.

Historically, separatism has also been a prominent strategy that harbours uneven features. Separate exercise classes, sport clubs and leagues may reflect women's self-empowerment. Yet these initiatives have often featured support for conservative gender norms and identities or have arisen because of women's exclusion from men-only sport organizations.

Evidently, co-operation affords the most practically and theoretically sophisticated policy. Shaped by Cultural Studies perspectives, it critiques women's marginalization in sport, recognizes how commodification underscores gender divisions, and enables the creation of opposing or alternative sporting models and identities. At the everyday level, compared to co-option and separatism, co-operation secures more space for women to adopt ironic, ambivalent, resistant, oppositional and transgressive positions within contemporary sport. Such cultural political relationships towards sport are also evident in regard to sexuality, to which I now turn.

LGBT cultural politics and sport

The cultural politics of sexuality have played a critical role in shaping the sport experiences of diverse individuals and social groups. Historically, in the context of patriarchal social relations, the organization of modern sport has been heavily heteronormative, in terms of being orientated towards normalizing and advancing heterosexual identities. Minority sexual identities – specifically, lesbian, gay, bisexual and transgender (LGBT) – have been largely oppressed, suppressed, marginalized and demonized. From the mid-nineteenth century onwards, British school teachers viewed games and sports as key fields for advancing 'heteronormativity' and as energy-sapping antidotes to homosexuality and masturbation (Mangan 1981). In male sport, in particular, modern sporting clubs and organizations across the world have long promoted deeply homophobic cultures. At the elite level, some of the most deliberately offensive insults from coaches and fans involve questioning the masculinity and hetero-sexuality of athletes; coaches and athletes continue to use derogatory and homophobic phrases and to opine that gay people should either not play the sport or be avoided as team-mates. Demonization of the LGBT community in sport often centres on popular myths; these include claims that lesbians promote lesbianism in all-female set-tings, act as sexual predators in locker rooms, are unfeminine and thus have unfair advantages in sport, and form cliques to control the governance of sports (Griffin 1998: 55–63; Brackenridge 2001). In some major sports, such as the NFL, team scouts have tested the heterosexuality of potential recruits with questions about interests in girls; or clubs have advocated a 'don't ask, don't tell' policy towards the issue of LGBT athletes or employees.

In such circumstances, to maintain their careers, contracts and public support, many professional athletes and officials have dis-guised their sexuality, often under pressure or following advice from agents, sport officials and fellow players. Indicatively, compared to other professions, elite sport continues to have far lower proportions of open members of sexual minorities. In elite team sports, only a few gay men have 'come out', such as John Amaechi and Jason Collins (NBA); Billy Bean, Glenn Burke and Kazuhito Tadano (MLB); Wade Davis, Kwame Harris, Roy Simmons and Michael Sam (NFL); Ian Roberts and Gareth Thomas (rugby codes); and Justin Fashanu, Robbie Rogers and Thomas Hitzlsperger (football). Some athletes (notably female tennis players such as Martina Navratilova, Billie Jean King and Amélie Mauresmo) came out after years of gossip that led to 'confession'.

What cultural political strategies may be employed by LGBT people to challenge their stigmatization, discrimination and margin-alization in sport? Three such strategies might be suggested here. First, at the everyday level, several sociological studies have high-lighted the importance of personal action and agency, particularly when individual LGBT athletes and coaches are publicly open about their sexuality. These actions pursue social justice by confronting sport's sexual politics (Anderson 2005; Cox and Thompson 2001; Griffin 1998).

Second, some LGBT athletes have formed their own sports clubs, leagues and associations. Perhaps the most successful separatist initiative has been the 'Gay Games', first staged in San Francisco in 1982 with 1,300 participants, which expanded to around 10,000 athletes at the Cologne event in 2010 (Symons 2010). On the positive side, these international events challenge prejudices and showcase alternative sport values, identities and forms of association. On the negative side, they may miss the opportunity to have the strongest social impacts by challenging and transforming dominant sport institutions and structures from the inside; they may lose some of their radical potential as they expand and become more corporate-friendly, and they may be weakened by internal disputes and breakaway movements (cf. Messner 1992: 159). At the national level, LGBT sport associations and tournaments have been founded, such as, in the United States, the New York City Gay Hockey Association and the San Francisco Gay Basketball Association. Perhaps the strongest impacts, in challenging negative treatment, are achieved by LGBT sport clubs which participate in established non-LGBT associations, tournaments and leagues: in football, these clubs include Stonewall (UK), the New York Ramblers (USA) and Paris Foot Gay (France).

Third, following long-term campaigning by LGBT individuals and groups, some sport organizations have introduced new policies and educational programmes that tackle homophobia. Examples of such initiatives are NBA adverts on anti-gay language and bullying; the NHL's partnership with the New York advocacy group 'You Can Play' in 2013; the American football players' union demanding that the NFL should prohibit scout or team questions on the sexual orientation of athletes; and, since 2006, collaborative work on homophobia leading to campaigns involving UEFA, FARE (Football Against Racism in Europe) and the European Gay and Lesbian Sport Federation (EGLSF). Compared to the culture and ethos of sport organizations in the 1990s, these campaigns represent significant advances in promoting basic civil rights for LGBT people within sport.

For some analysts, homophobia in sport is not as strong as in the past. Indeed, Anderson (2011) has claimed that American sport has been transformed, from 'intensely homophobic' in the 1980s to being far more willing to accept sexual minorities and more tactile masculine identities. Extensive research by Cashmore and Cleland (2012) in the UK revealed that football fans were explicitly opposed to homophobia in the game and were also critical of the failure of the sport's governing bodies, clubs and player agents to deal with the problem. However, in many parts of the world, institutionalized homophobia has direct impacts on sport at the everyday level: for example, Russia, host of the 2014 Winter Olympics and the 2018 World Cup, introduced laws banning 'gay propaganda' in 2013; in South Africa, 'corrective rape' is an everyday danger for women who are thought to be lesbians, and included the notorious gang-rape and murder of former international football player Eudy Simelane in 2008; and leading football officials in Croatia and Romania have advocated bans on gay players.

For some social scientists, the critical analysis of sexual politics in sport has been enhanced by turning to new theory. One influential approach in recent years has been 'queer theory' (Caudwell 2006; King 2008; Sykes 1998), which is derived particularly from critical and poststructuralist theories as well as social activism. In broad terms queer theory involves direct challenges to the normalization of heterosexuality within politics and culture, deconstructions of gender and sexual identities (including gay and lesbian ones), recognition of the fluidity and plurality of sexual identities, and explorations of how 'queer pleasure' may be gained from interpreting popular culture (such as films, television shows, music and sport) in homoerotic ways (Butler 1990). Perhaps most instructively, queer theory avoids the construction of 'grand theories' which would otherwise make the mistake of collapsing gender and sexual identities into a single set of experiences or one analytical framework. These themes of experiential, cultural and theoretical diversity within sexuality, which are raised specifically by queer theory, are also central to the analysis of constructions of masculinity within sport, to which I now turn.

Making men through sport: hegemony and diversity

Hegemonic masculinities

Academic critiques of masculinity within sport have revealed how physical culture serves to produce and to reproduce heterosexual male cultures and identities. Masculine ideals promoted through modern sport have tended to be highly restrictive and thus stigmatize or victimize many 'deviant' others, including women, gay men, the old, children and people with disabilities (Ingham 1997: 171). Extensive research by Messner (1994, 2007, 2009) in particular has highlighted how gender divisions and boundaries continue to shape sport at the everyday level. Moreover, sports media disseminate dominant masculine norms among boys and young men through a 'television sports manhood formula' built around themes of gender, race, militarism, aggression, violence and commercialism (Messner, Dunbar and Hunt 2000).

The Australian social scientist and theorist R. W. Connell (1987, 1990, 1995, 2000) has advanced a highly influential set of theories on masculinity which have had a major impact on critical, pro-feminist sociological studies of sport. Connell introduces the neo-Gramscian concept of 'hegemonic masculinity' to explain how dominant gender identities are established in part through gaining strong consent from men and women. Hegemonic masculinity represents the 'culturally idealized form of masculine character' which is centred on 'toughness and competitiveness', the subordination of women, and the 'marginalization of gay men' (McKay 1997: 17). A 'relational' rather than fixed identity, hegemonic masculinity registers the specific types of power relation that are at play among and between men and women. Thus, hegemonic masculine identities vary significantly in historical terms and between different cultures; in reality, these identities may not be the most common ones across all men or the most comfortable for men to experience (Connell 2000: 10–11).

The concept of hegemonic masculinity features in numerous sociological studies of sport–gender relations, for example on *Sports Illustrated*'s 'swimsuit issue', violent masculinities within sport, co-educational cheerleading, and media coverage of baseball stars (Davis 1997; Grindstaff and West 2006; Messner 1992; Trujillo 1991; cf. Connell 2000: 11, 188–9). Klein (1993) adapted Connell's theory to explore how male bodybuilding is driven in part by a subculture of 'femiphobia' – that is, 'the fear of appearing female, or effeminate', which 'fuels hypermasculinity, homophobia, and misogyny' and hyperconformity to masculine norms (ibid.: 269–73). This research also reveals how specific hegemonic masculine identities serve to damage men, for instance by advancing hopelessly unrealistic, idealized images of masculinity for boys and men to pursue; promoting aggressive and violent forms of sport that damage male bodies; and socializing boys and men into impoverished gender identities that damage relationships with other men and women.

Connell (1995) identified four dimensions that shape gender relations and thus provide the basis for establishing particular hegemonic masculinities. First, gender *power relations* are marked by the fluid reproduction of patriarchy, despite contestation by various movements. Second, the *production relations (division of labour)* of modern capitalism remain heavily gendered and continue to direct men and women into gender-specific roles. Third, *cathexis (emotional relations)* concerns the politics of desire and further defines gender relations through specific gendered objects of pleasure and the distributive justice of pleasure. Fourth, *symbolism* concerns human communication's role in reproducing the gender order.

We may apply this model to outline how gender relations are constructed in sport. First, men continue to dominate the organization and culture of most sports. Second, women's labour tends to be engaged gender-specifically in (typically unpaid) domestic or clerical work to support male-dominated sports clubs. Third, in modern sport-related advertisements, women continue to be objectified and portrayed as sexually available for the male heterosexual gaze. Fourth, males define themselves through tough play or post-match rituals against symbolic others (particularly women and gay men).

However, rather than fitting sport into these four areas, we may include sport within a new, fifth dimension that explicitly concerns *leisure (consumption) relations*. This fifth dimension would capture the centrality of sport and leisure for the making of gender identities in contemporary capitalism. Gender divisions in leisure share significant parallels and interconnections with the wider labour market. Since the 1950s, in most societies in the Global North, women have successfully fought for better employment rights and opportunities. More problematically, these gains have often been in gendered work (e.g., domestic and service orientated), with women functioning as a 'reserve army of labour' in economic booms and having greater levels of disposable income which is directed towards consuming heavily gendered products. Similarly, while more evident in sport and physical culture in general, women are often channelled into 'feminine' practices such as aerobics and act as a 'reserve army of leisure' to fill expensive stadium seats, sit in 'family ends', or purchase children's merchandise (Russell 1999). Overall, through establishing this fifth dimension in Connell's theory, we would be better placed to examine sport's key role in the contested reproduction of gender relations within the wider society.

Masculinities: historical and anthropological perspectives

Theories of hegemonic masculinity have the strongest explanatory power when they take full account of significant historical and cultural influences in shaping masculine identities in different ways. In some contexts, dominant masculine identities may be shaped with reference to different nostalgic and anti-modern mythologies: for example, in American football, old 'giant' players are sometimes portrayed as larger-than-life, inherently tough (and less technical) masculine figures (Oriard 2001: 332) or, in white New Zealand, rugby discourses and images make claims about a 'unified' nation embodied by tough rugby-playing farmers and workers (Phillips 1994). Conversely, 'new' and 'modern' masculinities may be advanced by dominant groups in societies undergoing rapid transformation – as in early revolutionary Cuba, where Castro's government sought to use sport to mould a socialist 'new man' personifying the socialist virtues of 'modesty, brotherhood, internationalism and a cooperative spirit' (Pye 1986: 122).

Anthropological approaches explore more fully the diversity of these dominant masculine and national identities within sport. The Argentinian anthropologist Eduardo Archetti (1998, 1999) advanced some of the most insightful studies of the masculinity–nationality nexus in sport. For example, his research at the 1992 Albertville Winter Olympics explored how the 'idealized masculinity' of elite athletes was reflected in public understandings of the skiers Vegard Ulvang and Alberto Tomba: the former was 'very Norwegian', undemonstrative, serene and close to nature, whereas 'Tomba La Bomba' became the boastful urban playboy, expressively Italian (loving pasta) and inspiring a new, football-type skiing fandom.

More expansively, Archetti (1998) demonstrated that, within one nation, different types of national masculine identity may be constructed and explored within physical culture through a comparison of polo (man–animal relations), tango (man–woman relations) and football (man–man relations) in Argentina. The dominant Argentinian playing style in 'gaucho' polo is 'manly' and risk-taking, in contrast to more conservative English styles (ibid.: 96, 104–5). In tango dance and song, alongside the dancers' vivid eroticism, a 'doubting masculinity' in relations with 'powerful women' is often revealed (ibid.: 155–7). In football, the dominant Argentinian playing style promotes individual expression, creativity and technical skill, in deliberate contrast to the perceived European, modern values of willpower and organization (ibid.: 70–2). In male Argentinian folklore, this *criollo* football style is embodied *not* by the physically large, aggressive and violent adult male but by the boy (*pibe*), who possesses a small body, high skill levels, a character filled with cunning, creativity and vulnerability, and a disorderly, risk-taking, carnivalesque lifestyle (ibid.: 182–4). Diego Maradona is, of course, the Argentinian *pibe par excellence*.

Archetti's point here has a deep significance for the analysis of masculinity in sport. Maradona may have some uniquely Argentinian cultural meanings, yet he is still regarded by millions of fans *worldwide* as one of football's greatest ever players on account of his extraordinary technical skill and artistry. Such qualities are in marked contrast to the violent, aggressive forms of hegemonic masculinity that are highlighted by Connell and others, particularly in the context of Australian and American sport. Moreover, in other sports we find that the greatest folk heroes tend not to be violent 'goons' (in ice-hockey) or destructive 'hammer-throwers' (in football); instead, they are far more likely to be gifted and graceful 'artists', often small and seemingly vulnerable in stature, such as Baggio (Italy), Best (Northern Ireland), Messi (Argentina), Platini (France), Zico and Neymar (Brazil) in football; great half-backs such as Cliff Morgan, Barry John, Phil Bennett and Jonathan Davies (all Wales) in rugby union; Wayne Gretsky in ice-hockey; and spectacular quarterbacks in the NFL such as Marino, Montana and Namath.

Two points follow from these observations on masculinity. First, we need to recognize the diversity of masculine identities that are constructed through sport and to appreciate that the most popular or favoured of these identities very often do not conform to the 'aggressive, tough or violent' features often associated with 'hegemonic masculinity'.

Second, these graceful sport artists are celebrated in popular culture for many reasons, particularly the aesthetic quality and technical excellence of their play. Part of their popular appeal also lies in the transgressive, carnivalesque qualities that they bring to the sport contest, as they outwit and outmanoeuvre opponents who are more aggressive and physically powerful but who are often left tackling thin air or sitting on their backsides by these evasive, skilful *pibes*. In this sense, if hegemonic masculinity is associated with power and aggression, then the sport field and sport stadium are often places in which this 'dominant' male identity is popularly and symbolically contested, evaded, disarmed and defeated to huge public acclaim, particularly among men.

Concluding comments

As we have seen, modern sporting disciplines and practices have played important roles in the systematic reproduction of gender divisions and domination. Historically, dominant groups have sought to construct modern sport cultures in accordance with patriarchal and other dominant ideologies, such as those supportive of capitalism, imperialism and militarized nationalism. Women and sexual minorities have endured powerful structural and cultural dynamics of exclusion or control in regard to their participation in sport. In many societies, the historical growth of women's involvement and acceptance in sport has been associated in part with their broader incorporation as consumers of gendered products and services. Sport remains a professional and cultural field in which many LGBT people, particularly gay men competing in elite team disciplines, seek to hide their sexual identities. Moreover, social scientists also point to how dominant or hegemonic masculine identities have damaging impacts upon boys and men.

However, like other fields of popular culture, sport does not function simply to reproduce patriarchal social relations. Sports that are practised by men and women contain diverse politico-cultural dimensions. Many aspects of sport reinforce gender divisions, some negotiate class and gender hierarchies, while some are significantly more radical. Historically, women and sexual minority groups have critically interpreted conventional gender roles and norms and fought to participate more fully and equitably within sport. Moreover, we should note also the diversity and plurality of gender and sexual identities, as registered for example in very different ways by queer theorists and anthropologists of sport. In many male team sports, the most publicly celebrated athletes tend not to be the most physically powerful, aggressive or violent in their style of play.

Different strategies have been advanced on how best to effect gender-focused social transformations within sport. I have argued here that the pro-feminist approach of co-operation, which should pursue equity in sport, provides the best way forward. For LGBT communities, strategies of individual action, alternative organization and public campaigns have been effective in challenging marginalization and stigmatization.

My final point here is that, as with other forms of social division and identity, the interface between gender and sport features substantial scope, not just for resistance and opposition but also for cultural political forms of ambivalence, irony and transgression with regard to dominant relations and ideologies of power. Irony and ambivalence are evident, for example, in how women and men often respond to the dominant bodily ideals of femininity and masculinity that are projected through sport. Events such as the Gay Games are surrounded by pageantry and carnival that involve the public transgression of dominant codes of clothing and attire, the sudden and colourful appropriation of urban space, and the exploration of alternative sporting identities and values. Aspects of the carnivalesque may also be identified in the popular culture that underpins elite sport at the broader level. Such carnivalesque impulses are perhaps illustrated when diverse social groups celebrate those athletes who display spectacular skills while outsmarting opponents who initially appear to personify the apparent 'ideal' of hegemonic masculinity.

Questions for discussion

1 How have sexist myths and assumptions shaped the experiences of women in sport?
2 What strategies have been used by women and by LGBT communities to improve their positions within sport?
3 How are masculine identities created within sport? How varied and diverse are these identities?
4 How might sport be transformed in order to remove its sexist and homophobic features?

7
The Body in Sport: Discipline, Experience and Risk

The body has been a major focus for sociological inquiry since at least the mid-1980s. The French social theorist Michel Foucault was most influential in directing sociologists towards a critical analysis of the body; the works of earlier phenomenologists such as Maurice Merleau-Ponty, as well as the different sociological theories of Pierre Bourdieu and Norbert Elias, have also had substantial impacts.

In this chapter, I examine four broad areas in which the body in sport may be examined by sociologists. First, I discuss the contribution of Foucault to the sociology of body and how his highly influential poststructuralist theories may be deployed by sociologists of sport. Second, I consider more agency-orientated, phenomenological perspectives on the body. Third, I turn to address specific bodily risks that are faced by sport participants in regard to violence, pain and injury, and doping. Fourth, I explore voluntary risk-taking in sport. I conclude by arguing for greater levels of interdisciplinary research in order to advance our understanding of the body in sport.

Foucault and the body: discipline and governmentality

The French poststructuralist Michel Foucault placed the body at the heart of his social theories (Foucault 1979, 1980, 1983). He argued that power and knowledge are not mutually exclusive, but interdependent; thus, struggles for power are closely tied to the emergence and spread of new frameworks of knowledge. In modern times, these power/knowledge relationships came to be dominated by states and governments and by the human and medical sciences. These relationships produced in turn various complex and sophisticated apparatuses for the regulation and disciplining of populations and their bodies. States and scientific 'experts' came to classify 'bad' bodies with reference to certain 'pathologies' or 'weaknesses': the more 'extreme' cases are defined as having, for example, mental illnesses, physical incapacities, criminal tendencies and forms of sexual deviance, though, more commonly, deviant bodies are classified as overweight, inactive or workshy, and unregulated in diet (such as in alcohol consumption, smoking). These bodies continue to be subjected to diverse, 'normalizing' interventions, perhaps through confinement within asylums, clinics and prisons; by way of special programmes and initiatives by government, corporations and voluntary agencies; and via everyday 'expert' guidance on how to behave, consume products and exercise.

From the Foucauldian standpoint, power is exercised on populations and their bodies in two key ways. First, *biopower* centres on political control of the key biological aspects of the human body and whole populations, notably in regard to birth, reproduction, illness and death. Among examples here have been state policies and scientific activity centred on 'race', including, most recently, medical research to map human genomes in part with reference to 'racial' makeup (Rabinow and Rose 2003). Second, *disciplinary power* is exercised by means of the everyday disciplining of bodies, particularly through controlling time and space, for example as prison inmates, hospital patients, factory workers or school pupils are confined within buildings and required to follow timetabled activities.

Modern disciplinary regimes have become diffuse, as entire populations are socialized within the heavily regulated environments of education, work, leisure and family. Thus, disciplinary regimes are constructed to produce *the body as object* – that is, as 'normalized', docile and obedient. To achieve these results, bodies are subjected to examination by 'experts' (such as medical doctors) who 'gaze' upon the revealed body. In addition, various apparatuses and techniques of surveillance following the logic of the Panopticon (such as watch-towers in prisons or CCTV systems in workplaces and public streets) are introduced in order to place the body under continuous observation. In turn, populations come to discipline their bodies and their conduct according to specific bodily 'norms'; in effect, each individual becomes his or her 'own overseer' (Foucault 1980: 155).

Foucault's analysis of disciplinary regimes may account for regimented or passive bodies, but how might his theories account for the construction of more active bodies (in other words, *the body as subject*)? The concept of *governmentality*, set out by Foucault in his final years, helps to answer this question. Governmentality refers to how power operates 'at a distance' by 'conducting the conduct' of different individuals and social groups (Rose 1999: 3–5; 1996: 43). Some social scientists have explored how neoliberal social policies are driven by specific forms of governmentality (cf. Rose 1996; Shamir 2008). According to neoliberalism, modern social issues relating to poverty, employment, crime and security, health, sexism and racism should not be dealt with through structural changes to society or state intervention. Instead, these issues should be tackled by social actors themselves, through forms of 'self-government' that promote individual responsibility and self-esteem (cf. Cruikshank 1999). Thus, contemporary consumer culture is replete with self-help manuals, diet plans and lifestyle checklists that both inspire and direct our subjectivities and choices.

The concept of governmentality encapsulates Foucault's claim that power is not simply a negative force; rather, 'power produces; it produces reality; it produces domains of objects and rituals of truth' (1977: 194). More vaguely, Foucault argued that power is everywhere, and that resistance to discipline or government always arises, often locally – for example when old and new systems of knowledge clash, or when particular bodies and selves refuse to be disciplined or to engage in self-government (Foucault 1983: 208). In his later work, as Morgan (2015) notes, Foucault (1985) turned to the idea of 'techniques of the self', thereby offsetting his emphasis on discipline or domination with some recognition of human agency and critical creativity. He indicated that the exploration of a new, ethical and aesthetic form of subjectivity might provide one escape from the disciplined and normalized self. Yet, against this hopeful claim, we might underline the point that neoliberal ideologies are adept at inspiring or colonizing techniques of the self: for instance, consumer culture constantly markets products that are intended to enhance our self-esteem and self-improvement, and armies of lifestyle 'experts' (particularly in the mass media) provide an endless stream of advice to individuals on how to improve themselves, particularly through how these products should be bought and used. Perhaps more plausible is Morgan's (2015) observation that, for Foucault, positive change is associated with transgression; that is, we should 'transgress what we have become in order to become something else, something new, something other than what we presently are'.

There are some notable continuities between Foucault and other leading theorists. While his poststructuralism builds upon Durkheim, Foucault's insights chime with Weber and Adorno on the dehumanizing effects of scientific rationalization. From a neo-Marxist standpoint, it may be argued that biopower, disciplinary regimes and governmentality have served to advance the interests of industrial capitalism, particularly in constructing well-regulated workers and energetic consumers. In addition, overlapping in part with Foucault, Elias's concept of the 'civilizing process' traces the long-term disciplining of the body through etiquette, manners and emotional management (see, for example, Brownell 1995); arguably, Foucault's analysis carries a more incisive theorization of power relations. Finally, Foucault's influence on Cultural Studies approaches has been very substantial. His exploration of themes surrounding the body, domination, resistance and the possibilities of transgression fits particularly well with Cultural Studies perspectives on sport.

Foucauldian sport

How might we draw on Foucault's theories to understand the body within sport? The most obvious starting point is on bodily discipline within sport. Thus, sporting *disciplines* tend to centre on specific physical actions – the serve in tennis, the swing in golf, the touch and pass in football – that are practised continually until they are performed instantly and intuitively by the body. Foucault's theories help to explain the historical development of modern sport, as disciplinary institutions such as schools and military services continue to organize games in order to 'mould men' into orderly, obedient civilians and soldiers.

In contemporary elite sport, coaches, scientists and other professionally accredited 'experts' gaze upon the bodies of athletes, identifying bodily weaknesses, and draw up training and dietary regimes in order to achieve peak performance. In the most advanced cases, prospective athletes are examined for physical flaws and 'character defects'; bodies that fail are screened out of future elite development, perhaps by being removed from training academies. Sport contests themselves represent bodily examinations in which athletes' performances are measured and compared, while also facilitating a wider array of surveillance that involves event officials and spectators (Markula and Pringle 2006: 41–2).

Disciplinary regimes in sport also point towards the homogenizing of sporting bodies. At the elite level, the diversity of body shapes appears to have declined significantly as athletes increasingly conform to relatively tall, muscled and highly fit physiques. More generally, modern sport and fitness industries seek to turn participants (especially women) into their own Panopticon, and to gaze critically at their own bodies vis-à-vis certain idealized (and increasingly unattainable) body shapes (cf. Duncan 1994). Thus, Foucault's theories here fit well with critical perspectives on the social construction of gender identities in sport and beyond. In sport stadiums, Foucauldian theories help to explain the disciplining and surveillance of spectators – for example as all-seated stands serve to restrict the freedom for movement and as crowd actions are continuously monitored by security officers and CCTV cameras.

We may note that modern governments seek to exercise biopower within sport and physical activity in order to shape public health. Governments and medical experts issue recurring warnings on rising obesity and diabetes and the need for mass participation in sport and physical activity to combat these health dangers. Governments also look to justify the enormous cost of hosting sport mega-events in part by pointing to the intended legacy of greater mass participation in sport and physical activity, although evidence from prior events suggests that the post-event take-up is rather low.

The concept of governmentality helps to explain the production of active subjectivities within contemporary sport, particularly at mass levels. In the neoliberal context, the sporting activities and conduct of different populations are directed towards self-monitoring and self-reliance. Individual consumers are encouraged to 'take responsibility' for their exercise and diet, usually by turning to the private sector in the form of the burgeoning leisure and health market, such as by joining gyms or purchasing various commercial 'technologies of the self' (such as workout videos or health plans) in order to get 'into shape'. And all of these activities are wrapped in consumerist clichés of personal pleasure and liberation: 'Look good, feel good!' or 'Discover the real you!' (cf. Johns and Johns 2000: 231–2). It is here that we see how, in sport and the wider leisure spheres, Foucault's hopeful comments on 'techniques of the self' actually point towards new forms of bodily discipline and government.

In other sport contexts, Foucault's theories may be used to explore the emergence of sport for people with disabilities and the development of the Paralympic movement (Howe 2008: 64–80). Early organized sport for people with disabilities was heavily influenced by medical discourses that favoured exercise to 'rehabilitate' the newly disabled, particularly those suffering spinal injuries in military conflict. Separate competitions for all disabled people grew internationally, enabling the Paralympic Games to take place in 1960 and in every Olympic year since, under direction of the International Paralympic

Committee (IPC). Encapsulating the workings of modern biopower, the basic differentiation between Olympian and Paralympian is premised upon the classification of bodies as 'able' and 'disabled'. Moreover, Paralympic sport competition is founded upon highly complex classifications of 'disabled populations' according to pre-determined categories of physical or intellectual impairment. For example, at the 2012 London Paralympic Games, there were six main classes of disability for athletics competitions, defined as blind/visually impaired, intellectually impaired, having cerebral palsy, 'les autres' (the others, including dwarfism), amputees, and those with spinal cord disabilities; most of these classes contained several subclasses that reflected different levels or types of impairment (for example, cerebral palsy featured eight such subclasses), producing a total of twenty-six categories of athletic competition. These classification systems have been highly contested in IPC sport, particularly when some categories are collapsed together in order to create a minimum number of competitors for a particular event. In addition, the focus within Paralympic sport on the use of expensive mobility technologies to assist athletes has created a major competitive divide between developed and developing societies largely on the grounds of cost (Howe 2011). Moreover, the tendency of the mass media 'gaze' to present successful Paralympians as 'supercrips' or 'superhumans' may appear as a positive celebration of those with disabilities; however, in effect, it serves to disempower people with disabilities through their presentation as 'freaks' and 'Others' (Silva and Howe 2012).

The broader Foucauldian points on resistance and transgression carry significant explanatory power with regard to sport and leisure cultures. Not all social groups are disciplined or governed in straightforward ways; acts of resistance do occur. In regard to biopower, we might point to those bodies – seemingly too large or too thin, or which rarely exercise, or which engage in excess or 'risky' health behaviours – that, despite continuous governmental or expert guidance, are not 'responsible' or engaged in careful self-management. There are also anti-disciplinary forms of carnivalesque, excessive behaviour that may be identified among particular sport subcultures, such as athletes renowned for their hedonism and disinclination to train, or spectators who prefer to stand rather than sit to watch sports events or to generate their own atmosphere rather than respond to the stadium public address systems. Historically, for many dominated social groups – notably women, non-white or 'disabled' people – actual participation in sport has constituted a form of corporeal transgression, in terms of putting their bodies in places where only white, male, able-bodied athletes were authorized or 'normally' expected to be present.

Finally, in this context, we might draw on Eichberg's (1994) theory of three sporting body types to highlight the differences between disciplined and undisciplined (or transgressive) bodies in sport. On the one side, there are the disciplined and controlled bodies; in Eichberg's terms, these are *streamlined* bodies associated with achievement sports and record setting and *straight, healthy* bodies associated with exercise and fitness such as gymnastic disciplines. On the other side, we find instead the undisciplined, *grotesque* body, which has its early history in pre-modern popular carnivals and folk games, such as traditional wrestling, the tug-of-war or the three-legged race. For Eichberg, the grotesque body is a source of laughter and pleasure; rather than being straight, disciplined and coordinated, this body comes in very different shapes and sizes and is often unbalanced and stumbling during play. In this context, the grotesque body transgresses the norms and conventions of modern sport. Yet we find still in modern sports that strong 'folk' impulses and subcultures continue to recognize and to celebrate the grotesque body and the associated carnivalesque – for example, when spectators cheer sport participants not for dexterity or record-setting but for their unusual size or gait or, during moments in sport contests, when streamlined or straight bodies are made to look grotesque, such as by stumbling or falling over when they are outwitted by lighter opponents. Thus, in line with Foucault, we might observe that disciplined bodies are not entirely dominant across diverse sporting populations.

The body, sport and phenomenology

In contrast to a Foucauldian, poststructuralist perspective on sport, I turn now to consider the rather different, phenomenological approach to understanding the sporting body. In broad terms, phenomenology is a philosophical tradition and research method which explores human consciousness, experience, sensuousness, subjectivity and intersubjectivity. Among leading theoretical influences within phenomenology are the philosophers Heidegger, Husserl, Merleau-Ponty and Sartre. In phenomenological sociology, the work of Schutz (1972) has been most influential, followed in particular by Berger and Luckmann (1966), notably in extending the interpretive legacy of Weber ([1922] 1978). Latterly, in line with a phenomenological approach, Crossley (1995) called for us to move away from a 'sociology of the body', which focuses on what is done to the body (such as in terms of discipline or regulation), and towards a 'carnal sociology', which explores instead what the body does.

If we adopt a phenomenological perspective, then we need to understand how our consciousness and subjectivity are fundamentally embodied; thus, we should view the body as a critical site for our 'lived experience', for our understanding of and engagement with the external world, and, in the phrase of Heidegger and Merleau-Ponty, for our 'being-in-the-world'.

In the field of sport research, phenomenology requires us to understand and to convey how specific moments and events are subjectively experienced and consciously 'lived' through the body. This approach also explores how we learn to play or to practise sports: to apply Merleau-Ponty (1962), the body is a crucial intermediary in this sense, as its movements serve to connect the 'being' of the player with outside 'things', such as sport fields of play, equipment and the bodies of opponents.

Drawing on a phenomenological approach, Hockey and Allen-Collinson (2007) have identified five key 'sensory activities' that are part of doing sport, primarily for 'able-bodied' participants.

1 *Movement and rhythm* Movement is essential for sport practice and may generate heightened experiences or 'flow' sensations. Competent and expert sport movements rely on timing, whereby body actions are skilfully sequenced and orchestrated to achieve specific, intended outcomes, such as the baseball bat striking a pitch for a home run or a high-jumper approaching and then clearing the bar.

2 *The aural and respiration* Sport participants 'listen' to their respiration, to their bodies, and to their external environments. For example, in the sport of biathlon, participants must undertake long-distance cross-country skiing and rifle-shooting. After their sprint on skis, participants stop to shoot at a distant target; in doing so, they must 'listen' to their bodies, to ensure their pulse and respiration is under some control, otherwise they are liable to miss their target.

3 *The visual* Sport participants 'see' their sports in different ways, usually according to different levels and types of experience. The most skilled participants 'see' openings and possibilities – the 'blindside run' in rugby, the defence-splitting pass in football, the space to turn in basketball – that are not envisioned by other players or spectators.

4 *The olfactory* Sport bodies are surrounded by aromas and odours, which intensify senses of 'being there' as participants or onlookers. For example, after sport participation, the changing rooms are filled with powerful smells, such as sweat, medical sprays and lotions, deodorant, and the outside environment (such as freshly cut grass).

5 *The touch line* 'Haptic' activity is central to most sport participation and is particularly important for making playing decisions. For example, golfers stroke the putting green to assess the line of their putt; boxers push out jabs to gauge their opponents' reflexes and distance; and cricketers examine, rub and shine the ball before deciding how to bowl.

The list is not exhaustive, and might also include taste, which would have a double meaning: first, as actual bodily sensation, such as for boxers who taste blood or injured athletes who suffer nausea; second, in the more metaphorical sense, for example as participants experience 'sickening' or 'bitter' defeats or savour the 'sweet taste' of victory.

Phenomenological approaches share significant continuities with some theories within human geography, notably the theory of topophilia ('love of place'), discussed in the next chapter. More broadly, the study of outdoor life draws substantially on phenomenology. Scandinavian researchers on *friluftsliv* ('open-air life') explore how walkers, hikers, skiers, climbers, sailors, boat-builders and others experience and engage with the natural environment, notably through their sensory activities but also as human agents who are constantly adjusting and adapting to an outdoor environment that is itself constantly changing (see, for example, Bischoff 2012; Tordsson 2010). In methodological terms, the phenomenological approach is ideally suited to qualitative research (Kerry and Armour 2000). In-depth interviews, participant observation, ethnography, auto-ethnography and textual analysis are all highly appropriate data-gathering techniques for capturing the embodied experiences and lifeworlds of social actors in sport or wider leisure activities.

The body and sporting risks

Sport participation is associated with a variety of bodily risks. Arguably, as sport has become more rationalized, professionalized and commodified, these risks have often increased, particularly in regard to medical-based dangers. In this next section, I turn to explore three types of sport-related risk, regarding violence, pain and injury, and doping, which have been examined by sociologists and other social scientists.

Violence in sport

Violent and aggressive practices are a constant feature of sport and are associated with substantial bodily risks. By way of definition, Coakley (2001: 174–5) has offered a useful distinction between these two keywords: violence is 'the use of excessive physical force, which causes or has the potential to cause harm or destruction', while aggression refers more broadly to 'verbal or physical behaviour grounded in an intent to dominate, control, or do harm to another person'. Aggression is a positively regarded aspect of play in most sports; athletes are encouraged to be more rather than less aggressive, and they receive highly favourable responses from spectators and media commentators when playing in such a way. Violence in sport is evidenced in many ways, notably among players and coaches – for example, in the stamping or elbowing of opponents in rugby or football, fights on the ice in hockey, or 'bench-clearing' melees in baseball; among sport fans, there are battles between rival groups of football supporters or fights that surround 'celebration rioting' at some North American sport fixtures. In contact sports, violence and aggression are also underpinned by hegemonic masculine cultures of play: when athletes seek to dominate their opponents in physical ways, the body is transformed into a tool of aggression and violence. Injuries are inevitable since, as Messner (1992: 71) notes, 'The body as weapon ultimately results in violence against one's own body.'

In a perceptive analysis that may be applied to many other sports, Finn (1994a: 102–5) has argued that, in football, players and supporters are socialized into a 'culture of quasi-violence' that contains different values to those of everyday life. This culture of quasi-violence is vaguely defined, as it 'accepts aggression and violence as central to the game but accompanies this acceptance with all manner of inconsistencies, uncertainties, qualifications and disagreements'. Thus, athletes, fans and media offer a wide range of interpretations on the acceptability or otherwise of specific violent actions or incidents in sport. Many societies and sport systems have sought to counter violent episodes through stricter policing and legal measures. Conversely, it remains rare for criminal prosecutions to be brought against on-field violence; sport governing bodies retain substantial juridical autonomy and discretion for regulating and policing such play.

One of the best ways of developing a sociological understanding of violence in sport is through detailed ethnographies of violent subcultures. The French sociologist Loïc Wacquant (1995a, 1995b, 2001, 2004) has produced several outstanding ethnographic studies of a Chicago boxing gym, which included training and fighting in the ring. For Wacquant (2005: 460), the gym constituted 'a place of respite and a temporary shield' for the young boxers, who were typically located at the foot of America's ethnic and class structures.

For the boxers that Wacquant studied, the fight game is double-edged. On the positive side, boxers pursue a 'glorified self' – winning fights, titles, status and wealth – by transforming their 'bodily capital' into 'pugilistic capital' (Wacquant 1995a: 66–7). On the other hand, boxers are only too familiar with their exploitation by managers; indeed, Wacquant (2001) outlined three self-descriptions of boxers that capture these circumstances: first, as *prostitutes*, boxers sell their bodies to profit the pimp/manager; second, as *slaves*, they are pushed to extreme violence, or are wrapped in conditions of contractual bondage, by their promoters;[17] and, third, as *stallions*, they are fed, housed, cleaned, exercised and farmed out to fight at management's discretion. Boxers recognize that their professional routine is one of continuous physical damage, in which they leave 'bits and pieces of their body in the ring' and live with the constant risk of a brain-scrambling or face-destroying single blow (Wacquant 1995b: 522). Yet they retain self-integrity through alternative, if ambivalent systems of corporeal self-knowledge. They deny that they will join the ranks of damaged fellow pugilists (Wacquant 2001). Climbing through the ropes, rolling punches, engaging opponents in intense combat, and embracing rivals at the end are experiences often described by pugilists in highly excited terms. Pain, injury and corporeal deterioration may be intrinsic to boxing, but fighters 'construct a heroic, transcendent self' within the 'skilled body craft' of their 'sweet science'. More broadly, there is the crucial issue of how violent sport subcultures are underpinned by deeper social structures. Wacquant's research, in this case, indicates that boxers view the risks surrounding this most violent of sports as relatively empowering, particularly given the wider and uncontrolled exploitation that is endured by lower-class social groups in other areas of life.

Pain and injury

The subject of pain and injury in sport, particularly for male athletes, has attracted substantial study by social scientists. Howe (2004: 74) has defined injury as a 'breakdown in the structure of the body . . . that may affect its function', whereas pain 'is the marker of an injury and is an unpleasant sensory and emotional experience associated with actual or potential tissue damage'.

In early research, Nixon (1993) argued that various structural, cultural and social factors lead to athletes being presented with the message, particularly through the media, that pain and injury should be accepted as an inevitable part of sport. Athletes who show willingness to play 'through the pain barrier' are positively valued; conversely, those who lack such 'bravery' and 'give in' to pain have their moral characters questioned, by being deemed unreliable, weak, lazy, cowardly and unpatriotic (cf. McKay and Roderick 2010). Athletes in pain come under constant pressure to continue competing, such as through stigmatization by coaches and team-mates or the threat of losing their team places (Roderick 2006). In addition to the problematic ethics of requiring athletes to endure substantial pain, there is the real risk that the accumulation of minor injuries will result in more serious, long-term injury. Moreover, elite sport puts a high premium on having athletes passed 'fit' in order to compete. Medical staff, management, coaches, and even the athletes themselves may look to patch up or to gloss over secondary injuries, again with long-term consequences for fitness and health (Howe 2004).

At the same time, the social agency of athletes needs to be considered. Young, McTeer and White (1994) initially found that male athletes did not question the physical risks associated with sport, and that serious injuries tended to be viewed positively in enhancing masculine identity. Theberge (2008) later observed that athletes viewed their bodies as 'disembodied' – as objects to be managed – and thought of health in terms of athletic capacity, with reference to their 'immediate competitive careers'. Howe (2004), in some contrast, found that athletes are substantially aware of cultures of risk in sport and negotiate the extent to which they will risk pain, injury and long-term health in the pursuit of improved performances. Similar questions are increasingly relevant to mass sport, as participants may take specific risks (such as with illegal training supplements or unusual forms of cosmetic surgery) in order to pursue the idealized body types that are promoted through consumer culture.

Two areas of substantial public concern regarding pain and injury in sport have centred on children and American football. First, for children, the dangers of excessive exercise were recognized as far back as the ancient world: Aristotle (1981: 460) observed that boys in Olympic competitions would 'lose their strength' as men as a result of overtraining. In modern times, diverse protective standards for the rights of children are enshrined within national and international laws and conventions. However, David (2005: 7) has estimated that, in children's competitive sports, while 70 per cent of participants have positive and empowering experiences, 20 per cent are at risk of violent or other abuse, and 10 per cent experience violations of their human rights. Sports such as gymnastics, swimming and tennis remain subjects of substantial concern over the pain, injury, long-term health problems and 'burnout' suffered by child athletes through intense training (Ryan 1996: 11).[18] It needs to be recognized that children are vulnerable citizens who, particularly in pre-adolescence, are not able to give full 'informed consent' to such physical exercise and, indeed, may experience familial pressure to submit to such regimes. In addition, children's involvement in elite sport should be treated as a form of 'child labour' and thus come under full legal protection (Donnelly and Petherick 2006).

Second, in American football, there has been a growing legal, medical and public focus on the health protection of elite players. A mid-1990s report found that around half of NFL players required club-prescribed painkillers or anti-inflammatory drugs each season (*Sports Illustrated*, 27 May 1996). Insider reports and legal actions drew attention to how some team doctors would patch up injured players rather than allow proper healing, thereby increasing risks of long-term damage (Huizenga 1995; *New York Times*, 28 July 2002).

The biggest controversy over injuries in American football has centred on instances of player concussion, which leads to various cognitive or neurological impairments, such as early-onset and severe dementia, Parkinson's, and motor neurone disease (or 'Lou Gehrig's disease'). The NFL downplayed the issue through much of the 1990s and 2000s until many high-profile cases emerged of ex-NFL players (such as Mike Webster, Tony Dorsett and Jim McMahon) with serious degenerative brain conditions, including several who had committed suicide (notably Terry Long, Andre Waters and Junior Seau). Over 4,000 ex-NFL players who had suffered debilitating head injuries brought a collective lawsuit against the league; in August 2013, lawyers representing both sides agreed a $760 million compensation settlement to the ex-players, but the deal was rejected later by the courts, partly on the grounds that players might receive insufficient compensation. In the meantime, the issue of brain injuries has become established in wider social discussions of the NFL. While having a long-standing significance in boxing, brain injuries have also become a growing issue in other sports in recent years, notably rugby, ice-hockey and football, putting pressure on sport governing bodies to do more to safeguard participants, for example through education programmes, changes in rules, and the introduction of new equipment. Information from medical science on sport-related brain injuries will inevitably proliferate, thereby increasing the prospect of future litigation by participants, and thus raising the significance of this issue for many sport governing bodies.

Doping

Doping refers to the use of performance-enhancing drugs (PEDs) in sport. Most sport organizations view the use of PEDs as contrary to the ethos of sport and thus impose prohibitions on the stated grounds of fairness of competition and athlete health.

Athletes have always used stimulants to enhance performance. Ancient Olympians consumed specific herbal concoctions, while, in early modern sports, athletes such as the 1904 Olympic marathon champion Thomas Hicks took such stimulants as strychnine and amphetamine to improve competitiveness. In the 1950s and 1960s, a growing anti-doping lobby began to have influence within the politics of sports, despite limited initial hard evidence emerging on the actual prevalence of the problem (Møller 2015). Several sport governing bodies introduced testing for prohibited substances, and the list was later extended in many sports to encompass anabolic steroids, blood doping and the use of EPO (erythropoietin).

Several notable doping controversies have arisen in global sport. First, in what was then the biggest case by far, at the 1988 Seoul Olympic Games, the 100-metre men's champion, Ben Johnson, tested positive for anabolic steroids. Yet a delve into recent Olympic history highlights the scale of doping offences since testing was first introduced in 1968, with athletics and weightlifting in particular seeing many competitors caught. The 2004 Athens games produced a particularly high number of identified doping violations: thirty-three cases. Second, in elite cycling, particularly at the Tour de France, separate investigations by police forces, journalists and sport officials uncovered a culture of systematic doping across leading cyclists and their teams. Ultimately, only one original winner of the Tour de France from 1996 to 2010 had not tested positive or admitted to doping; the guilty list included six-time Tour winner Lance Armstrong, who was stripped of all his titles. Third, there is widespread evidence of systematic state-sponsored doping in the former communist bloc of East European nations from the 1960s through to their collapse over the years 1989 to 1992. In the former East Germany – winner of over 150 gold medals at five summer Olympics in the period 1968–88 – a highly organized apparatus of doping contributed substantially to an exceptional record of success. Fourth, in American baseball, numerous players have admitted to PED use, including José Canseco and Mark McGwire (who broke the MLB record for single-season home runs, with 70 in 1998), while others such as Barry Bonds (who broke the same record with 73 in 2001) have been accused of involvement. After the MLB was pressed to toughen its testing, over thirty players received bans between 2006 and 2013 for PED use, among them top stars such as Alex Rodriguez, Melky Cabrera, Ryan Braun, Bartolo Colon and Manny Ramirez (twice).

Since the late 1990s, there has been a growth of governmental organizations and activities that focus on tackling doping within sport. The World Anti-Doping Agency, WADA, was founded in 1999 with full support from the IOC, while many national sport systems have introduced their own anti-doping agencies; meanwhile, UNESCO (the United Nations Educational, Scientific and Cultural Organization), the Council of Europe and other intergovernmental organizations have established conventions and treaties against doping in sport. This transnational apparatus of testing and regulation may be far more systematic and powerful than early anti-doping initiatives. However, such measures will not entirely eradicate doping, so long as some sport systems, subcultures and key social actors are able to take calculated risks in using PEDs in ways that are likely to go undetected.

★ ★ ★

Overall, violence, pain and injury, and doping are three key research fields for the sociological study of bodily risk-taking within sport. One overarching theoretical approach which may be used to explain such risk-taking is provided by the German sociologist Ulrich Beck (1992) through his work on *risk society*. For Beck, modern life is shaped by the growing significance and increasing public awareness of, as well as anxiety towards, different kinds of transnational risk. Examples of such risks are global warming, radiation leaks at nuclear power stations, potential attacks by international terrorist organizations, food-related risks such as 'mad cow disease' in the UK, and the global spread of highly infectious diseases such as HIV/AIDS or avian flu. These risks are essentially 'man-made' – for example in being the unintended side effects of industrial and scientific development or of greater levels of migration and global travel. In the risk society, the wider public come to view scientists and other 'expert systems' more critically, 'not only as a source of solutions to problems, but also as a cause of problems' (ibid.: 155–6). The emergence of a contemporary risk society is tied only in part to class divisions: more risks are endured by lower-class social groups, but 'boomerang effects' occur, so that risk-producers are also adversely affected (for instance, chemical companies which pollute rivers are also adversely affected by pollution).

The main aspects of Beck's theory of risk society are applicable to our discussion of risk-taking in sport. First, sport organizations, athletes and wider publics have a greater awareness of the physical risks with regard to injuries, violence and doping, as demonstrated by the fact that these aspects of sport have become major public issues in recent times. Second, these risks are widely viewed as 'man-made' or socially constructed, in part through the activities of sport 'expert systems', such as coaches who downplay or ignore athlete injuries and scientists and physicians who manufacture PEDs and guide athletes into usage. Third, the greatest risks in sport tend to be endured by the weakest and most vulnerable social groups, such as lower-class boxers in societies with high levels of social inequality and young people under the direction of elite-performance coaches. (However, the risks of serious sport injuries reach other such groups, such as elite rugby union players who might be drawn from middle-class backgrounds.) 'Boomerang effects' occur, for example, when these experts produce too many risks and there is a backlash within the sport or wider social system, as occurred in response to doping programmes in athletics and in cycling, and as also happens in boxing when fighters suffer fatal injuries. Overall, Beck's theory of risk society provides us with a useful analytical framework for examining critically the contemporary social context for bodily risk-taking in sport.

Sport, voluntary risk-taking and 'peak experiences'

We turn now to consider a particular field of voluntary risk-taking in sporting activities, where the emphasis is on the pursuit of excitement and 'peak experiences'. Such activities include climbing, water-skiing, skydiving, kayaking, surfing and snowboarding. In recent years, many of these activities have come to be viewed as part of the expanding field of 'extreme sports' or 'action sports' (Rinehart and Sydnor 2003; Thorpe 2014).

Given their emphasis on excitement, we might begin to discuss these sports with reference to social psychological approaches. Participants in these types of activity may be understood as having distinctive 'paratelic' personalities, which are playful and enjoy high arousal (Apter 1982) and thus seek out peak experience from their sport participation, such as through senses of ecstasy and euphoria, temporal confusion, increased energy and physical power, and environmental unity (McInman and Grove 1991; Lyng 1990: 882). Such pleasurable 'flow' sensations are maximized when there is an appropriate balance between the level of challenge within the sport and the specific skill level of the participant (Csikszentmihalyi 1975; Csikszentmihalyi and Csikszentmihalyi 1988). Extreme sports – such as long-distance running, rock-face climbing, skydiving and BASE jumping – may generate senses of vertiginous excitement or 'voluptuous panic' that are literally sensational. As one participant explained, shortly before being killed in an attempt to complete a trapeze-like manoeuvre across two gliders, 'I only feel right when I have goose pimples running over my skin. It's a gut need. It's a sort of drug. In fact I have to frighten myself' (Le Breton 2000: 8–9).

Social psychological approaches help us to understand the motivations behind sport-related risk-taking, but sociological perspectives are more effective in explaining social factors and influences. For example, we might consider how participants enter and are socialized into these sporting pastimes, particularly through the influence of wider subcultural groupings. We may also examine the social demographics of these sports, notably the high levels of participation among white middle-class professionals (Fletcher 2008; Kay and Laberge 2002; Lyng 1990).

In an insightful sociological analysis, Langseth (2011) has argued that social scientific explanations of voluntary risk sports have tended to fall into two broad categories. First, *compensation* approaches argue that risk sports provide compensatory, escape experiences for social groups whose lives have otherwise become overly regulated, routinized and boring. In his classic study of skydiving, Lyng (1990) found that participants were seeking an exciting refuge from the excessive rationalization and bureaucratization of white-collar work. From a Northern European perspective, Møller (2007) has argued that strong social welfare systems serve to remove the 'fear-factor' of everyday life, hence extreme sports serve to compensate for overly secure social lives. Second, and in some contrast, *adaptation* perspectives view exciting risk sports as embedded within the 'cultural imperatives of late modernity'. Thus risk-takers are understood as embodying the dominant values of contemporary modern culture, 'such as individualism, authenticity, creativity, spontaneity, anti-conventionalism, flexibility, self-realization and the search for an interesting and exciting life' (Langseth 2011: 632–3). Viewed in this way, the act of participating in risk sports represents a lifestyle identity statement within an individualistic consumer culture (cf. Featherstone 1991). Moreover, the adaptation perspective may link the rise of risk-taking sports with neoliberalism and the perceived decline of social welfare systems. The point here is that risk-taking sports are associated with individual qualities and skills (such as resourcefulness, or effectiveness in risk assessment and crisis management) that are particularly valuable in neoliberal contexts, where old forms of personal and social security (such as strong welfare systems or the opportunity to enjoy lifetime employment) have been greatly weakened. For Langseth, participation in risk sports is driven by both compensation and adaptation: social actors escape one set of social structures and cultural norms that are associated with boring over-regulation, but turn to another set that emphasize individualism and lifestyle consumerism. Given these social factors and influences, we may expect the participant numbers in extreme or action sports to continue to grow, particularly in developed countries.

Concluding comments

In this chapter I have examined the diverse ways in which sociologists might study the body within sport. Foucauldian theories enable us not only to understand how the body has been central to power relations in modern sport and other social spheres through forms of corporeal discipline, control and government but also to recognize the scope for alternative, resistant and transgressive forms of bodily knowledge and practice. Phenomenological perspectives are particularly valuable in capturing the bodily experience of sport, especially in sensory terms. The phenomenological insights by scholars of outdoor life (or, in Scandinavian terms, *friluftsliv*) may be fruitfully reapplied to explain sport. Modern sport places the body at risk in a variety of ways, and sociologists have been particularly active in exploring this point with reference to the issues of pain and injury, violence (such as in boxing) and doping. Beck's theory of the 'risk society' may be utilized to explain risk-taking within these contexts. Voluntary risk-taking in extreme or action sports may be examined through a mix of social psychological and sociological perspectives; theories of 'peak experience', 'flow', subcultural socialization and 'compensation/ adaptation' are particularly useful here. Notably, power differentials within advanced capitalist societies are reflected in the correlations between the middle classes and relatively new, voluntary risk-taking activities (where the 'escape' tends to be from an over-rationalized life) and between the lower classes and more 'required' forms of risk-taking in long-established sports such as boxing (where the 'escape' attempt, usually unsuccessful, is from poverty and low social status).

The concluding point that I wish to make relates to the need for much more substantial and extensive interdisciplinary research on the body in sport. Over fifty years ago, the British novelist and scientist C. P. Snow (1959) complained that modern Western intellectuals had divided themselves into two cultures, centring on the liberal arts and the natural sciences respectively. Dialogue across this divide has tended to be deaf and mutually destructive. Arguably, this division is reflected in the separation between the arts and social sciences, on one side, and the natural sciences, on the other, in the study of sport and many other social fields and issues. The study of the human body in sport represents one research focus that is shared by the social and natural scientists, and thus provides potentially the best study area for bringing the 'two cultures' together in order to undertake genuinely interdisciplinary work. Such research would certainly generate more comprehensive explanations and understanding of the body in sport. It may also demonstrate how the social and natural sciences may be most effectively combined in order to advance our knowledge of sport and many other research topics.

Questions for discussion

1 How has modern sport been used to exercise discipline and control over the body?
2 What particular sensory experiences are facilitated by participation in different sports?
3 What bodily risks are associated with violence and doping in sport? Are these sport-based risks linked to specific social classes or ethnic groups?
4 What reasons might be given for the participation of different groups in voluntary risk-taking activities such as BASE jumping and skydiving?
5 How might sport be restructured in order to extend the pleasurable experiences of participants while reducing bodily risks?

8

Sporting Places and Spaces: Fields of Affection, Commerce and Fantasy

On one of his numerous comeback albums, Frank Sinatra crooned a poignant and nostalgic tribute to his old baseball team, the Brooklyn Dodgers, and to their Ebbets Field stadium in Brooklyn, New York. The song – written by Joe Raposo and entitled 'There used to be a ballpark right here' – recalled the sounds and smells, the crowds and occasion, of sunny summer days at the stadium. All of that came to an end in 1958 when the owner of the Dodgers, in search of bigger revenues, relocated the club to the other side of the United States: the Brooklyn Dodgers became the Los Angeles Dodgers, and the vacated Ebbets Field was demolished two years later. Sinatra's song and the wider story of Ebbets Field demonstrate how we generate particular emotional and popular cultural ties to recreational landscapes. The story also underscores how, in capitalist societies, sport and leisure spaces are commercial entities where, in most circumstances, money may be used to trump sentiment and community. Thus, in the context of American sport, and unlike Sinatra's own career, there was to be no comeback for Brooklyn's baseball team.

In this chapter, I examine the major sociological questions surrounding sport's spatial dimensions. First, with particular reference to the work of John Bale, I discuss the emotional attachments and special meanings that people give to specific sporting spaces. Second, I assess the political economy of sporting landscapes, notably with regard to processes of 'hypercommodification', the construction of stadiums in North America using public money, the hosting of sport mega-events, and the relationship of sport to environmental issues. Third, I explore the postmodern aspects of sport arenas, with reference to processes of rationalization and commercialization and the rise of virtual culture. Fourth, I turn to discuss the social control of sporting spaces – a subject that has gained greater significance for social scientists since the late 1990s. I conclude by interrelating these different arguments to consider the balance between political economic and socio-cultural factors in shaping sporting spaces.

Sport places and emotional attachments

Sport places often possess strong social and cultural meanings for different publics. John Bale, who pioneered the field of sport geography within the social sciences, has made a major contribution to explaining these forms of popular attachment.[19]

Drawing on the work of Tuan (1974), Bale (1994: 120) used the concept of 'topophilia' to capture the 'love of place' that different publics may have for specific sport settings. In the same vein, Bale (1991a) applied five metaphors, with strong Durkheimian overtones, to capture the heightened public meanings that sport settings (in this case, football stadiums) may have for different people.

- First, the stadium appears as a *sacred place* with heightened spiritual meanings for its 'congregation'. Quasi-religious ceremonies are enacted in stadiums, such as the scattering of the ashes of deceased fans or turning some sections into 'shrines' in memory of people who have recently died. For example, following the 1989 Hillsborough stadium disaster in Sheffield, at which ninety-six Liverpool fans were fatally injured, football supporters covered many sections of the stadiums in both cities with wreaths, flowers and diverse football memorabilia.[20]
- Second, the stadium may have *scenic* qualities that provide athletes and spectators with distinctive visual pleasures, particularly when 'complex landscape ensembles' are evident, such as the local cathedrals, old trees, and nearby hillsides that may be viewed from some English cricket grounds (Bale 1995: 81).
- Third, the stadium is a *home* to players and fans, reflecting deep senses of familiarity and attachment while promoting collective psychological advantages for the 'home' club over visiting opponents during games.
- Fourth, the stadium may be a *tourist place* or heritage site that offers visitors guided tours.
- Fifth, the stadium may engender *deep local pride*; the team which plays at home may be 'a focus for community bonding and the source of "reconstruction" of some former *Gemeinschaft*' (Bale

1991a: 135). Strong examples here are old, inner-city stadiums which are still attended by large groups of fans who previously lived in the local area.

To add to this fivefold model, I would suggest that sport stadiums acquire further symbolic meaning through their 'patina' – in other words, the signs of age that they might carry which, nevertheless, point to their distinctive identity and community history (Ritzer and Stillman 2001). Illustrations of this patina might include discoloured brickwork, frayed signs, worn seating, and faded graffiti in and around the stadium.

Viewed in this way, the stadium emerges as a critical site for the construction and expression of particular kinds of personal and collective identity. Spectators may have favourite standing positions or seats from which to watch their favoured team, and where they may meet with friends, family or acquaintances. Different parts of the stadium may have their own habitus in Bourdieu's sense (see chapter 10), in terms of attracting spectators who have particular social backgrounds (as regards age and class), cultural tastes and predispositions. Distinctive spectator subcultures may congregate in some parts of the stadium; for example, in many sports we find long-standing supporters who have identified strongly with particular ground sections, claiming these places as 'their own', where they 'belong', and from where they generate loud, expressive, and often raucous and spectacular displays of support for their team. Football stadiums typically accommodate these intense forms of identification within the ground 'ends' (or *curvas* in Italy). Similar fan groups tend to gather in specific sections in other football codes, such as Gaelic football, Australian Rules football and American football – for example, fans in the 'bleacher' seats at college level or supporters in the old 'Dawg Pound' section in the Cleveland Browns stadium.

Not every social group or community may accord positive meanings to specific sport places. In some instances, the stadium may inspire 'topophobia' – that is, negative emotional meanings such as fear or hostility (Bale 1994: 145–6). For example, residents or businesses located near to stadiums may be badly affected by 'spillover' problems or 'negative externalities' such as raucous singing, drinking, urinating, vandalism and fighting among fans (Bale 1990; Mason and Roberts 1991). Topophobia may be associated particularly with vulnerable social groups, who are, perhaps, more likely to fear any crime and disorder that might be linked potentially to a specific place of sport.

Yet, as a whole, the themes of topophilia rather than topophobia tend to resonate more within other sociological perspectives on places of sport and leisure. Wearing (1998: 134–5), for example, has employed the concept of *chora*, initially advanced by Grosz (1995), to describe how people (or 'chorasters') engage fully and informally with popular recreational areas, using the example of an old saltwater swimming pool in Manly, Sydney. Extending this concept, it might be argued that sports fans act as chorasters when they develop distinctive ties with stadiums. On sport in Argentina, Archetti (1998: 180–1) discussed the symbolic significance of *potreros* (undeveloped urban wastelands) where, according to popular folklore, young boys (*pibes*) learn to play football in the Argentinian way, with an emphasis on dribbling skills and a style rooted in 'freshness, spontaneity and freedom'. In this way, the topophilic meaning of *potreros* is closely associated with the making of masculine national identities through sport.

Overall, emotional investments in sport places are complex and multi-faceted; they may be negative as well as positive and may intensify over time. For fans in particular, sporting places are also important reference points in the production and reproduction of strong social solidarities through sport. Yet, as I discuss in the next section, these socio-cultural meanings and qualities of sporting places are apt to be reshaped or challenged by powerful political economic forces.

Political economy and sport arenas

In this section, I explore the political economic aspects of sport with reference to four critical issues that affect sporting publics: the hypercommodification of sport spaces, stadium building in North America, the hosting of sport mega-events, and environmental issues.

The hypercommodification of sport spaces

In most societies, nearly all sport venues are what Reiss (1991: 4) calls 'semipublic sports facilities' – in other words, they are privately owned (whether by individuals, private associations or local authorities), and the public are charged fees in order to enter and to use these facilities. At the elite level, modern sport stadiums have been developed largely to maximize their commercial value. In much of Europe and North America during the nineteenth and early twentieth centuries, large stadiums were constructed in order to stage and to enclose popular sport events, ensuring that spectators would need to pay admission charges to watch. In turn, in sports such as baseball and football, stadium gate-money played the critical role in financing the professionalization of athletes.

The stadium quickly mirrored the wider spatial division of city populations into class-based 'segments' or 'molecules': more expensive, prime-viewing seated areas were reserved for the bourgeoisie; more distant stands (such as the 'bleacher' seats in North American stadiums) or larger standing terraces were dominated by working-class spectators (see Sennett 1977: 135). Since the 1970s, the socio-economic structure of advanced modern societies has become more varied, and so the class composition and price differentiation of stadium sections has tended to become more complex. Thus, professional sport arenas are increasingly filled with commercial sections and facilities, such as executive boxes primarily for corporate groups and sponsors; specific 'member' stands that offer exclusive lounge areas inside the ground and other perks; more space for national and international media; and 'family stands', offering cut-price seating but aiming to secure the long-term reproduction of spectator numbers.

I noted in chapter 3 that elite professional sport has undergone processes of hypercommodification. Two critical socio-spatial issues have arisen from this process.

First, in many elite professional sports, the commercialization of stadiums has raised issues regarding *the politics of access*. In this sense, we have a classic sociological problem to consider: how insufficient resources (in this instance, tickets to gain access to sport events) should be distributed across different social groups. For elite sport events, those resources have become increasingly scarce and have tended to be distributed along the lines of market criteria (that is, who can afford and is willing to pay for tickets) rather than other principles (such as who has longest-standing commitment to supporting the relevant team).

Hypercommodification of access to elite sport is reflected in escalating ticket prices. In the English Premier League, over the period 1990 to 2010, season ticket prices at clubs rose by many times more (in some cases, ten times more) than the rate of inflation (*The Guardian*, 16 August 2011). Prices for international cricket in Australia have also been criticized as high, as dedicated fans are required to spend a greater proportion of their disposable income on match attendance (*Sydney Morning Herald*, 26 December 2011). In American football, average ticket prices rose over the 2003–13 period by more than 5 per cent and parking costs more than doubled, while in recent times stadium attendance figures have declined (CNN, 7 September 2013). In San Francisco, some of the oldest fans of the 49ers football team were unable to maintain their season tickets after the club moved to a new stadium, resulting in a tripling of admission prices and demands for 'seat licence' payments of US$30,000 (*San Francisco Chronicle*, 18 April 2012).

The distribution of tickets to elite events such as 'Cup Finals' or sport mega-events is also heavily premised upon market principles: thus, priority access tends to be accorded to corporate sponsors or those with high-price 'membership' packages, as well as political elites, particularly within the sport system. A further, murkier layer of commodification has been added by the vast 'secondary market' which has mushroomed since the 1990s, involving the *de facto* 'touting' or 'scalping' of elite sport event tickets, notably through the corruption of officials in sport governing bodies. For example, Brazilian police at the 2014 World Cup finals found initial evidence of a US$90 million scam for the illegal reselling of match tickets involving a gang with high connections among football officials and thought to have been active also at three earlier tournaments (*The Guardian*, 8 July 2014). The overall result is that, *ceteris paribus*, non-corporate long-term supporters of different clubs or national sport teams have found it increasingly difficult and expensive to gain tickets to attend these prestige events. Thus, for the London 2012 Olympics, large proportions of tickets were allocated to Olympic sponsors and to members and associates of the 'Olympic family', while UK citizens often had access to relatively few seats for the most important occasions: for example, only 44 per cent of tickets for the opening ceremony, 43 per cent for some cycling finals, 3 per cent for some tennis fixtures, and a measly 0.12 per cent for one sailing final went on sale to the general public (Giulianotti et al. 2014b).

A second issue arising from hypercommodification relates to the *politics of stadium identities*. For example, we may explore how, as stadiums become more corporate and expensive, there is relatively less capacity to accommodate comparatively younger and working-class supporter subcultures. Ironically, marginalization of these groups may impact negatively on stadium atmosphere, which otherwise makes the sport 'product' more appealing to television viewers. Thus, we have the famous comment by Roy Keane, then captain of Manchester United, that too many spectators were focused more on consuming 'prawn sandwiches' and other corporate hospitality than on events on the field of play. Intensified stadium security, discussed later in this chapter, may also undermine these fan identities by restricting more boisterous or spectacular supporter activities; in European football, these restrictions have included prohibitions on fireworks, which had otherwise become integral to the spectacles mounted by fan subcultures. At the same time, we find occasions when sport clubs appropriate the spatially specific identities of supporter subcultures for commercial ends. For instance, in American football, the Cleveland Browns have been criticized by some fan groups for the commodification of the 'Dawg Pound' section, where more raucous, 'blue-collar' supporters gathered, in terms of higher ticket prices and a more corporate atmosphere, and through 'trademarking' of this particular fan identity, leading to the marketing of 'Dawg Pound' 'official' apparel.

A further issue concerns the widespread practice of commodifying the 'naming rights' of stadiums. To select but a few examples, among sport grounds with corporate names are the Allianz Arena (home to Bayern Munich football club), Allianz Parque (Palmeiras of Sao Paulo football club), ANZ Stadium (Sydney), Red Bull Arena (home to Red Bull Salzburg), Rogers Centre (Toronto Blue Jays baseball team, Toronto Argonauts Canadian football team), BIDVest Wanderers Stadium (Johannesburg), Emirates Stadium (home to Arsenal of London), Lincoln Financial Field (Philadelphia Eagles) and Mall of America Field at the Hubert H. Humphrey Metrodome (Minnesota Vikings). While generating substantial revenues for the relevant sport clubs, the selling of naming rights may undermine the extent to which stadiums generate topophilia among spectators or encapsulate the distinctive identities of the wider community of fans.

Overall, the hypercommodification of stadiums provides us with many case studies in how the free-market political economy of sport may serve to challenge or to undermine its 'bottom-up' socio-cultural aspects. As I have indicated here, the key cultural political issues centre on stadium access and identities.

North American sports: the politics of stadium construction

A second set of critical issues on the political economy of sport spaces relates to public subsidies for stadium construction, primarily in the North American context. In major North American sports leagues such as the NFL, MLB, NHL and NBA, each competing team is in effect a privately owned 'franchise'; if they so wish, franchise owners are largely free to relocate their team to a new 'home' city. The Brooklyn Dodgers, mentioned at the start of this chapter, is only one of more than sixty such relocations that have occurred in the leading four North American sports since the 1900s. Sport leagues are also free to grant new memberships (or 'expansion' franchises) to cities and club owners in locations which offer strong commercial opportunities.

Many civic authorities in North America have built expensive new sport stadiums over the years in order to attract or to retain major league clubs. Some argue that these sport teams have commercial benefits for host cities in terms of offering employment and associated revenues such as consumer spending when games are staged (see Euchner 1993: 68–70); sport teams are portrayed as 'civic flagships', particularly for post-industrial cities seeking new investment, tourism and leisure spending (see Bélanger 2000); and sport teams are seen as powerful vehicles for building social capital and civic identification in host cities.

However, powerful critiques may be advanced on the politics and economics of stadium construction in North America. In effect, stadium subsidies constitute a form of 'corporate welfarism', wherein public money is actually directed towards protecting the commercial interests or 'welfare' of the billionaires who privately own and control these sport clubs. Sports economists argue that the public costs of stadium building tend far to outweigh the financial benefits (Noll and Zimbalist 1997; Rosentraub 1999). Indeed, such spending inevitably means that hundreds of millions of dollars of public money cannot go towards key public services such as education, health, policing and transport (see Delaney and Eckstein 2003; deMause and Cagan 2008). Moreover, civic authorities lose some US$4billion in the tax exemptions that they grant to club owners (Bloomberg, 5 September 2012). In addition, the real costs of stadium construction are usually far higher than initial estimates; the difference here totalled some US$10 billion for all major sport arenas in use in 2010 (Long 2012). New sport facilities often lead to higher ticket prices for supporters; thus, poorer spectators may be priced out of attendance or be required to forgo more of their limited disposable income in order to gain admission. We may also query whether even a winning local team will by itself redefine the public image or commercial status of a host city (Rowe and McGuirk 1999). Overall, the evidence indicates that North American cities lose rather than gain financially from hosting sport teams, although there are clear commercial benefits for the 'franchise' owners and the sport leagues.

The politics of hosting sport mega-events

A third set of political economic issues surrounding sport spaces relates to the hosting of mega-events such as the Olympic Games or the World Cup finals. Cities and nations bidding to host these events need to win public support for such massive projects. Thus, the bidding committees and their backers argue that these events will create new jobs, business and tourism opportunities; new or enhanced sport facilities; improved infrastructure in roads, railways and airports; better public health through more sport participation and physical activity among the host population; and major urban transformations, such as the gentrification and regeneration of declining inner-city areas (Hall 2006; Malfas, Theodoraki and Houlihan 2004; Preuss 2006). The 1992 Barcelona Olympics is often presented as the ideal role model here in generating many of these benefits while transforming the hosts into a 'global city' (Degen 2004).

Yet critical social research tends to point to other, less positive impacts of event hosting. Many mega-events produce 'white elephants' – extremely expensive sport facilities that are grossly under-utilized afterwards; examples here are the Olympic stadiums in Montreal (1976), Seoul (1988), Sydney (2000), Athens (2004) and Beijing (2008). Clear evidence that these events have provided host cities and nations with significant economic boosts is also difficult to identify. Meanwhile, international governing bodies such as FIFA require the hosts, first, to bear the multi-billion-dollar costs of staging the event and, second, to grant these bodies and their corporate partners a full exemption from taxes on any profits – for the 2014 Brazil World Cup, this entailed an estimated loss of US$250 million in revenues for the Brazilian government (*Forbes*, 16 June 2014).

Sport mega-events may serve to disempower the poorer members of host communities, with wealthier parts of the city or nation being the main beneficiaries. For example, at the London 2012 Olympics, most events were staged at venues in the Olympic Park, located in the poor East End. Yet many residents, business people and politicians reported that few job opportunities were available locally in regard to building or working in the venues. Due in large part to the transport system imposed on the area, many local businesses suffered losses in trade during the games; conversely, the large shopping mall next to Olympic Park, privately owned by an Australian corporation and filled with leading transnational companies, enjoyed unprecedented numbers of visitors (Giulianotti et al. 2014a, 2014b). East London also lost its best opportunity to reach global television audiences when the Olympic organizers relocated the marathon events from the Olympic Park area to central London. After the Olympics, the privately owned local football team West Ham United won the right to move into the Olympic stadium; the local council agreed to borrow £40 million to help fund the stadium's conversion for football purposes – at the same time, the council, representing one of the UK's poorest areas, was set to suffer overall budget cuts of £100 million (Giulianotti et al. 2014b).

The most disempowering social impacts of sport mega-events may relate to the redevelopment and privatization of land. In some instances, unwanted poor populations are evicted to make way for the construction of sanitized, neoliberal spaces for new, wealthier residents and businesses. Prior to the Commonwealth Games in Delhi, India, an estimated 250,000 poor people were evicted (*The Hindu*, 13 October 2010); other such social clearing occurred at the 2008 Beijing Olympics, the 2010 World Cup finals in South Africa and the 2010 Winter Olympics in Vancouver (*USA Today*, 5 June 2007; *The Guardian*, 3 February 2010, 1 April 2010).

Corruption is also a concern, notably misappropriation of public funds for the event; for example, the budget for the 2014 Sochi Winter Olympics multiplied from US$12 billion to US$51 billion, with an alleged US$30 billion going on corrupt 'kickbacks and embezzlement' (*The Guardian*, 9 October 2013). Further criticisms have been directed towards human rights abuses by event hosts. Western media and politicians have accused Russia, host of the 2014 Winter Olympics and the 2018 football World Cup finals, of state-backed abuse of the LGBT community. The Gulf state of Qatar, which won the right to host the 2022 football World Cup finals, was widely criticized in the West for the abuse and mistreatment of migrant workers; one international trade union report estimated that up to 4,000 workers would die during the country's preparations for the event (*The Guardian*, 26 September 2013). In this context, we might consider the position of the host cities and nations vis-à-vis international society. These hosts aim to use the event in part to strengthen their civic or national 'brands' and to increase their 'soft power' (that is, their attractiveness and influence) among global audiences. However, such events also place host cities and nations in the international spotlight, so that critical media reports and human rights campaigns may serve to 'disempower' them in terms of reputation or 'brand' identity (Brannagan and Giulianotti 2014).

Environmental issues

A fourth set of issues, commonly underpinned by substantial political economic influences, relates to the environmental impacts of sport. To begin we may note that environmentalism has become embedded in the official ideologies of many sport organizations, tournaments and associated sponsors. For example, after the 1994 Lillehammer Winter Olympics in Norway, the IOC added the environment as the 'third dimension of Olympism' (sport and culture being the other two), so that future games should have a clear environmental agenda and secure a 'green legacy' (cf. Klausen 1999: 34).

Yet elite sport tends to be environmentally problematic in four main senses. First, major sport events leave a huge 'ecological footprint', notably through the air travel of athletes, coaches, officials, media, VIPs and spectators. Second, commercial sport invariably puts economic interests ahead of environmental and community concerns. For example, environmental campaigners criticize the global golf industry for harming delicate eco-systems, as well as for its high use of water and pesticides (Wilson and Millington 2015). Third, the 'green' ideals and statements of sport event organizers may jar with local community experiences. At the 2000 Sydney Olympics, 'green' criteria were said to have influenced stadium planning, yet many locals complained about local environmental impacts, such as the erection of a temporary beach volleyball stadium on Bondi Beach (Prasad 1999: 92; Lenskyj 2002). The London 2012 Olympics organizers highlighted the creation of the green 500-acre Olympic Park as a lasting environmental legacy. Yet several community groups protested against the imposition of Olympic events and facilities on local green spaces. Fourth, green messages from sport governing bodies and event organizers may be contrasted with the environmental records of corporate sponsors and 'partners'. Environmental groups protested at the 2012 London Olympics against several event sponsors, including the oil company BP (which had caused the Deepwater Horizon oil spill in the Gulf of Mexico), the mining company Rio Tinto (accused of various human rights and environmental abuses, particularly in the Global South) and Dow Chemical (one of whose subsidiaries is the Union Carbide company, which had caused the 1984 Bhopal gas leak disaster in India, estimated to have fatally injured over 16,000 people). Thus, overall, notwithstanding the initial recognition of 'green' issues, sport tends to have a highly problematic relationship to the environment, particularly when political economic factors are taken fully into account.

Political criticism and opposition

These political economic issues surrounding sporting spaces have attracted diverse criticisms and opposition. Some social movements within sport – notably football fan organizations in Europe and South America – have mobilized against rising ticket prices alongside the broader commercialization of sport culture (cf. Gaffney 2013; Giulianotti 2011a; Kennedy and Kennedy 2012). Critics of excessive admission prices may point also to alternative models for organizing sport; in the UK media, for example, there is regular reference to German football stadiums, which attract more spectators and have much lower admission prices.

The renaming of sport stadiums represents a prioritization of commercial interests over the socio-cultural identity of the club and its 'home'. In some circumstances, supporters resist by using the stadium's old name, directly ignoring the new commercial title, as occurred among baseball and American football fans at Candlestick Park in San Francisco. Elsewhere, in north-east England in 2011, the unpopular owner of the Newcastle United football club temporarily renamed the home stadium, St James' Park, after his main company, to become the 'Sport Direct Arena'; the move drew widespread criticism by fans, media and politicians and was subsequently reversed.

In regard to the public costs of hosting sport stadiums and sport events, significant forms of popular opposition have emerged in different social contexts. In the United States, various political figures, journalists, academics and social movements have opposed the vast expenditures of public money on building stadiums for privately owned clubs (*The Atlantic*, 18 September 2013; deMause and Cagan 2008). Opposition groups also surface in cities that are hosting, or seeking to host, sport mega-events. A notable example was the 'Bread Not Circuses' movement opposing Toronto's 2008 Olympics bid (Lenskyj 2008). The largest mass opposition movements in recent years emerged in Brazil in 2013, when hundreds of thousands of protestors took to the streets during football's 'Confederations Cup' tournament; initially focused on rising public transportation costs, the mass protests soon embraced many popular issues, including corruption, rising living costs, and the multi-billion-dollar spending on hosting the 2014 football World Cup finals and the 2016 Olympics. At London 2012, diverse public criticisms, complaints and forms of opposition were directed at the event in terms of high costs, security measures (such as positioning surface-to-air missiles on tower blocks), the local environment, civil rights (such as legal restrictions on freedom of expression), Olympic transport strategies, the practices of event sponsors (such as the treatment of workers in Adidas production factories), and human rights campaigns against competing nations such as Russia and Sri Lanka. Finally, some cities organize public votes to decide if they will bid to host mega-events, and at this point popular opposition may be successful; for example, in 2013, Munich's citizens voted against bidding to host the 2022 Winter Olympics on the grounds of high costs and environmental concerns.

Overall, political economic forces play a pivotal role in shaping sport spaces; in so doing, they may have significant negative impacts on popular cultures within sport, which in turn may resist aspects of the commercialization of these settings. Political economic forces are also highly influential in the making of 'postmodern' sport stadiums, to which I now turn.

Postmodern sport stadiums

Postmodern sport stadiums may be understood as having significant differences from modern sport settings. Three aspects of the sport stadium are relevant here – their rationalization and commodification, association with 'fantasy cities', and privileging of virtual culture – which I consider in turn. These arguments anticipate some of the key points on 'postmodern sport' that are discussed in chapter 11.

Rationalized stadiums

Postmodern stadiums have a complex relationship to processes of rationalization in sport. This is illuminated when considering baseball stadiums in North America. Drawing on the 'McDonaldization thesis' (discussed in chapter 2), Ritzer and Stillman (2001) have argued that baseball stadiums fall into three historical categories.

First, *early modern* stadiums – such as Boston's Fenway Park or Chicago's Wrigley Field – were built in the early twentieth century and are usually associated with strongly topophilic qualities for five main reasons: their small size, allowing good views and intimacy; their quirky individual features, such as unusual wind channels that influence play; more iconic features, such as distinctive walls or vegetation that inspire fan affection; their urban location; and having played host to epic moments in baseball history, thereby inspiring nostalgia.

Second, *late modern* ballparks, such as Houston's Astrodome, were built in the mid-1960s through to the late 1980s and are largely functional in four particular ways (Ritzer 1993): their efficiency, such as in multi-use design; predictability, such as through fixed roofs, to control playing conditions, and consistent artificial turf; quantity over quality, thus prioritizing stadium capacity over the viewing angles from different seats; and use of automation instead of workers, such as with electronic ticketing machines. Late modern stadiums are relatively charmless and 'lose the magical qualities that attract consumers' (Ritzer and Stillman 2001: 100); during the heyday of these stadiums, baseball attendances declined significantly.

Third, *postmodern* ballparks, such as Baltimore's Camden Yards and Atlanta's Turner Field, have been constructed since the early 1990s. Postmodern stadiums feature 'simulated de-McDonaldization'; in effect, this softens the visibility and impact of stadium rationalization and seeks to re-enchant supporters in subtle ways. For example, some park owners stage 'extravaganzas' that have little relevance to the game in order to attract and distract supporters, such as by using high-tech and entertaining scoreboards or by putting on firework displays. Postmodern stadiums host other major businesses and commercial leisure activities – such as shopping malls, museums, video arcades and food courts – that increase spectacle and ballpark profitability. I note in chapter 11 how postmodern culture is marked in part by playful cultural pastiche and by breaking down taken-for-granted categories and boundaries. In this vein, postmodern ballparks simulate some features of early modern stadiums – such as downtown locations, old-fashioned facades, stylized old technology (beer pumps and mini-trains) and monuments to former players – that confuse time and space categories, playing on nostalgia, and giving the arena 'the aura of the old'. Re-enchantment is also sought through associating the stadium with distinctive local cultural symbols, such as through special backdrops or selling products with local themes. Yet, beneath these attempts to re-enchant the stadium, we find much bigger processes of rationalization (McDonaldization) and commercialization still holding court: thus, for instance, the stadium's layout is carefully designed to maximize the sale of products and profitability. Arguably, this model of the postmodern stadium might be extended to explain other sporting spaces.

Fantasy stadiums

According to Hannigan (1998), North America is producing post-modern 'fantasy cities' in which the middle classes are able to enjoy new experiences while having minimal interaction with the lower social classes. Hannigan identifies six key characteristics of the fantasy city, and these may be applied to explain the 'fantasy sport stadium'. The fantasy city is:

- *theme-o-centric*, in advancing a scripted theme or themes. For example, in some cities there may be a strong focus on the theme of popular culture, which includes references to specific sport stadiums, music venues, and nightclubs.
- *aggressively branded*, often involving 'synergy' partnerships with transnational corporations. In sport, as noted earlier, numerous stadiums have sold their naming rights to major corporations.
- *a 24/7 enterprise*, running day and night, offering flexible consumption outlets to fit with new, varied employment routines. The fantasy stadium might be part of a wider multiplex facility comprising restaurants, shops, cinema houses, bars, bowling alleys, hotels and car parks.
- *modular*, mixing many standardized consumer outlets. Fantasy sport stadiums might have food and merchandise outlets in modularized sale points.
- *solipsistic*, emphasizing illusion and disregarding social problems and injustices in local neighbourhoods. The fantasy stadium might be located within a poor residential area, but its internal themes will entirely ignore outside civic issues and social problems.
- *postmodern* as a cultural form, in terms of emphasizing architectural pastiche, virtual reality and the 'pure entertainment' of theme parks (Rojek 1993; Baudrillard 1996a). Contemporary sport spaces may be experienced as theme parks, where the old differences between fantasy and reality, past and present, local and global, are increasingly blurred. Inside the fantasy stadium, spectators may encounter life-size cartoon characters, play at interactive exhibits in the stadium museum, spend more time buying products or watching giant screens rather than the field of play, and exit at the end through faux art-deco gates.

For Hannigan, the fantasy city promotes three types of consumer activity which are largely self-explanatory: 'shopertainment', 'eatertainment' and 'edutainment'. In effect, according to the logic of this model, the postmodern stadium is rooted in the entertainment-based intersection of fantasy environments and consumerism. In broad terms, this analysis also chimes strongly with Ritzer and Stillman, in producing fantasy locations that are heavily focused on profitable consumerism.

Virtual sport stadiums and settings

A third perspective explores how postmodern sport settings interconnect with the rise of *virtual*, mediated cultures and social experiences. The French social theorist Jean Baudrillard considered the virtual world to be the 'fourth dimension' (*la quatrième dimension*) for human life (*Liberation*, 4 March 1996). In sport, Baudrillard would encourage us to examine how the virtual world has taken precedence over the real; thus, for example, football stadiums may come to be filled with television cameras rather than 'live' spectators (Baudrillard 1993: 79). For Eichberg (1995), the rise of virtual culture is reflected in the *zapping* model of contemporary sport; thus, in the stadium, we find spectators constantly switching their attention from events on the field of play to the giant screens that constantly replay key moments, to their radios that provide running commentaries, and to their various electronic devices (smart phones, tablets, laptops, and so on) which provide links with countless other social environments and realities.

These observations underline how sport is experienced in multifarious virtual ways. Sport games are an important constituent of the global video-game industry, which is predicted to be valued at US$82 billion by 2017 (*Forbes*, 7 August 2012). Video games represent the principal ways in which many sport fans 'play' sport. Moreover, in most nations, sport events soak up a large proportion of the content of television networks, particularly on subscription-based channels. During sport mega-events, such as the World Cup finals, millions of fans congregate in public squares and parks to watch the events on giant television screens.

Overall, these different analyses and premonitions of the postmodern help to reveal the influences of advanced rationalization, commercialization and virtual culture in contemporary and future sport spaces. Several of these approaches advance theoretical models that may be used to assess how close current stadiums are to these particular visions of postmodern sport spaces.

We may also note that the postmodern aspects of sport settings intermingle with other, modern and, indeed, pre-modern aspects of sport culture. For example, watching live sport in public squares on giant screens appears initially to be a virtual, postmodern experience. Pre-modern folk culture is also evident here, for instance through heavy drinking and partisan support for a specific team, and perhaps in the setting for the giant screen, such as a historic park or piazza that has old topophilic significance for local publics. In modern terms, the event may be rationally organized, with alcohol outlets, portable toilets and public transport, and commodified, such as through corporate sponsorship, advertising and VIP sections for corporate guests (cf. Bale 1998; Giulianotti 2011a; Hagemann 2010). In chapter 11, I explore more fully the postmodern aspects of contemporary sport and their interplay with modern and postmodern culture. In the next section, I turn to a subject of growing importance for sport stadiums: security and social control.

Sport stadiums, security and social control

Since the turn of the millennium, social scientists have directed greater attention to the regulation, surveillance and social control of sport stadiums and other sporting spaces.[21] An early inspiration for this research was provided by Foucault's (1977) theory of 'panopticism', which pointed to how populations undergo modern forms of spatial surveillance, discipline and regulation. Foucault drew his theory from Bentham's ([1791] 2010) model of the Panopticon, in which, in a prison context, a central watchtower is positioned to view and to monitor a surrounding ring of cells; prisoners in these cells must assume that they are under constant surveillance, and so they are more likely to follow prison rules and regulations. More broadly, we may consider that the logic of the Panopticon has become central to everyday life, as reflected in the design of public spaces to maximize the monitoring and surveillance of diverse populations.

Sport has played a significant role in advancing the public Panopticon. In the UK during the 1980s, CCTV systems were installed in most football stadiums, primarily as an anti-hooligan measure, in order to monitor crowds. In effect, these stadiums became social laboratories for testing CCTV systems, which were then installed in urban centres in many towns and cities, as well as in most elite-level sport stadiums throughout the world (Armstrong and Giulianotti 1998). Panoptical surveillance and control are achieved inside stadiums in other ways. For example, all-seated stands provide greater comfort than standing areas and are often presented as appealing to broader audiences, including more women, young fans and older spectators; however, seating also restricts the movement of fans and serves to differentiate sport crowds into individual spectators. Thus, security personnel may better observe spectator activities and may identify and remove those deemed to be misbehaving.

Since the 9/11 attacks on the United States in 2001, there has been a substantial expansion in the surveillance and social control of sport-related spaces, as reflected in much greater spending on security. Thus, for summer Olympic Games before 9/11, official security spending was estimated at US$66.3 million (Barcelona, 1992), $108.2 million (Atlanta, 1996), and $180 million (Sydney, 2000); after 9/11, spending multiplied to $1.5 billion (Athens, 2004), $6.5 billion (Beijing, 2008) and an estimated $2 billion (London, 2012) (Houlihan and Giulianotti 2012). In addition, if their bids are to be successful, cities seeking to host major events such as the NFL Super Bowl must demonstrate to the relevant sport governing bodies that they are 'terrorist-ready' in terms of security personnel, technology and overall spending (Schimmel 2011).

The security and surveillance technologies at sport mega-events go on to become part of the *security legacy* from these events (Giulianotti and Klauser 2010). For example, for the Beijing Olympics, among new security technologies were CCTV systems, surveillance systems that registered unusual crowd patterns and movements, two-wheeled electric scooters, and event tickets containing RFID (radio-frequency identification) chips to monitor ticket-holder movements. In Delhi, around 2,000 CCTV cameras were installed during the build-up to the Commonwealth Games. In Germany, for the 2006 World Cup finals, the first national use of CCTV cameras with facial-recognition software occurred, allowing images of those being filmed to be checked against 'hooligan databases'. Some cities such as Stuttgart and Munich also installed hundreds of new public CCTV systems. Other new security technologies were RFID chips, bar codes and holographic images for match tickets (Eick 2011; Klauser 2008). The common expectation is that these technologies will stay in place after the mega-event in order to monitor ordinary citizens at the everyday level.

Sport events also provide the basis for the sharing and transfer of security knowledge and expertise. Further partnerships arise within the security system, for example through new links between private and public security providers, or between the police, the armed forces and the intelligence services. Moreover, these events produce a transnational shadow industry, involving nation-states, security companies and sport governing bodies: for the 2008 Beijing Olympics, almost all of the spending on security technology was directed towards business with foreign corporations such as Honeywell, GE, IBM, Siemens and Panasonic (Giulianotti and Klauser 2010).

Overall, many of these security technologies and strategies extend beyond the Foucauldian model of the Panopticon, in terms of being orientated towards anticipating potential breaches in security, while also routinely gathering data and intelligence on individuals that may be stored for future use. For some scholars, the security legacies at some sport mega-events have anti-democratic impacts and longer-term effects, in terms of eroding civil liberties, while erecting and normalizing systems of surveillance without gaining public approval or establishing sufficient legal safeguards (Eick 2011; Samatas 2011).

We should also underline the deep interconnections between these 'surveillant assemblages' and dominant, neoliberal political economic influences within sport (cf. Haggerty and Ericson 2000). The establishment of relatively controlled, sanitized and pacified spaces inside and outside sport arenas contributes strongly to the neoliberal project of commercializing sport in order to attract wealthier, more bourgeois audiences (Giulianotti 2011b).

Do significant forms of opposition or protest arise with regard to these processes? In the context of social control at sports, we might identify aspects of transgression (if not explicit resistance) as lurking in any rowdy or disorderly behaviour that occurs in stadiums and which is deemed to be offensive to 'respectable' or corporate spectators. For example, at the Sydney Cricket Ground, until the late 1980s, the 'Hill' was a large, undeveloped grassy area, with strong topophilic associations, and populated mainly by working-class fans given to raucous conduct (Lynch 1992). After its redevelopment as a more expensive seated area, disorderly and unruly incidents occurred which might be interpreted as 'reactions' against the 'sanitization' and 'corporatization' of sport and 'against being placed in a plastic seat and enclosed' (ibid.: 44). Elsewhere, since at least the 1960s, different subcultures of young male football supporters have sought to evade security measures in order to engage in violent clashes with their rival peers (Giulianotti and Armstrong 2002). More routine forms of resistance may occur when, at football fixtures in different nations, spectators refuse to sit in allocated seats and instead stand to watch the game. Finally, explicit protests sometimes take place against constrictive security measures at sport events, for example among football supporters in the UK, Germany and Italy and for the Olympics in Beijing, Vancouver and London. However, security 'lockdowns' at sport mega-events may be such that the scope for protest is substantially curtailed. Overall, given these political economic and technological drivers, elite-level sport will continue to experience intensified and more elaborate forms of securitization in and around stadiums.

Concluding comments

The critical academic study of sport spaces is a highly vibrant interdisciplinary field for sociologists of sport. The socio-cultural meanings and identities of sport arenas may be underpinned by strong forms of topophilia and social solidarity. These deep attachments are potentially threatened by political economic processes, notably the hypercommodification of sporting spaces, which in turn has direct impact on public access to, and cultural identities within, sport stadiums; local publics are further squeezed by the political economy of stadium relocations and the hosting of sport mega-events. Theories of postmodern sport settings help us to recognize both the social impacts of the rise of virtual culture and how commercialization and rationalization shape fantasy sporting environments. Finally, through their rapid expansion in sport, security and surveillance systems have had wider societal influences and lasting social legacies, particularly at mega-events, while also creating more orderly, commercialized stadium environments. Ironically, in line with Ritzer's thesis, such processes may serve to de-humanize the stadium by marginalizing the raucous, participatory atmospheres that otherwise appeal to live and television audiences.

Diverse forms of public opposition and criticism have at times sprung up – in episodes of transgression and resistance in stadiums and in popular campaigns and mass demonstrations by social movements. Mirroring the position of some oppositional movements, a critical sociological standpoint would point towards alternative models for the socio-spatial organization of sport. However, as the fate of the Brooklyn Dodgers might remind us, the cultural politics of sport settings seem to boil down to an uneven contest: on the one hand, there are dominant political economic forces of commodification, rationalization and securitization; on the other, we find sport's subordinate grassroots folk cultures that celebrate forms of topophilia, social solidarity and the carnivalesque expression. To protect the latter, sport settings would require forms of political, social and cultural intervention to override purely commercial interests. Such measures would have clear social benefits, although admittedly would come too late to save great former clubs such as the Brooklyn Dodgers.

Questions for discussion

1 In what ways do different sport places inspire particular kinds of love and affection?
2 What impacts do commercial interests and factors have on sport stadiums and their wider communities?
3 How are postmodern stadiums designed? What impacts do they have on the experiences of sport audiences?
4 How are sport stadiums and their wider environs designed to allow for the surveillance and social control of sport audiences?
5 How might we change our use and design of sport stadiums and other sporting spaces to ensure wider public participation and inclusion?

9

Elias on Sport: Figurations, Civilization and Interdependence

In the early 1980s and 1990s, the work of Norbert Elias, and his figurational or 'process sociology' perspective, acquired a prominent position within sociology, particularly in England and the Netherlands. Elias's wide sociological influence came late: his great work, *The Civilizing Process*, had been published first in German in 1939, but was translated and published in English (in two volumes) only between 1969 and 1982. Unlike many sociological schools of thought, Elias and his followers regard sport as an important field of inquiry and research. Most work was undertaken at the University of Leicester, where Elias co-authored (with Eric Dunning) his major statement on sport and leisure, *Quest for Excitement* (1986), and where figurational sociology exerted different influences on future scholars such as Joseph Maguire, Dominic Malcolm, Patrick Murphy, Chris Rojek, Ivan Waddington and Kevin Young. Arguably, the figurational approach has had its strongest impact among English sociologists of sport; in most other branches of sociology, and in most other nations, it is relatively marginal or overlooked, being little known for example in North American sociology.

In this chapter, I examine the figurational standpoint in five main parts. First, I set out how Elias theorized social life through his concept of human figurations, which leads into discussion of his view of sport as 'mimesis' within the 'spare-time spectrum'. Second, I consider Elias's theory of the 'civilizing process' and how this may explain the historical development and 'sportization' of games. Third, I examine how figurational sociologists have attempted to explain violence in sport, in particular modern football hooliganism, with reference to the civilizing process. Fourth, I consider several other fields within sport studies in which the figurational standpoint has been active. I conclude by arguing that figurational sociology should be deployed critically and selectively, in conjunction with other sociological standpoints, in order to examine different aspects of sport.

Human figurations, mimesis and the spare-time spectrum

Elias's sociological standpoint understands societies as being made up of different figurations of interdependent people. Elias (1987: 85) defined figuration as a 'generic concept for the pattern which inter-dependent human beings, as groups or as individuals, form with each other'; examples here might be families, leisure associations, work teams and sport clubs. For Elias, power relations within figurations are highly fluid and mobile rather than being fixed or heavily structured. In addition, he argued that individuals within figurations are 'open beings' (or *homines aperti*) and must not be seen as *homo clausus* (that is, as somehow standing apart from the wider society) (1978b: 115–25). Elias further rejected the 'dualist' approach within much of modern social science, which centres for example on the binary oppositions of the macro and the micro, or between social structures and social action. Conversely, his approach is sometimes presented as 'post-dualist', wherein the concept of figuration combines both the structural/macro and action/micro components of social life. Moreover, Elias extended his points on figurational interdependencies when arguing for the breaking down of disciplinary barriers within the academic field; hence, scholars should draw on the social and natural sciences in order to produce more 'reality-congruent' knowledge on human life (cf. ibid.: 96).

Like Bourdieu, Elias frequently referred to games and sport in order to develop and illustrate his arguments. Games serve to reveal the interdependencies within human figurations and the flux and 'progressive interweaving of moves' (Elias 1978b: 97):

> If one watches the players standing and moving on the field in constant interdependence, one can actually see them forming a continuously changing figuration. In groups or societies at large, one usually cannot see the figurations their individual members form with one another. Nevertheless, in these cases too people form figurations with each other – a city, a church, a political party, a state – which are no less real than the one formed by players on a football field, even though one cannot take them in at a glance. (Elias and Dunning 1986: 199)

Social interdependencies are omnipresent within games and sports, and the figurations within sport are interconnected with other figurations. Thus, sport-related figurations include, for example, the two teams of players, referees and umpires, spectators, administrators, business sponsors, media personnel, a great variety of officials (such as from clubs, governing bodies, and local and national government), workers and employers with equipment manufacturers, and so on (cf. Dunning in Elias and Dunning 1986: 207). In the most complex societies, these 'chains of interdependency' stretch further and further beyond sport and are increasingly international in scope. Moreover, games and sports also illustrate how power is founded upon interdependence within social figurations; even in ancient civilizations, games such as gladiatorial contests were based on interdependencies between the combatants as well as among a much wider array of social actors.

Elias located sport and leisure activities within a 'spare-time spectrum', which basically encompasses social practices outside the realm of paid work. In contrast to other, more routinized activities (such as household chores or voluntary work), the area of 'leisure' offers substantial scope for de-routinization, such as in 'mimetic' or play activities (Elias and Dunning 1986: 96–8).

For figurational sociologists, mimetic activities cover a wide range of pastimes in sport, the arts, wider entertainment and leisure (Dunning 1999: 26). Crucially, mimetic activities arouse excitement, which may be experienced and shown 'with the approval of one's fellows and of one's own conscience as long as it does not overstep certain limits' (Elias and Dunning 1986: 125). Conversely, in non-mimetic activities (notably in work), the public display of emotion is greatly restricted by social controls as well as by individual conscience (Dunning 1999: 26; Elias and Dunning 1986: 125). The most successful and popular modern mimetic activities enable participants to 'de-routinize' by escaping from such low-arousal routines. However, mimetic activities are neither limitless nor unrestrained in their emotional arousal but, instead, allow for a 'controlled de-controlling of emotions' (ibid.: 44). Mimetic activities also generate important 'tension balances' among participants and spectators: if tension is too high or low, then levels of pleasurable excitement are greatly reduced, and there is always the danger that mimetic activities may lose their tension balances by becoming overly routinized.

It might be argued that many sport organizations have been established to produce and reproduce mimetic activities, in terms of staging emotionally exciting events that both facilitate sociability among participants and spectators and provide an escape from more routinized and emotionally restrictive public spaces. Successful sport events inspire the 'controlled de-control' of emotions, where spectators may experience and express substantial excitement without, say, engaging in violence (Dunning 1999: 30). Less exciting sport events may be overly routinized or have weak tension balances – for example, if the contest is too one-sided and predictable. As these points indicate, the emotions play a prominent role in Elias's perspective on sport and leisure; to consider how he explained the historical control of the emotions, I turn now to discuss his theory of the civilizing process.

The civilizing process

The Civilizing Process is the major sociological statement by Elias ([1939] 1978a, 1982) and the seminal text for figurational sociologists. The book itself consists of two volumes: the first addresses the 'history of manners' in regard to the long-term development of bodily controls and broader social etiquette, while the second examines state formation and more macrosociological issues regarding the emergence and transformation of different social institutions and structures. The empirical focus is on England, Germany and France from the Middle Ages onwards.

On the civilizing of manners, Elias traced how European societies moved historically away from the toleration and acceptance of relatively unrestrained and expressive behaviour and towards a greater focus on bodily control and personal comportment. This civilizing process included, for example, increasingly specific table manners; a growing sense of embarrassment, shame and repugnance towards bodily functions or display; and more constrictive codes of conduct within the bedroom, notably hiding of the naked body and establishing private sleeping spaces. The civilizing process was also marked both by growing expectations of individual self-restraint and by less tolerance towards emotional outbursts and expressivity or towards aggression and violence.

Yet, as the rise of modern sport demonstrates, forms of public excitement and emotional expression have not been eradicated. Hence, tension balances continue to arise in different societies between civilizing codes of self-control and desires for emotional fulfilment. In the long term, the civilizing of manners began primarily in European aristocratic and court societies, then influenced the emerging bourgeoisie and latterly was taken on by the 'respectable' working classes. Empirically, Elias's arguments on this civilizing process were drawn particularly from civility and etiquette books, which functioned as pedagogical texts for social elites after the Middle Ages.

In order for this civilizing of manners to take hold, social actors needed to live in reasonably stable political figurations, in which forms of authority were relatively established. In English court society, the old violent warriors of the Middle Ages were civilized in part by being drawn into different court circles, while aristocrats, military figures and religious leaders established their own court circles, which sought to acquire and control information in order to extend their political influences more widely. Cycles of violence did erupt between rival court figurations, but in England the Civil War in the mid-seventeenth century led to the 'parliamentarization' of politics; as a result, military conflicts were replaced by political debate and persuasion, involving more orderly, predictable and non-violent conduct.

According to Elias, 'a civilizing spurt' occurred in England, in large part through parliamentary state formation alongside other societal processes. The latter included a stronger state monopoly on taxation and violence, which functioned to reduce violent conflict (Elias [1939] 1982: 235–6); the rise of monetary relationships and economic growth; processes of rationalization; increased self-control, as individuals competed for influence through calculation and argument rather than force; and more complex divisions of labour and 'functional democratization', which made people more reliant on each other (Elias 1987: 76–7).

As the long-term civilizing process took hold in Western European societies, power differences between different social classes were reduced. 'Established' powerful groups needed to exercise restraint, as weaker 'outsider' groups (such as the middle and working classes) exerted greater influence and adopted many 'civilized' values, manners and habits of their social superiors. Struggles arose (and continue to do so) between established and outsider groups, for example along class, gender and ethnic lines. Yet, overall, Elias argued that modern, urban, industrialized parliamentary democracies have produced more civilized, complex human figurations in which 'people become more sensitive to what inspires others' and 'the mutual urge of people to take each other into account grows' (Elias [1939] 1982: 114).

Elias did qualify his arguments by indicating that the long-term civilizing process is not linear or unidirectional; hence, 'decivilizing spurts' occur when people show greater tolerance or enjoyment towards expressive emotions or violence, and where disturbances arise over state formation. One extreme decivilizing spurt occurred with the rise of Nazism in Germany in the early twentieth century; Elias (1996) attributed this development to a variety of factors, such as long-term self-perceptions of national threat and isolation, the failure to pacify Germany's warrior nobility, the inculcation of violent mores among the urban bourgeoisie, and German citizens' child-like dependency upon authority figures.

Alongside the concepts of mimesis and the spare-time spectrum, the theory of the civilizing process spotlights sport's expanding socio-cultural importance. Modern societies are required to find a solution to the dilemma of enabling people to enjoy pleasurable excitement while maintaining particular levels of physical restraint and self-control. Modern sports appear to provide that solution by offering 'the liberating excitement of a struggle involving physical exertion and skill while limiting to a minimum the chance that anyone will get seriously hurt in its course' (Elias, in Elias and Dunning 1986: 165).

We may examine how games and sporting pastimes emerged during and through the civilizing process, notably in England from the seventeenth century onwards. The 'sportization' of games involved establishing specific rules and conventions within play, which served to reflect a growing public repugnance towards violence and to necessitate forms of self-discipline for participants and spectators (Elias and Dunning 1986: 151). Indeed, Elias (ibid.: 34, 48) identified direct connections between the parliamentarization of English politics and the advanced 'sportization' of English game contests:

> One could see there that rules for non-violent combat between rival factions in Parliament and for peaceful handing over of governmental power to a victorious faction or party emerged more or less at the same time as the stricter constraint on violence, the greater demands on personal self-control and on sublimatory skill which gave leisure-contests involving muscle power and agility the characteristics of sports.

Thus, for example, fox-hunting was 'civilized' by the landed classes during the eighteenth and nineteenth centuries: the huntsman's enjoyment of killing the fox was replaced by his more civilized appreciation of the pleasures of the chase, and his hands were no longer bloodied as the actual kill was delegated to the hounds. In pugilism, sportization occurred through the introduction of the Queensbury rules, the use of gloves to reduce bloodshed, and an aesthetic code centring on 'the noble art' of self-defence.

Figurational sociologists also employed the theory of the civilizing process to explain football's transformation from folk pastime to modern sport (Elias and Dunning 1986: 175–90). Medieval 'folk football' games were characterized by 'riotousness and the relatively high level of socially tolerated physical violence': old scores were violently settled, bones regularly broken, and deaths not unknown (ibid.: 184). Further signs of folk football's uncivilized nature were found in the absence of equal numbers between rival sides, ideas of 'fairness' or competitive balance, clear divisions between spectators and players, and a sufficiently powerful state able to curb the violence (cf. Dunning and Sheard 1979).

Football games underwent a civilizing 'sportization' during the nineteenth century when they were adapted by English public schools to include specific rules and principles of fair play, although levels of violence were still markedly higher than today. The new sports fulfilled civilizing functions by promoting self-restraint and social order in schools that had previously been marked by riotous behaviour (Dunning 1977). Meanwhile, British society was undergoing broader civilizing processes of functional democratization: the aristocracy and bourgeoisie entered into longer interdependency chains, and significant sections of the working classes were later incorporated into 'respectable' society. Significant class differences were still evident, reflected in different rules for football: the most established, aristocratic classes showed 'higher orders of self-restraint' by favouring the soccer-style sport that prohibited ball-handling; middle-class and upper-middle-class males tended instead to favour the more violent game of rugby (Dunning and Sheard 1979: 128-9). And it is football, in seeking to explain spectator violence or 'hooliganism', that provided the figurational perspective with its more significant and contested research focus.

Figurational sociology and football hooliganism

In the 1980s and early 1990s, a team of figurational sociologists at the University of Leicester produced several books and research papers which sought to explain football spectator violence and disorder with reference to Elias's theory of the civilizing process (see in particular Dunning, Murphy and Williams 1988; Murphy, Dunning and Williams 1990). Drawing on English Football Association records and local newspaper reports, they argued that, until the First World War, the violence and disorder that occurred within football crowds was considered by people at the time to be largely part and parcel of attending games. Crowd violence was viewed as mainly expressive, in response to events on the field of play, as reflected in attacks or threats aimed at football officials and players. Such incidents, it was argued, reflected the relatively low levels of emotional restraint and greater tolerance of open aggression and violence to be found among largely working-class crowds at this time. In significant contrast, after 1945 and until the early 1960s, and despite their record sizes, English football crowds were markedly more peaceful or 'civilized': violent or disorderly incidents were less evident, and greater self-restraint was apparent as higher thresholds of repugnance towards public disturbances took hold among spectators. The researchers attributed this relative peacefulness to the growing presence within football crowds of 'respectable' working-class people who had been 'incorporated' into the more civil norms and values of their social betters, while benefiting from greater functional democratization within work and politics (Dunning, Murphy and Williams 1988: 126–8). Greater numbers of women, along with middle- and upper-class males, were also attending matches, and these 'feminizing' and civilizing influences served further to restrain football crowds.

The emergence of modern football hooliganism in England, from the early 1960s onwards, was explained by the figurational sociologists according to a number of interdependent factors. Notably, the 'respectable' working classes became less prominent within football crowds, partly because of alternative leisure activities, as well as the off-putting experiences, and often sensationalized media reports, of violence and disorder among young spectators (Dunning, Murphy and Williams 1988: 235–6). Most significantly, the figurational researchers argued that consistent incidents of violence and disorder (or 'hooliganism') in English football were caused, and continue to be caused, primarily by 'rough', lower-working-class youths. Crucially, the researchers maintained, these 'rough hooligans' are not incorporated into 'respectable', civilized standards of conduct but socialized instead on the streets, where violent and aggressive behaviour is routine and normal. Lower-working-class locales are, it was argued, characterized by many single-parent families, petty crime and delinquency, and high unemployment and welfare dependency. Local people have limited contact with other communities and cultures, leading to strong 'we-group' identification with kin, neighbourhood and the 'home turf' (cf. ibid.: 205–6). These communities also play limited roles within the growing chains of interdependency across complex industrial societies (ibid.: 228–9).

The researchers contended that football hooligan groups are formed when young males from these different neighbourhoods combine, as followers of a specific club, to fight against equivalent groups that support rival teams. Intergroup violence is different to earlier forms of football-related disorder, being more instrumental than expressive, less connected to events on the field, and more premeditated in terms of targeting opposing supporters (Dunning, Murphy and Williams 1988: 236–8). From the 1960s onwards, as violent incidents increased at football, more and more 'rough' young men were attracted to fixtures, including some from the higher social classes (ibid.: 215). As evidence, the figurational sociologists referred to police arrest figures, a television documentary, some interviews with young people in Leicester, and research by Suttles (1968, 1972) in a multi-ethnic Chicago neighbourhood.

The theory of the civilizing process also suggests we consider the broader context of rising football hooliganism in England, particularly during the 1970s and 1980s, when arguably a serious 'decivilizing spurt' was underway across the UK, as reflected in inner-city riots, intensified sectarian violence in Northern Ireland, bitter industrial disputes such as the 1984–5 Miners' Strike, and widening social inequalities and divisions. Indicating the radical possibilities of their approach, the figurational researchers argued that football-related violence and other forms of public disorder may only be tackled effectively by reducing these deeper social problems (Dunning, Murphy and Williams 1988: 243–5). The researchers also pointed towards more practical strategies for tackling hooliganism, such as the increased participation of women and families, which would reduce 'aggressive masculinity' and help to 'feminize' football crowds (Murphy, Dunning and Williams 1990: 78, 224–5).

Figurational research on football history and spectator violence has been challenged by subsequent research. Several historical studies indicate that 'folk football' and early football crowds were far less disorderly, and that upper-class sport was far more violent, than the figurational sociologists had claimed (Goulstone 1974, 2000: 135–6; Harvey 1999: 114; Mason 1980: 166–7; Lewis 1996; Tranter 1998: 47–8). Research in England and Scotland indicates that contemporary football hooliganism has tended to feature relatively 'incorporated' young men, with upper-working- or lower-middle-class profiles, and not the most marginalized, 'rough', lower-working classes, as claimed by the figurational sociologists (Armstrong 1998;

Giulianotti 1999: 46–52; Giulianotti and Armstrong 2002: 215–17). The figurational proposal – to 'feminize' disorderly fans by attracting more female supporters – has a dubious ethical basis, in that such a measure effectively utilizes women as objects of sport policy in order to resolve a male problem (Clarke 1992: 217). Finally, it was significant that the figurational sociologists' chief researcher, John Williams (1991), withdrew from this paradigm and argued that more politically radical strategies should be introduced in order to tackle hooliganism (P. Smith 1997: 119–20).

Figurational sociology and the sociology of sport

Looking beyond the earlier work of Dunning and his colleagues on the historical development of sport, figurational sociologists have been active in other fields of sport-related research. Two main areas stand out. First, in relation to globalization and sport, Maguire (1999) advanced a figurational sociological perspective to explore the long-term historical diffusion of sport, the migration of athletes, and the interrelationships between sport and the mass media. Important themes within this analysis are the notions of 'inter-civilizational' relations and exchanges, which point beyond Elias's focus on largely European civilizing processes, and power networks and relations that are constructed and negotiated across this global sport terrain. Latterly, Malcolm (2013) has advanced a figurational study of cricket and global processes, with a particular focus on the historical development of the game vis-à-vis civilizing processes, Englishness and empire.

A second field of study for figurational sociologists has been in the interrelated areas of health, illness, injury and pain within sport. Waddington (2000), for example, explains doping in part with reference to theories of the civilizing process and 'sportization'. Thus, the wider socio-historical context for doping includes the long-term move away from playing 'for fun' and towards competing to win on behalf of bigger units (e.g., cities, nations); meanwhile, the promotion of an 'English ethos of fairness', as part of the civilizing process in sport, leads governing bodies in sport to challenge doping with the aim of removing 'cheating' rather than protecting the health of athletes (ibid.: 106–8, 123–5). Elsewhere, an early paper by Roderick (1998) advocates the use of a figurational perspective to examine pain and injury within sport. For Roderick, particular attention should be paid to the interdependencies between athletes, medical personnel, coaches and others within the sport figuration and to the long-term development of the figuration (in effect, the occupational subculture) of athletes, which includes internal expectations and pressures to avoid talking about or reporting injury or pain.

Other research fields that draw on figurational sociology include the analysis of blood sports and the violent treatment of animals such as greyhounds in racing sports (Atkinson and Young 2005, 2008); changes in the organization of sport development in England (Bloyce et al. 2008); and the use of Elias's established-outsider theory in order to explain gender relations within Irish sport (Liston 2005). Overall, these original contributions point to the continuing presence of figurational sociology in the study of sport, albeit in more selective ways or with much smaller research programmes than was evidenced by the Leicester-based scholars two or three decades earlier.

Concluding comments

In concluding this chapter, I turn now to evaluate the figurational paradigm in terms of strengths and limitations. Certainly, to begin, figurational sociology has several attractive, insightful and persuasive aspects for sociologists of sport. The figurational approach advances a set of accessible, cogent and apparently comprehensive explanations of different aspects of sport. Most notably, figurational sociology is to be commended for taking sport seriously through a strong location within the paradigm's overall analytical framework. Moreover, the concepts of figuration and social interdependency serve both to underline the centrality of social connections and ties to the human condition and to provide a powerful basis for rejecting political ideologies of pure individualism. However, the figurational paradigm does harbour some major weaknesses, many of which have been highlighted by earlier commentators.[22]

First, figurational theories tend to be set up descriptively and to defy proper testing. For example, it seems to be impossible to test the civilizing process, as the theory claims to explain both 'civilizing' *and* 'decivilizing' spurts, in past, present or future. Thus, we have the scientifically strange situation in which, if the next Olympic Games are a site for major public rioting or for the signing of international peace treaties, the figurational sociologists would try to persuade us that either eventuality would be fully explained by their theory.

Second, a related problem here is in method: figurational sociologists have tended to engage with sport in order to showcase rather than to test (and thus improve) their theories. For Elias, sport was a 'comparatively manageable field' 'to show how I think it [figurational sociology] should be used' (Elias, in Elias and Dunning 1986: 154). Thus, to try to 'prove' that football hooligans came from 'rough' lower-working-class backgrounds, they went to gather data in 'rough' lower-working-class areas or did research with fans of a famously working-class football club (West Ham United). It would have been far more persuasive if they had conducted research across a wider range of football hooligan groups connected to one or more clubs. Elsewhere, Rojek (1995: 54–5) argues that the figurational approach lacks an adequate method on which to base its claims that it is more 'objectively adequate' or able to conduct more 'detached scientific research' than other social scientific perspectives.

Third, the theory of the civilizing process is, at least in part, Eurocentric, evolutionist and ethnocentric (cf. Blake 1995: 48–50; Robertson 1992: 120). It does not account for Asian civilizations. Nor does it provide anything like a sufficiently strong basis for critiquing Western European 'civilizations' in their genocidal colonization of other continents (cf. Armstrong 1998: 305). Moreover, anthropologists have queried Elias's grasp of what he calls 'simpler societies'; they would also question his evolutionary view that different societies have different knowledge levels but share the same knowledge staircase (cf. Goody 2002). Finally, on this point, there is certainly a lot of scope for the figurational standpoint to consider John Williams's observation, noted earlier, on the need to explore more fully and critically how sport might be radically reformed in order to become more democratic, egalitarian and socially just.

Fourth, a significant number of figurational sociologists insist upon an excessively singular and faithful devotion to Elias and his work: as Smith (2001: 14) puts it, they 'wall him up in a temple to be tended only by the faithful'; those who would use his work more selectively are deemed to be 'not "good enough" to be true Eliasians'. There is an acute irony in this deification, given Elias's emphasis on human interdependence and his rejection of the *homo clausus* idea of human life. Much more problematically, this unswerving loyalty also restricts the scope for creative and critical adaptation of existing theories to explain sport or other social phenomena. The figurational explanation of football hooliganism is a case in point. The figurational researchers rigidly applied the civilizing process thesis by seeking out 'confirming' evidence that hooligans are drawn overwhelmingly from the lower working classes. Alternatively, proper fieldwork by these researchers should have uncovered the large involvement of young upper-working- and lower-middle-class males in hooligan subcultures. To explain the involvement of such 'respectable' groups, the researchers might have turned instead to a creative adaptation of the theory of 'informalization', which was initially forwarded by Elias and then substantially developed by Wouters (1986, 1990).[23]

While the figurational approach is still utilized by sociologists of sport, there is little doubt that its influence has declined since the 1980s. Indicatively, one recent comprehensive volume of papers on the sociology of sport barely mentions the figurational standpoint (Andrews and Carrington 2013). The paradigm's best-known sociologists of sport have become less active or have retired, other approaches (such as Cultural Studies and poststructuralism) have become more established, and there is the strong sense that the major applications of Elias's work to sport have already been made.

In this context, the future challenge for sociologists of sport working with the figurational approach, or indeed with any other sociological paradigm, is to do so in an original and critical manner: ideally, that requires identifying clearly the paradigm's strengths and weaknesses and working creatively to develop or transform it where possible. Crucially, this work must also engage fully and imaginatively with other sociological approaches to produce more robust theoretical frameworks and thus better explanations of the social world. Such an endeavour may lead in turn to the production of 'neo-figurational' approaches, in the way that neo-Marxist, neo-functionalist, neo-Weberian and other such 'neo-' perspectives have been creatively developed. Such a conceptual undertaking also makes explicit and constructive use of the deep interdependencies between figurational sociology and other sociological standpoints.

In the study of sport, there have been some signs of cross-theoretical activity involving figurational approaches. Initial comments on possible links between figurational and Cultural Studies approaches were promising but did not result in any significant programmes of research (see, for example, Maguire 1999: 216). More substantially, Rojek's (1985, 1993, 1995, 2006) extensive work on sport and leisure frequently draws on figurational sociology and many other modern and postmodern social theories. For instance, when examining contemporary sport celebrity, Rojek (2006) creatively applies Elias's theory of 'functional democratization' alongside other sociological approaches, particularly a Durkheimian analysis of how famous 'role models' contribute to the 'moral regulation' of societies. Elsewhere, Brownell (1995) draws on Foucault's theory of 'discipline' and Elias's concept of 'civilization' to examine sport in China;

both keywords are central to Chinese state discourses and cultural understandings of the body; hence, combining the two theorists to facilitate analysis makes a lot of sense.

As the work of Rojek and Brownell demonstrates, this sort of selective and integrative engagement with figurational sociology does not, by itself, require scholars to create an entire neo-figurational approach. But, such activity does point to how the figurational stand-point may be used more successfully by future generations of scholars who are looking to undertake original, stimulating and influential work within the sociology of sport.

Questions for discussion

1 How might we use the concept of 'figurations' to examine sport groups?
2 How might we use the concept of the civilizing process to explain the history of different sports, such as fox-hunting, boxing and football?
3 What are the strengths and limitations in the figurational explanation of football hooliganism?
4 How might figurational standpoints be usefully combined with other theories and perspectives to explain sport?

10

Bourdieu on Sport: Domination, Distinction and the Public Intellectual

Pierre Bourdieu, who died in January 2002, was one of the world's leading post-war sociologists. His work has been most influential in France, but several of his books, in particular his masterpiece *Distinction*, have gained global renown. A prominent 'public intellectual' in the full sense of the term, Bourdieu argued that sociologists have a crucial role to play in challenging different forms of social domination. Towards the end of his life, he was increasingly critical of the neoliberal policies of Western governments for producing greater social inequalities, job insecurity, crime, social stress and disregard for the developing world (Wacquant 2002: 556).

Bourdieu recognized the social importance of sport and wrote several papers on the subject; sport and physical culture also feature prominently in *Distinction*. He was concerned not with sport *per se*, but with behind-the-scenes factors of socialization and social differentiation that serve to engender different sporting tastes:

> How is the demand for 'sports products' produced, how do people acquire the 'taste' for sport, and for one sport rather than another, whether as an activity or as a spectacle? . . . More precisely, according to what principles do agents choose between the different sports activities or entertainments which, at a given moment in time, are offered to them as being possible? (Bourdieu 1978: 819–20)

As I shall argue here, this research agenda has many sociological strengths but may oversimplify sport's social and cultural complexities.

I consider Bourdieu's relevance to the sociology of sport in three main parts. First, I discuss his key concepts, specifically on subject–object dualism, habitus, capital, field, and symbolic violence.

Second, I examine the sports-related research findings of Bourdieu and his followers, focusing principally on *Distinction*. Third, I assess Bourdieu's more explicitly political writings and their relevance to the sociology of sport. I conclude with a critical assessment of Bourdieu's contribution to the study of sport.

Bourdieu's theoretical framework

Subject–object dualism

Like many influential 'grand theorists', from Parsons to Giddens, Bourdieu claimed that his sociological approach served to dissolve sociology's traditional 'dualism' or binary opposition of social action (associated with 'subjectivism') and social structure ('objectivism'). 'Objectivism' is, in effect, structuralist social theory, defined by a 'top-down' theoretical perspective that understands all societies as having underlying logical structures or patterns which exist beyond the consciousness of society members, but which are open to identification by social scientists. Conversely, 'subjectivism' is a 'bottom-up' theory and method, focused on social action and interpretation, which seeks to understand the social world through the subjective meanings, motives and understandings of social actors at the everyday level. Both objectivism and subjectivism have inherent weaknesses: structuralism does not account adequately for the critical and creative faculties of social actors; action-orientated and interpretive perspectives pay too little attention to how social structures shape and constrain social actions.

Bourdieu sought to move beyond this theoretical dualism, while also retaining the keywords 'action' and 'structure' within his conceptual framework (Bourdieu and Wacquant 1992: 121–2). However, perhaps inevitably, any such 'post-dualist' approach might still be seen as leaning more towards the structure side or the action side. In Bourdieu's case, the emphasis was mainly towards a structuralist approach, as reflected partly in his theory of 'genetic structuralism' (1990a: 125–6).

Bourdieu's 'genetic structuralism' is a theoretical approach that seeks to provide a more action-focused version of structuralism, revealing how social structures are constituted and reconstituted through everyday 'practices'.[24] Bourdieu argued that 'practice' discloses both people's practical understanding of the social world and how social reality is made. Through social practice, people seek to master (rather than consciously theorize) their everyday activities. Practical comprehension of the world is embedded in subjectivity because the world 'comprises me' and 'has produced me'. The world generates the subject's categories of thought; hence, the world has a 'self-evident' appearance, which gives rise to a stronger concern with practical mastery rather than withdrawn, objectifying reflection (Bourdieu and Wacquant 1992: 127–8).

The body is central to the practical mastery of the world. Sport is 'perhaps the terrain *par excellence*' in which this prioritization of practical mastery is most apparent:

> There are heaps of things that we understand only with our bodies, outside conscious awareness, without being able to put our understanding into words. The silence of sportspeople . . . stems partly from the fact that, when you are not a professional analyst, there are certain things you can't say, and sporting practices are practices in which understanding is bodily. (Bourdieu 1990a: 166)

In addition, Bourdieu understood social reality as being intrinsically 'relational': it is created out of the social relations between social groups rather than from the substance qualities of individuals in themselves.

Bourdieu advanced a range of important methodological arguments for social scientists. He sought to dispense with the binary opposition that separates theory and evidence, insisting instead that the 'logic of research' is 'inseparably empirical and theoretical' (Bourdieu and Wacquant 1992: 160). His own sociological work combined substantial data (both detailed surveys and sophisticated ethnography) and theoretical reflection, for example when examining Berber households or French academia.

Bourdieu argued that sociological practice must be intensely reflexive and self-critical. When doing fieldwork, sociologists should show a 'reflex reflexivity', exercising their sociological 'feel' for what they encounter and making connections between 'on the spot' events and wider social structures (Bourdieu et al. 1999: 608). Sociologists should formulate scientific 'objectifications' about the social world and also reflect upon the socio-historical conditions for their own knowledge production; in other words, they need to objectify their objectifications, in effect by turning the critical tools of their trade back upon themselves, in order to remove biases (Bourdieu 2000: 121; Bourdieu and Wacquant 1992: 67–8).[25]

Bourdieu identified three levels of bias that may undermine the sociological perspective (Bourdieu and Wacquant 1992: 39):

- the researcher's specific social background;
- the researcher's position within the academic field and the general position of social scientists within wider social relations of domination;
- the researcher's superior intellectual status, which leads to social practices being perceived not as practical activities involving social actors but as spectacles for an objective, withdrawn kind of interpretation.

These biases may apply in the sociology of sport in the following ways. First, the sociologist's privileged economic and cultural background may lead to an ambivalence or disdain towards particular sport subcultures. Second, the researcher may 'play the academic game' to secure a successful career, for example by positively citing other sociologists and their works to ensure publication in good journals and research grant income. Third, the researcher may produce a detached, speculative, even dismissive account of the research group under study, rather than seeking to understand fully the meanings and contexts of social practices.

To elaborate Bourdieu's theoretical positions, I turn now to his concepts of habitus, capital and field.

Habitus, capital and field

Bourdieu's theory of *habitus* refers to the 'socialized subjectivity' of social actors. The habitus of social actors represents their systems of classification that shape their practices, beliefs, habits, 'tastes' and bodily techniques (see Fowler 1997: 17). The habitus tends to operate outside of individual self-awareness and is 'always orientated towards practical functions'; it also possesses 'an infinite capacity for generating products – thoughts, perceptions, expressions and actions – whose limits are set by the historically and socially situated conditions of its production' (Bourdieu 1990b: 52–5). For Bourdieu, the habitus 'expresses first the *result of an organizing action*, with a meaning close to that of words such as structure; it also designates a way of being, a habitual state (especially of the body) and, in particular, a *predisposition, tendency, propensity* or *inclination*' (1984: 562, cited in Tomlinson 2004).

Bourdieu also understood that social actors have different types and different volumes of *capital*. Four types of capital may be highlighted here: economic capital relates to material wealth, cultural capital to cultural resources such as educational qualifications and artistic knowledge, social capital to social networks across friends, families, workmates and wider circles, and symbolic capital to honours, prestige and other such valorized forms of accreditation.

The concept of *field* refers to 'a configuration of positions comprising agents (individuals, groups of actors or institutions) struggling to maximize their position' (Maton 2005: 689). These agents exercise their different types and volumes of capital in order to strengthen their position and influence within the field. Dominant groups seek to define what is legitimate and valuable within each field and also where the boundaries lie between different fields; weaker groups invariably seek to challenge these definitions in order to improve their field positions. It is also common to find fields in complex interrelations with each other, especially in the way of large overlaps and intersections.

Habitus, capital and field are interdependent terms within Bourdieu's theoretical framework. A person's habitus, combined with her capital and added to her field position, will determine her particular social practices. This interplay is captured through the 'generative' formula: (habitus × capital) + field = practice. Although there is an 'ontological complicity' between the two terms, habitus and field carry different respective weightings of the 'subjective' and 'objective' (Bourdieu and Wacquant 1992: 127–8). The habitus is a form of subjectivity, but a socialized one; the field, in some contrast, is an objective construct which is constituted from the contested relations of different social actors.

The field also possesses a specific *doxa*, which is made up of common sense or tacitly accepted ideals, or 'everything that goes without saying' (Bourdieu 1993: 51). The *doxa* is internalized unquestioningly by both dominant and dominated groups. For dominated groups, the *doxa* may be akin to a dominant ideology, in constituting 'the most absolute form of conservatism' whereby the conditions of their oppression are viewed as inevitable, as central to their taken-for-granted world (Bourdieu and Wacquant 1992: 73–4). Crucially, for Bourdieu, sociologists must move beyond the *doxa* to produce challenging 'para-doxal modes of thought' that destabilize this common or practical sense among both dominant and dominated groups.

Bourdieu (2000: 151–3; Bourdieu and Wacquant 1992: 98–100) understood the field as being a kind of competitive 'game'. Each game relies on the commitment of social agents to participate. While game positions taken by each player are never entirely predictable, they are largely shaped by her specific habitus, which defines her different interpretations, types of 'feel', and levels of 'comfort' within the game. The social agent will also act with respect to her specific volumes and types of capital, which may be used to secure or improve her positions vis-à-vis other game players.

Bourdieu pictured capital as game tokens with different colours to designate each player's varied capabilities within the field. To understand strategies and positions within games, we need to examine the actual volume of tokens/capital that the player possesses and how that capital has increased or decreased over time. Players adopt different tactics to protect and augment their capital. For example, they may play 'trump' or master cards whose capital values vary over time; or, playing more radically, they may seek to 'transform, partially or completely, the immanent rules of the game', such as by changing token colours or devaluing the colour of tokens held by opponents (Bourdieu and Wacquant 1992: 99).

New players must acquire practical understandings of the game and its history. Interpretive workers – biographers, historians and archivists – play a crucial role in protecting the game and thus their own positions (Bourdieu 1993: 73–4). Prior investments by players in learning and gaining distinctive positions within the game ensure that its destruction is 'unthinkable'. Each game has its own definitive interests and stakes that mark differences between players; those seeking to protect their pre-established positions in the game tend to resist the attempts by players from other games to transfer themselves and their capital into the new field.[26]

Bourdieu's game/field model has notable applicability to sport. To begin, we may see sport as a kind of field/game that is 'relatively autonomous' to other such games, in that it 'has its own tempo, its own evolutionary laws, its own crises, in short, its specific chronology' (Bourdieu 1993: 118). Sport as a whole is a field which comprises diverse intersecting fields, particularly in the form of different sport categories. Olympic sport is one such field that is made up of diverse groups of competing players (athletes, coaches, officials, media workers and producers, sponsors, and so on) who possess different types and volumes of capital. Olympic sport has its own taken-for-granted *doxa*, notably centring on the stated power of the Olympic movement to promote health, education, culture, peace and environmental sustainability.[27] Interpretive workers such as public relations officials and journalists help to sustain the Olympic field by constructing its history and advocating its *doxa*. 'Para-doxal' perspectives are provided by critical politicians, social scientists and social movements, for example by highlighting the close historical

ties between the Olympic movement and nation-states or corporate sponsors which undermine peace, the environment, health and
wider human rights (cf. Lenskyj 2008). To reshape the field (in
other words, to redefine the Olympic movement), new and relatively
weak players must increase their capital levels, notably in economic,
social and symbolic terms. Most attempts to transform the Olympic
movement tend to be strongly resisted by dominant players who, in
Bourdieu's terms, are seeking to safeguard their field positions and
the value of their existing capital.

One major transformation within the Olympic field involved the
official switch of Olympic sports from 'amateur' to 'professional'
status during the 1980s. The move reflected the growing field
influence of those with large amounts of economic capital, notably
television corporations, sponsors, and full-time elite sports workers
(coaches and athletes). Those pro-amateur IOC members and officials who might have been threatened by this change were largely
able to re-establish their strong field positions, in part by asserting
control over the growing volumes of economic capital that entered
the Olympic field.

Across the Olympic field, the list of recognized Olympic sports
reflects the different field positions, habitus and types and volumes
of capital that are held by dominant social groups. Sports such as
archery, equestrian disciplines, fencing, the modern pentathlon,
rowing, sailing and shooting have long-standing Olympic recognition. These sports are embedded within the habitus of elite social
groups, who are dominant within sport and many wider fields of
international society. These elite groups also have the different
types of capital required to participate in such sports. For example,
equestrianism may require economic capital to buy horses and land;
cultural capital follows from elite riding-school training; and social
capital, such as family connections, may give access to the best
equestrian clubs. In turn, dominant social groups claim status or distinction through participation in these sports and by securing official
Olympic recognition for them. Conversely, either dominated social
groups lack the economic and social capital to pursue these sports or,
when initially participating, their habitus will lead them to feel culturally and socially 'out of place'. Dominated social groups also lack the
appropriate capital in order to press for other sports to be included
within the field of Olympism – for example, for the working-class
'pub sports' of darts and pool to replace archery or shooting or for the
mainly women's sport of netball to gain admission. Two new sports
which were introduced for the 2016 Olympics in Rio were golf and

rugby union; indicatively, both are associated with the habitus and types of capital that are held by dominant male social groups.

Social divisions and symbolic violence

Social class was central to Bourdieu's analysis of social stratification. Bourdieu understood a social class to be a group of agents who 'share the same interests, social experiences, traditions, and value system, and who tend to act as a class and define themselves in relation to other groups of agents' (Clément 1995: 149). Each class endeavours to impose its habitus on the collective habitus of other social classes in order to dominate across a specific field (Urry 1990: 88). The habitus of each social class is revealed through specific tastes for particular sports and other cultural pursuits; thus, social agents follow their habitus to find sports that are 'just right' for them (Bourdieu 1993: 129–30).

Sport is closely tied to the structure of class relations, in being socially 'classified and classifying, rank-ordered and rank-ordering' (Bourdieu 1984: 223). Class distinctions also have spatial dimensions; exclusive social spaces possess a 'club effect' that excludes those with different habitus (Bourdieu 1993: 129). Thus exclusive sport clubs restrict membership to those with high capital levels, whether this is economic (annual fees), social (member contacts), cultural (such as education, dress, language, ethnicity and general demeanour) or symbolic (sport title-winners).

Bourdieu used the concept of *symbolic violence* to explain how disadvantages within the field are systematically and harmfully imposed upon dominated social groups. Echoing Gramsci's theory of hegemony, as domination by consent, he indicates that symbolic violence is 'exercised upon a social agent with his or her complicity' (Bourdieu and Wacquant 1992: 167; Bourdieu 2000: 170).

For example, educational institutions exercise symbolic violence upon dominated groups. Schools actively privilege the habitus of dominant groups, such as through language and cultural tastes; in turn, through attending and seeking education in schools, dominated groups are effectively reduced to *collaboration* in their symbolic coercion (Bourdieu and Passeron 1977). In sport, symbolic violence is manifested in a variety of ways. On the one hand, many educational systems have practised symbolic violence through racist assumptions that specific dominated groups are intellectually limited but 'naturally' athletic. On the other hand, other dominated groups have been excluded from sport participation through the assumption that they are not 'natural' athletes or that certain sports are 'not for them', thus undermining their participation. Symbolic violence is further evidenced in how dominated social groups internalize and act on this *doxa*.

* * *

Overall, Bourdieu's sociological approach is concerned with social practices and committed to reflexive research that blends empirical content and theoretical strength. Four aspects of Bourdieu's theories are particularly appealing. First, his rather structuralist reading of social action (or practice) is satisfyingly sociological and registers the force of power relations in the enactment of everyday social life. Second, the concept of field enables us to examine social relations and social struggles through game models. Third, Bourdieu advocated the critical reflexivity of sociologists in order both to confront their underlying biases and to produce critical 'para-doxal' research. Fourth, the term 'symbolic violence' graphically registers the harmful consequences of systematic social domination for dominated social groups. In the next section, I develop further Bourdieu's approach by exploring how his theory of distinction may be applied to explain sport.

Distinction: the stratification of sporting tastes

Key arguments

In the book *Distinction*, Bourdieu (1984) elaborated the thesis that culture is a vast, complex field in which different social groups struggle for distinction through different types of status contest. As an essentially relational field, each group advances its collective claims to distinction and, through cultural snobbery, 'expresses disgust for the taste of other groups' (Defrance 1995: 126).[28]

Bourdieu identified the links between social stratification and cultural taste as occurring across three dimensions. The *vertical* dimension measures differences in capital volume (economic and cultural), from richest to the most impoverished. The *horizontal* dimension differentiates between kinds of capital, specifically economic and cultural. The *temporal* dimension traces the general historical trajectory (rising or falling) of each specific group.

In the UK, for example, the 'old-money' upper classes are vertically high in their volumes of capital; in horizontal terms, they tend to have slightly more cultural than economic capital (high education, etiquette, control of major cultural institutions, high property ownership, but rarely in the billionaire category) and, in temporal terms, their capital strengths may go back several centuries. Hence, the old-money elites prefer distinguished 'traditional' sports such as equestrianism, which require landed property and are associated with rural and pre-modern 'ways of life' (in which these elites are and were at their most powerful). Notably, these old elites are rarely involved in the ownership of major professional sport clubs, a competitive 'game' now dominated by billionaires in which very high levels of economic capital are required.

Moreover, Bourdieu indicated that cultural activities such as sports may be demarcated by the different levels and kinds of 'social profit' that they offer to participants, and which contribute in turn to the 'distributional significance' between different classes (Bourdieu 1984: 35). For example, golf may have healthy 'intrinsic profits' regarding exercise, but it may offer high social profits for members of middle-class golf clubs, such as through social connections that may advance social standing, business interests or careers. Access to these forms of social capital serves to strengthen further the differences between 'clubbable' dominant groups and excluded dominated groups.

Sport and class habitus

Bourdieu emphasized the very deep connections between the particular sporting tastes of social agents and their specific class habitus. The habitus of the dominant classes favours 'aesthetic', 'contemplative' and 'healthy' sports; examples here are 'golf, tennis, sailing, riding (or show-jumping), skiing (especially its most distinctive forms, such as cross-country) or fencing' (Bourdieu 1984: 215). Compared to football and boxing, which are favoured by dominated classes, the sports of dominant groups are usually less intense, are less likely to involve strong bodily contact between players, have greater association with health and lifelong participation, and often have the ambience of social encounters.

Sport also serves to differentiate groups *within* the dominant class. The dominant groups within the dominant class might include aristocrats and managerial or business elites, who are high in both economic and cultural capital. In contrast, dominated groups within the dominant class would include university teachers, artists and other cultural workers, who tend to have far higher levels (indeed, often the very highest levels) of cultural capital but significantly less economic capital. For dominant groups within the dominant class, there is a glorification of sport (for example, with rugby) that also 'implies a certain anti-intellectualism', marking off these groups from dominated groups within the dominant class who have more intellectual or avant-garde forms of cultural capital. Rugby is defined as manly, virile, character-building and to be practised through willpower, in contrast to the passive, effeminate and self-critical attributes of intellectuals and artists (Bourdieu 1993: 122).

Bourdieu indicated that, when we drill down further into dominant groups, we find that sporting tastes connect closely to the particular habitus of different groups and their different volumes and types of capital (Bourdieu 1984: 219). For example, teachers have an 'aristocratic asceticism' in their taste for mountaineering, cycling and rambling, thereby fitting their high cultural capital to low economic costs. Doctors and modern executives pursue a 'health-oriented hedonism', escaping the masses through exotic, expensive pastimes such as yachting or skiing. Business employers favour sports such as golf that connect to consumerist lifestyles while offering social profits.

The difference between social classes in their tastes for sport is tied further to how they view the body. For the dominant classes, the body is an end in itself, wherein sports practices are associated with physical health. The lower middle classes take this corporeal philosophy to literal extremes: thus, their taste for gymnastics embodies both their 'ascetic exaltation of sobriety and dietetic rigour' and their habitual tendency to embrace scientific theories that link practical actions towards predetermined ends (Bourdieu 1993: 130).

In contrast, the dominated classes (particularly males) take a more 'instrumental' approach to the body. Sports such as boxing or weightlifting reflect the experience of manual work, 'building' the body-object through painful exertion and subjugation. The excitement of 'gambling with the body' arises in boxing, motorcycling, and violent play in football or rugby league. Though ignoring working-class women in sport, Bourdieu did point to their instrumental use of the body in regard to dieting or beauty care.

Bourdieu (1984: 217) observed that different sporting tastes are not caused simply by material divisions. Skiing, golf and cricket require relatively expensive equipment, yet 'more hidden entry requirements' ensure social closure for potential working-class practitioners. Family habits, childhood sports experiences, initiation into the correct bodily habitus, and socializing techniques are some of the important cultural and social factors that imbue these sports with the dominant class habitus. Thus, there is a lot more to golf than sinking a few putts.

Individuals with high levels of proficiency in sport may gain specialist cultural capital (such as coaching certificates), along with economic (salary) and social (contacts, elite circles) capital; symbolic capital (awards, titles, media fame) may also follow. For dominated groups, however, sport is an insecure, capricious career path that is reliant on physical fitness. Bourdieu (Bourdieu and Balazs, in Bourdieu et al. 1999: 361–9) recounted the case of a Portuguese family that appeared to integrate successfully within a small French town, partly through the father's football skills. However, after being injured, the father's social and symbolic capital evaporated; old friends disappeared and the French state offered no welfare security.

The sport tastes of different classes have diverse impacts across the life course (Bourdieu 1984: 212). 'Popular', energetic sports correlate strongly with youth. Rugby league, football and boxing are usually abandoned by working-class males upon entering adulthood, as 'excess' physical, libidinal or playful energies are diverted into marriage and domestic provision (Bourdieu 1993: 129). Conversely, bourgeois sports such as golf or tennis require less physical exertion, enabling longer life-course participation, healthy exercise and the social profits of local club membership. Learning and playing golf also fit with the bourgeois habitus in terms of drawing on accredited expertise to improve performance – for example through one-on-one professional tuition or using coaching videos to enhance technique or playing strategies.

Bourdieu (1990a: 163) further contended that the sporting field is not static. The dominant meanings and types of distinction offered by different sports may be transformed through social struggle, in the same way that musical compositions acquire different social meanings over time (see Buch 2003). Other sports may emerge and squeeze into the overall sport field, perhaps by reflecting the distinctive habitus of new class fractions. For example, through his initial research in the 1960s and early 1970s, Bourdieu identified the rise of 'Californian', 'counter-cultural' sports that favoured 'authentic' natural products or crafted attire and which harboured a social and somatic weightlessness, as in hang-gliding, trekking and windsurfing. These sports are favoured by the 'new petite bourgeoisie', notably employed in 'cultural intermediary' professions of commercial seduction, such as in fashion, advertising, photography, journalism and design (Featherstone 1991). Whereas the old petite bourgeoisie advocate duty, self-restraint, modesty and self-control, the new petite bourgeoisie regard the pursuit of pleasure as a personal and ethical imperative (Bourdieu 1984: 367).

Bourdieu's influence in the sociology of sport

Bourdieu has been hugely influential within the French sociology of sport, inspiring work that connects sport's meanings and practices to social identities and divisions (see Vigarello 1995: 225). His regular collaborator, Loïc Wacquant (1995a, 1995b, 2004), utilized particularly the concept of capital to produce several outstanding studies of Chicago's boxing culture. Drawing on Bourdieu, Defrance (1976, 1987) traced the social history of French gymnastics and other sports from the late eighteenth century onwards. In combat sports, class habitus is reflected through different tastes: the established bourgeoisie appreciate aesthetic body shape and economic movement (such as in aikido), while the lower classes favour bodily contact, physical exchanges and strength (such as in wrestling) (Clément 1985).

Outside France, others have used Bourdieu's theories to examine the social stratification and culture of sports participation. One American study found that youth football club membership demarcated the white, suburban culture from the 'urban depravity and difference' of non-white, lower-class locales (Andrews et al. 1997: 271–2). In Canada, sociologists reinterpreted Bourdieu's classifications to examine physical activity and general leisure among 180 local francophone women with different class backgrounds. The results confirmed the correlation between physical activity and class habitus. Middle-class women favoured workouts, aerobics and swimming, reflecting both 'self-imposed rules of behaviour' to stay slim and look healthy and their labour market subordination to the dominant norms surrounding female body shape. Working-class women were least active because exercise had few instrumental benefits, particularly for their routine manual labour. The intellectual bourgeoisie preferred 'liberating', new (but not 'popular') physical activities, such as orienteering or 'body awareness through movement' programmes that required educational and cultural capital. Finally, upper-class women enjoyed luxurious consumption associated with particular kinds of social and cultural capital, as instanced by membership of exclusive golf or skiing clubs with 'après-sport' opportunities (Laberge and Sankoff 1988).

Overall, Bourdieu's approach debunks the social innocence and sacred aura of sport. Instead, sport is viewed as one of many cultural means through which social classes distinguish themselves from one another (Clément 1995: 149). I explore criticisms of this approach towards the end of this chapter, but first I turn to consider how Bourdieu understood the politics of social research.

The politics of research

Bourdieu was an *intellectuel engagé* in the French tradition of Voltaire, Zola and Sartre, and as such he held firm ideas on the public and political role of the sociologist. He viewed sociology as a 'combat sport' which should directly critique the forms of domination that are uncovered by sociological research (Müller 2002).

In his book *Acts of Resistance*, Bourdieu (1998a) attacked Western-led neoliberal economic and social policies, which have produced greater inequalities and social insecurity (especially among the young) through unemployment, low wages and criminalization. Culture was considered to have been infected by 'the reign of commerce' that undermines social scientific critical inquiry and artistic creativity. Bourdieu advocated instead an 'economics of happiness' that recognizes non-material, symbolic profits and losses. This paradigm would take full account of the social costs and benefits of different economic policies and decisions, including the 'violence' of neoliberal measures such as mass job cuts by companies. As Bourdieu (1998a: 40) put it,

> All violence is paid for, and, for example, the structural violence exerted by the financial markets, in the form of layoffs, loss of security, etc., is matched sooner or later in the form of suicides, crime and delinquency, drug addiction, alcoholism, a whole host of minor and major everyday acts of violence.

Chiming with Bourdieu's approach, subsequent research has shown that societies with high levels of economic and social inequalities are also blighted by high levels of major social problems (presented here by Bourdieu as social violence) (Wilkinson and Pickett 2010). The *doxa* of neoliberal societies serves to 'legitimize' the different forms of violence that are visited on dominated groups. The latter are portrayed as immoral, degenerate, stupid and unworthy of political influence. The educational system further inculcates these false perceptions of self-evident worthlessness..

In response, Bourdieu (1998a: 52–9) advocated a reflexive battle against neoliberal forces alongside a 'transnational struggle' across Europe. New social movements (e.g., environmental groups) effect social resistance but cannot match the symbolic power of dominant groups in communicating their messages. Social researchers should help through dialogue with activists and by advancing 'para-doxal' critiques of conservative media. Bourdieu berated his intellectual colleagues for their political 'ambiguity', their constant 'surrenders' and 'collaborations' in dealings with neoliberalism. Intellectuals are a dominated element within the dominant group, but, for Bourdieu, their tendency to remain 'uncommitted' in politics, to hide behind the alibi of 'professional competence', was viewed as unacceptable. For sociologists, Bourdieu's arguments here have significant continuities with diverging, later calls for a 'public sociology' that engages directly with public issues and pursues structural social change (Agger 2000; Burawoy 2005).

Bourdieu's politics have direct consequences for sociologists of sport. Researchers should engage with new social movements within sport, publicizing scientific studies that critique transnational corporations and governing bodies. Lenskyj's (2000, 2002, 2003, 2008) participation in social movements that oppose the expensive hosting of the Olympic Games, together with her wider sociological work on the Olympics, exemplifies the kind of publicly engaged (in Gramsci's terms, 'organic') intellectual work that Bourdieu advocated. Sociologists of sport might engage with campaign groups and new social movements on a variety of other issues, several of which have been discussed in earlier chapters, including the role of commodification and rationalization in alienating or disenfranchising many long-standing communities; the public costs of hosting sport mega-events; and the partnerships between sport governing bodies and transnational corporations or nation-states that have poor human and civil rights records.

In terms of sports policy, Bourdieu advocated a 'realistic utopia' that would, in effect, remove commodification and instrumental rationality. The aim here was to restore to sport 'those values which the world of sport proclaims and which are very like the values of art and science (non-commercial, ends in themselves, disinterested, valuing fair play and the 'way the game is played' as opposed to sacrificing everything for results)' (Bourdieu 1998b: 21).

Bourdieu recommended a 'coherent and universal model' with several policy features, to promote:

• sport's educational dimension
• state support for unpaid sports officials
• anti-corruption initiatives

- greater coaching and development of young players
- tightened links between grassroots and elite-level sport
- realistic forms of identification among young people towards elite professionals
- integrating immigrants socially through sport
- establishing a sports charter governing all athletes, officials and media analysts, enabling sport journalists to act as the 'critical conscience for the sporting world'.

These are highly laudable recommendations for the future of sport. For Bourdieu, they also register a switch in sociological emphasis. The earlier Bourdieu adopted a comparatively objectivist stance to explain how cultural preferences and practices functioned to distinguish social groups within specific cultural fields. The later, politically engaged Bourdieu advanced a more subjectivist position that staked out a particular critical spot within the sport field, while arguing that sporting preferences and practices are social goods *in themselves*. In this way, Bourdieu came to counterbalance his often dense sociological theorizing with the pragmatic, critical politics required of a public intellectual.

Concluding comments

Bourdieu's work has many sociological virtues. He advanced a potential solution to the structure–agency division while (in my view, correctly) favouring a more structuralist focus on power relations and divisions. His sociological keywords – habitus, field, capital, practice and distinction – became highly influential and beneficial conceptual tools for social researchers. His sociological blend of theory and evidence is 'good to think with' and invites elucidation in such research fields as sport (Jenkins 1992: 61, 98). The resultant research findings, notably in *Distinction*, may trace a rather familiar story about class taste and patterns of cultural snobbery, but this work is also a model of comprehensive, systematic analysis. Bourdieu's concern with the potential biases and critical responsibilities of sociologists is an important, underrated contribution to research methodology that must be read alongside his critique of education. His conception of symbolic violence, to expose the patterns and experiences of symbolic subjugation, is extremely important, and it also enables a more sophisticated and comprehensive understanding of violence *qua* many varieties of social harm. Bourdieu's argument that social scientists should actively expose and challenge systems of domination is hard to contest and fits with his wider sociological theories. Finally, his political legacy compares rather well when set against that of his English contemporary Anthony Giddens, whose 'third way' social theory was too closely tied to the policies of the former UK prime minister Tony Blair.

Bourdieu's approach does have some significant weaknesses, and here I shall highlight three. First, it allows us little scope to explore in their own terms the complex meanings, pleasures and aesthetics of sport. Instead, for Bourdieu, these aspects of sport appear to be used by social actors merely as means towards securing a more fundamental end (that is, claiming distinction). If we followed Bourdieu on this point, we would tend to overlook, wrongly in my view, the capacity of sport to produce what Canclini (1995: 20–1) has called 'autonomous nonutilitarian forms of beauty'.

Second, although he trumpets the 'relative autonomy' of the field of sport vis-à-vis other fields, Bourdieu's approach effectively reduces sporting tastes and practices to the dominant influence of other, larger, more influential fields. For example, the sport culture of working-class males is viewed as being largely derived from the industrial conditioning of this social group: thus, manual work in effect produces preferences for highly physical sports. Similarly, playing golf becomes a sign that the golfer wants to 'look like' a member of the established bourgeoisie (Bourdieu 1990a: 132).

The result is that Bourdieu's analytical framework provides us with little scope to examine the important symbolic differences and cultural conflicts that occur *within* specific sporting fields. These differences and conflicts are important within sport and cannot easily be reduced to broader forms of class habitus or claims to cultural distinction. For example, in many sports, there are intense debates within different clubs, nations and regions over the best playing tactics, techniques and styles that should be employed by teams. These debates often make reference to how styles of play help to construct and to explore particular forms of civic, regional or national identity. To pick another example, we might explore surfing, in particular how its meaning has been subject to struggles across different groups, including orthodox life-saving groups, hedonistic surfers, consumer-focused surfers, triathletes, and those promoting surfing's general professionalization (Booth 2001). Bourdieu's approach would offer us little encouragement to explore in depth these debates and developments, unless we were looking to connect each perspective to a specific class habitus.

Third, and following from the above, some criticisms might be advanced on Bourdieu's theory of social structure and social action. In short, social actors appear to be 'over-socialized', so that their sporting tastes and practices may be read off from class location. The problem here is that Bourdieu's approach tends to present sporting tastes as 'over-determined', as though 'everything seems decided in advance' (Boltanski 2011: 22). Thus, Bourdieu rather underestimated the critical capacities of social actors, notably in regard to how they may reflect on their position within different social fields; he also underplayed their scope to move in and out of different sporting activities and preferences.

Accordingly, Bourdieu's empirical claims linking class and cultural practice have been challenged. In the United States, Gans (1999: 19) insisted that people in elite occupations use cultural practices as 'status indicators' and not as forms of capital that are 'virtual job requirements', as Bourdieu implied. Moreover, 'mass culture' – such as fast or convenience food and mass-produced furniture – is rather more cross-class than Bourdieu's theory might allow (Gartman 1991). In Finland, sports interests cross class boundaries, although some pastimes (e.g., golf and surfing) carry distinction between and within classes (Heinilä 1998). Other Scandinavian research found that socio-economic capital, but not cultural capital, influences patterns of sport spectatorship (Thrane 2001).

To overcome some of these weaknesses, a Bourdieusian approach might develop a research programme that contains a more culturally flexible, sports-focused and transnational version of *Distinction*. In terms of method, such a programme would follow Bourdieu by conducting quantitative and qualitative research into sporting practices and tastes. The project would allow for regional, national and international variations in how each sporting field is constituted and contested while recognizing the 'relative autonomy' of every 'game'. The project might go beyond Bourdieu's fourfold model of capital; indeed, various scholars have advanced theories of 'human', 'health', 'subcultural', and 'sexual' or 'erotic' capital, in part to indicate the wider diversity of resources which social actors might utilize in order to gain distinction or better social outcomes within different social fields (Becker 1964; Grossman 1972; Hakim 2011; Thornton 1995).

Sociologists examining contemporary subcultures have hinted inadvertently at this need to soften Bourdieu's framework, to concentrate on struggles for distinction *within* specific cultural practices. Thornton (1995: 11–14), for example, argued that young people often claim 'subcultural capital' within their main subcultures.

Thompson (1995: 223) found that contemporary fan cultures have their own power hierarchies and sets of conventions by which amateurs and the cognoscenti are differentiated. In both instances, distinction is gained through possessing mixtures of capital that are specifically meaningful within the relevant subcultural field. A similar point comes into play regarding sport. Sport fans employ numerous interactive strategies to identify and evaluate the subcultural capital of one another. Do other fans recall key moments in major sports events? Can they identify specific techniques or individual players? To what extent did they grow up with the sport? Answers to these questions are often found in the distinctive social and historical relations within each sporting field rather than in any dominant influence from wider social fields.

Questions for discussion

1 According to Bourdieu, how are our sporting 'tastes' linked to our wider class positions? What roles are played by our habitus and different types of capital?
2 To what extent do we practise particular sports in order to distinguish ourselves from other individuals and social groups?
3 According to Bourdieu, how should we reform sport and challenge neo-liberal policies? What role should be played by sociologists?
4 Overall, what are the strengths and limitations of Bourdieu's perspective on sport?

11

Postmodern Sport: Fragmentation, Consumption and Hyperreality

During the 1980s and 1990s, postmodern social theories provided some of the most important keywords and areas of debate across the social sciences. A disparate array of theorists have been associated with 'the postmodern', including Nietzsche, Foucault, Derrida, Baudrillard, Lyotard, Rorty and many others. Supporters and sympathizers argued that a 'postmodern turn' had occurred in social science and that theories of the postmodern equipped sociologists to make sense of an increasingly post-industrial, consumerist, sign-saturated, globalizing world. Sceptics countered that postmodernism was a sociological fad, lacking rational principles or critical foundations, while exaggerating the degree of social change across modern societies. By the late 1990s, the 'postmodern debate' in social science had declined substantially, although other research areas have continued to be influenced by many of the arising themes and issues.

Debates on the postmodern have tended to be complicated by the notoriously elusive and contested meanings of the keywords. The discussion that follows here will be based on two important definitions. First, the word *postmodernity* will be taken to refer to relatively new forms of social organization, particularly in terms of new kinds of social stratification, relationship and reflexivity within increasingly post-industrial societies. In sport, postmodernity may refer, for example, to the influence of new social classes in interpreting and presenting sporting events or to a much wider array of social identities (beyond white, heterosexual males) that are targeted in marketing for sport-related consumption. Second, the word *postmodernism* will refer to relatively new cultural movements and philosophies, such as in television and film, music, art, literature, dance and sport. The birthdates of these postmodern cultural styles tend to be disputed, though in sport we might point in particular to new styles of mass-media coverage of sport that took hold from the 1980s onwards. More broadly, postmodern cultural styles may refer, for instance, to the architectural design of stadiums or the production techniques of sport-related films. While being differentiated in these ways, the keywords 'postmodernity' and 'postmodernism' both represent significant departures or breaks from modernity and modernism respectively.

To examine the sport and postmodern debate, this chapter is separated into six parts. The opening three parts set out the main components of postmodern social theory and poststructuralist theory, as well as their relevance to sport. Parts four and five examine how sociological approaches seek to explain postmodernity and how these perspectives may be harnessed to examine sport. Part six focuses on the important contributions of Jean Baudrillard, a highly influential French social theorist, and his potential relevance for explaining sport. I conclude by considering key critical and political questions concerning the issue of postmodern sport.

Postmodern and poststructuralist social theories

To begin, I turn to examine the main claims of postmodern and poststructuralist theories. A useful starting point is to identify the contrasts between modern and postmodern social theories. Postmodern approaches reject what they take to be the main claims of modern theories, that modern scientific knowledge is based on universal and rational 'truths', that it transcends local customs and other belief systems, and that it is capable of delivering long-term human progress and emancipation (Best and Kellner 1991). The postmodern standpoint argues instead that, while these modern 'meta-narratives' or grand theories of knowledge may promise such progress and emancipation, they tend to overreach themselves and to have disastrous consequences (cf. Lyotard 1984, 1993). Consider, for example, the case of Marxist theory, which promised revolutionary emancipation for the working classes, but which has led primarily to Stalinist forms of state socialism and to the deaths of tens of millions of citizens. Consider also the case of advanced scientific knowledge, which, through atomic and nuclear technologies, has produced disastrous radiation leaks, the deaths of hundreds of thousands of civilians during and after the Second World War, and the permanent threat of complete world destruction.

Postmodernists dismiss the modern assumption that knowledge might be universally 'true' or that there are universal ethics and norms (such as universal human rights) which should apply in all societies. Alternatively, for postmodernists such as Lyotard and Rorty, knowledge is relative or specific to different cultures; in effect, knowledge is organized into different cultural 'language games', each of which has its own rules, standards and principles (Kellner and Best 2001). To outsiders, some of these language games may look strange, irrational or unethical. However, as outsiders, we cannot properly understand these knowledge systems or language games. On that basis we are in no position to judge these societies or to intervene when we find their practices to be offensive.

How might these postmodernist claims be applied to sport? We may begin by exploring the modern meta-narrative that sport produces stronger, healthier, happier, more competitive, 'better' bodies and thus contributes positively to physical development and social emancipation. The postmodern standpoint might point instead at the much darker sides of sport and sport science: consider, for example, the costs of sport in regard to injuries and pain among athletes, the systematic use of scientific knowledge for doping, and the violence and harassment among participants and spectators. We might point at how modern Western sport has been forcibly inserted into diverse cultural contexts since at least the late nineteenth century; one direct consequence has been the decline and eradication of many non-Western physical or movement cultures (in other words, non-Western physical 'language games'). Additionally, the postmodernist stance might challenge the large 'sport for development and peace' (SDP) sector which has emerged strongly since the mid-1990s (see chapter 12 for more discussion). A large proportion of SDP work involves using sport to promote particular forms of development (such as education and human rights) in non-Western societies, particularly in sub-Saharan Africa. One postmodernist position would critique the SDP sector as a classic case of the arrogance of modern Western thinking, in terms of using sport to impose the Western 'language game' of development upon non-Western societies (Giulianotti 2004b).

Poststructuralist social theories, notably advanced by Derrida and Foucault, represent an important strain of postmodernist theorizing. A poststructuralist argument is that power and knowledge are inseparable and deeply entwined; for example, for Foucault, powerful bourgeois groups have produced scientific discourses on the body, such as through medical science or modern penology, which have served to discipline and to govern diverse populations, particularly the 'danger-ous' lower classes and women. Another poststructuralist standpoint, provided by Derrida (1978) in the field of literary theory, critiques the assumption that authors have the power to control the mean-ings and interpretations of their texts; writing instead is presented as highly contextual, unstable, and forever open to critical 'deconstruc-tions'. In line with Lyotard, Derrida (1978) also challenges the 'logo-centrism' of Western rationality and the claim that it is based upon objective, eternal, scientific, universal foundations.

In the sociology of sport, the poststructuralist influence has been dominated by Foucauldian theory, notably in the analysis of bodily discipline and government, care of the self, and surveillance in and around sport grounds (see chapters 7 and 8). Derridean theory has had little impact, but may have some fruitful applications to sport – for instance, the 'logocentrism' of many sporting rule-books and governing bodies refers to values such as 'gentlemanly behaviour', 'fair play' and 'sporting conduct'. Poststructuralist analysis enables us to deconstruct these keywords, to reveal their inherent biases in terms of gender, ethnicity and class, which in turn shed light on the underlying political roots of modern sport institutions. The mission statements and constitutions of sport governing bodies may also be deconstructed in this way.[29] More broadly, the relativist aspects of postmodern and poststructuralist theories enable us to recognize, and indeed to celebrate, deep cultural differences within sport, for example in how the rules and customs of specific sports are under-stood and manifested in very diverse ways.

Turning to criticisms, we might highlight two broad problems within postmodern standpoints. First, the relativist position of post-modern standpoints is ultimately illogical: you cannot make a 'truth claim' which denies the possibility of any universal truth. Even if we did momentarily suspend belief in truth claims, we would leave ourselves no grounds on which to judge the quality of any claim or argument; if that were the case, social science would close tomorrow, as its statements would be no more valid than those from any other source.

Second, as a result, postmodern cultural relativism appears to abandon political hope and moral critique. One concern here is that some postmodern social theories attempt to relativize the fun-damental or universal points on our moral compass, for example by giving up entirely on the idea of universal human rights. Such a stance means that we would have to ignore the conditions of desper-ate peoples living under oppressive regimes, on the grounds that we are not in a position to understand or to intervene within these other cultures. In sport, this might mean that Western organizations would have to stop their use of sport to promote development and peace, even in contexts where the human rights of women seemed to be flagrantly abused or where violent conflicts were causing widespread suffering. The postmodernist stance might also mean failing to intervene if athletes are subjected to systematic abuse by the relevant authorities within sport or beyond. In such circumstances, we might argue that the adoption of a postmodern stance seems to be more socially harmful than helpful; indeed, this stance of 'tolerant open-mindedness' towards other cultures seems to result merely in our moral scruples falling out of our heads (Morgan 1998: 362–3, via Rorty 1991).

Notwithstanding these critical points, I would argue that a selective use of postmodern social theories has benefits for the sociology of sport. We saw earlier how Foucauldian poststructuralist theory helps to explain the exercise of power on the sporting body. Here, I would add that postmodern theory encourages the constant critical interrogation of the constitution and 'universal ethics' of different sports. For example, in the case of the SDP sector, a partial postmodernist standpoint would encourage Western organizations and researchers to pause and to reflect critically on their work; a key question here concerns the extent to which they engage fully with local peoples and cultures in order to avoid the blank imposition of Western values, development agendas, and sport practices within these different contexts. Moreover, postmodernists and poststructuralists correctly sense that there is a growing public interest in cultural diversity and alternative knowledge systems, whether in sport or in other social fields. I build on these themes in the next section in exploring the postmodern idea of dedifferentiation.

The postmodern world and dedifferentiation

According to Lash (1990: 11–15, 173–4), the modern world was characterized by the increasing differentiation of most aspects of modern life; thus, different social structures, organizations, institutions and social identities came to be more and more separated and differentiated from one another. Conversely, the postmodern world is associated with processes of 'dedifferentiation' – that is, the breaking down or collapse of these modern boundaries and distinctions. Thus, complex modern societies saw the growing separation of cultural, economic, political and social spheres; conversely, postmodernity may be viewed as marked by greater overlaps and interplay between these spheres. Sports are part of the cultural sphere but also increasingly embedded within the economy (through greater commercialization), within the social sphere (such as through contemporary social media) and within politics (as politicians engage constantly with sport to boost their popular appeal).

The postmodern dedifferentiation of boundaries is also reflected in the apparent collapse of high/low cultural divisions. Modern culture had been divided into two basic domains. First, 'low' or 'popular' culture featured expressive, participatory, relatively physical working-class activities, such as popular music or traditional folk events; in sport and physical culture, these might include rugby league, boxing, wrestling and football in working-class communities. Second, 'high' or official culture featured more intellectual, critically detached, bourgeois pursuits, such as the performing arts or literature; in sport, this might include English cricket, in which there is a focus on strategy and audience detachment from play.

Cultural postmodernism, it is argued, breaks down these modern boundaries between high and low culture: hence, we find poets penning verses on rugby league, prize-winning authors writing on 'bad-boy' football players, and composers writing operas on football (Rowe 1995: 165). We also find signifiers of 'high' and 'low' culture being playfully juxtaposed and interconnected, particularly in the mass media. For example, British television coverage of football's 1990 World Cup finals in Italy included substantial use of operatic arias, as well as a televised concert by 'the three tenors' (Carreras, Domingo, Pavarotti). Later, a BBC television advert for the 2004 European Championships in Portugal presented a variety of leading international players in the painting style of their major national artists (thus, Italy's Buffon was portrayed in the style of Modigliani, France's Zidane in the style of Monet, Spain's Raul in the style of Picasso, and so on). In such cases, we see how, in the pastiche style of postmodernism, a previously 'low' cultural form (football) is brought into playful contact with high culture forms (opera, painting).

Arguably, the old modern boundaries between audience and author (or performer) have undergone partial dedifferentiation (Lash 1990: 173). The modern development of sport had been marked by the strong spatial differentiation and segregation of audience and athlete. Postmodern dedifferentiation arises in a variety of ways: through marketing discourses that make spectators 'part of the show'; through team mascots who mix with crowds; through the entry of individual spectators onto the field of play to participate in shoot-out competitions; through cameras on racing cars, cricket stumps, skiers and other competitors that place viewers 'inside the action'; and in social media, such as Twitter and Facebook, that bring athletes and audiences into continual virtual contact with each other.

Postmodern culture is also assumed to compress (or to dedifferentiate) time–space boundaries (Harvey 1991). Contemporary technology and institutionalized forms of globalization enable images and capital to move globally in an instant. An evening's television can cover sport in all continents through mixtures of recorded and live content (see Gottdiener 1995: 50–1). Some television coverage of sport serves to compress time by flitting across decades or by integrating images of athletes from yesteryear and today into a single film (see Rail 1998: 154). Further time–space compression is evidenced at the everyday level, as sport clubs employ elite athletes from across the globe, while sport mega-events 'bring the world to one city' as competitors and spectators from many nations meet in a single urban space.

Finally, we might identify processes of postmodern dedifferentiation as having occurred across different sports and other cultural fields. Much stronger interconnections exist between sport and wider leisure cultures, for example through the use of sport disciplines and training methods (such as running, rowing, weightlifting, 'boxercise') as part of the workout or fitness boom since the 1980s. In much of the Global North, there has also been a rapid growth in 'lifestyle sports' – such as surfing, snowboarding and paragliding – which often reject the modern competitive model of sport. Since the early 1970s, we have witnessed a collapse in the boundaries between Western sport and Eastern martial arts, notably as the latter have often developed more competitive formats while being taken up by millions of new participants in the West (Guttmann 1988: 179–1). We also find Western sports being interpreted and analysed with reference to Eastern forms of spiritual knowledge – as illustrated by book titles such as *The Zen of Muhammad Ali and Other Obsessions* by Davis Miller and *The Tao of Golf* by Leland T. Lewis – in ways that suggest a postmodern engagement with Eastern belief systems.

Overall, the concept of dedifferentiation is extremely useful in registering significant structural and cultural changes within postmodernity – that is, the many ways in which modern forms of differentiation are being weakened and challenged through the breaking down of barriers and the interpenetration of diverse spheres. These processes of dedifferentiation also surface in the making of postmodern social identities, which I turn to consider now.

Postmodernity and social identities

Postmodernity has been associated with the emergence of new types of social identity. To begin, it may be argued that, in postmodern society, social identities are no longer as 'fixed' as during modern times but, instead, have become much more complex and fluid. Thus, the old modern 'container categories' of identity – such as class, gender and nationality – are much more blurred and may have lost a substantial part of their social significance. For example, gender roles and identities have become more complex and diverse, notably in relation to sexuality, while women have gained significantly stronger presences in old male-dominated public spaces. The idea of a singular 'national identity' that is tied strongly to a fixed nation-state has become less and less relevant; immigration and rapid geographical mobility have produced more complex forms of national identity (such as dual, hyphenated and multiple national identities). In addition, regional and 'subnational' identities have intensified, for instance in Spain (through Basque and Catalan identities) and the UK (notably in Scotland and Wales). Moreover, modern identities were largely tied to production processes, notably in terms of social class and types of employment; postmodern identities, by contrast, are linked more to consumption, in terms of particular consumer tastes and leisure preferences. In turn, the postmodern 'habitus' of social actors is more fluid and fragmented than in modern times. Postmodern consumers are more likely to hold diverse cultural tastes that cut across modern categories (notably social class); thus, it might be argued, postmodern cultural tastes are more eclectic and harder to pin to old class identities – after all, some individuals may combine enjoyment of punk and operatic music or ballet and American football.

Some scholars argue that social identities and relations have been transformed in more radical ways. Maffesoli (1996) posits that social life is now largely shaped by 'neo-tribes' – that is, transitory and postmodern gatherings of individuals who move fluidly in and out of participation in particular affective spaces (Bauman 1992: 137). Neo-tribalism is particularly evident in consumer and popular culture. For example, the old modern subcultures – notably the youth styles skinhead, mod, punk, soccer casual, goth, and so forth – tended to have relatively fixed and comprehensive identities. Conversely, postmodern identities are more neo-tribal or 'mix and match', often involving a creative, pastiche combination of signs and styles from earlier, competing subcultures.

Neo-tribal identity signs and markers also tend to be more aesthetic and transitory and less fixed to specific forms of strong or 'hot' solidarity. Consider tattoos: previously, these body markings tended to show the deep and fixed ties of individuals (especially working-class men) to particular social formations (such as family, home town or nation); today, postmodern tattoos point to more aesthetic and transnational identities, perhaps in featuring Chinese calligraphy while often being located on less exposed areas of the body (e.g., the foot, the back shoulder) and worn by different classes and genders (Turner 1999).

We may locate some of these aspects of the postmodernization of social identity within sport. In regard to national identities, for example, sport participants and athletes are increasingly likely to hold not one single national affiliation but, instead, a range of such ties, in part through their multi-layered ethnicities; meanwhile, 'national' sport teams are also more likely to be highly poly-ethnic, featuring participants who have been born abroad, who speak different languages, or who have grown up with different national loyalties.

For some spectator groups, team loyalties and affiliations have become more fluid. I have argued elsewhere that sport spectator identities fall into four categories: supporters, followers, fans and *flâneurs* (Giulianotti 2002; note: for the purposes of that particular article, these four keywords were defined in very specific ways). In this context, we might argue that the most striking contrast is between 'supporters' and postmodern *flâneurs*: 'supporters' have relatively fixed forms of team identification, particularly towards local clubs. *Flâneurs* do not have these 'hot' forms of solidarity and instead shift their sport interests and allegiances quite freely; they tend to buy into the commodity signifiers of sport teams through consumer culture, such as by wearing the New York baseball hat, the Chicago Bulls T-shirt, the Brazil football jersey, the tracksuit top with 'Italia' emblazoned across the chest, and so forth. *Flâneur* identities thus embody a fluid, neo-tribal transnational consumerism which at least points to the potential breakdown of sports team identification.

This particular study on different types of sport spectator registers a further, more fundamental point: that we should focus on the modern/postmodern debate less in either/or terms and more in terms of the complex interplay and co-existence of these two categories. (Indeed, this observation fits with postmodern theory, which otherwise celebrates the collapse of such boundaries.) For example, in elite sport, we may see how leading clubs endeavour to build and extend their modern ties with supporters while seeking to sell products to transnational *flâneurs*. We might also see how modern, fixed, sub-cultural ties in sport co-exist with more fluid, neo-tribal identities. For example, my research into football hooliganism in Scotland and England suggests that both of these identities are evident: hard-core hooligans are evidently subcultural in terms of regular and committed participation, whereas neo-tribal groups drift in and out of hooligan activity (Giulianotti 1999). However, it is worth noting that modern types of sport identity provide the crucial social preconditions and contexts which allow for the entry of more fluid, postmodern types of social participant; for example, sport supporters and subcultures establish the social spaces and forms of social identity which *flâneurs* and neo-tribal groups may then enter and explore, albeit temporar-ily. In addition, depending on context, we may find individuals flit-ting between these broad categorical identities – for instance as local supporters of English football teams also act as *flâneurs* in buying fashionable sport-related merchandise.

Overall, these points on the postmodernization of social identity have substantial value for the sociological analysis of sport, notably with reference to what might be termed 'post-subcultural' identi-ties, the importance of consumption-based identities, neo-tribalism, and *flâneur* social types in sport. However, we need to recognize the continuing roles played by modern social identities in enabling the construction or exploration of postmodern identities. Moreover, as discussed in the next section, the role of social class in shaping post-modern identities and cultural practices needs also to be registered.

Postmodern sport and the new middle classes

As I noted in the last section, postmodern identities might be associ-ated with consumption (leisure) rather than production (work). It is possible to extend this focus by exploring how postmodern identities are associated also with transformations in the production process and with the breaking down of boundaries between production and consumption within postmodern societies.

In broad terms, in regard to political economy, postmodernity is associated with the decline of modern manufacturing and heavy industry and the rise of post-industrial, service-led, 'knowledge-based' fields of employment. As a consequence, postmodernity is marked by major changes in the class structures of advanced societies in the Global North. These structural changes have seen the old working class decline greatly in number and also splinter into many different fractions; we have also witnessed the growth of white-collar employment, often in relatively routine and low-paid areas of work, such as in telesales. In many nations in the Global North – notably the UK and the United States – 'New Right', neoliberal governments offered little social support for deindustrializing towns and regions. These governments also presided over growing levels of social inequality through much of the 1980s and 1990s: at the bottom, there was an expanding lower-working class trapped in unemployment or low pay, with low educational attainment and few opportunities for social mobility; at the top stood a small elite which had benefited greatly from free-market government policies such as tax cuts, welfare cuts, and the rise of a new, unregulated global financial sector.

Amidst these social changes, the class that is most associated with postmodern culture tends to be the new 'service class' or 'new middle classes', who are heavily involved in sales and marketing, media, and other knowledge or lifestyle industries (Lash and Urry 1994: 164). The new middle classes are the social engine of postmodern culture, driving cultural tastes, habits, and new types of employment. Bridging many of the old divides between high and low culture, and unlike the traditional bourgeoisie, the new middle classes embrace rather than dismiss popular culture and are trained to engage critically (not passively) with consumer products. These classes also enjoy the 'aestheticization of everyday life', in which more and more aspects of day-to-day social life are subjected to appearance improvement and beautification (Featherstone 1991: 35, 44–5).

These societal transformations have had substantial impacts on sport. The economic and cultural importance of elite professional sport has mushroomed since the late 1980s. For example, professional leagues such as the EPL, MLB, NFL, AFL and IPL are increasingly important features of service-sector economies, as reflected in the long-term growth in their media coverage, commercial aspects and centrality to consumer culture. The new middle classes have played a key part here and in driving other aspects of the new sport economy, such as in the design and marketing of sport-related merchandise and fashion or the production of sport media content for print and electronic media. Moreover, the new middle classes have a relatively cosmopolitan, critical and culturally engaged habitus, which has served to advance the writing and the sale of sport-related literature and wider media content. This media content is also far more informed, literate, transnational and voluminous than was the case before the late 1980s. Sport fanzines and online blogs illustrate this development.

It might be argued that processes of class postmodernization have substantial influences upon how particular social groups engage with sport and the wider fields of leisure and recreation. For example, we may consider the case of tourism. Feifer (1985) advances the concept of the 'post-tourist', which was subsequently developed by Urry (1990: 90–2), in order to explain the partial shift from modern mass tourism towards forms of 'post-tourism' that are associated with cool detachment, irony, choice, flexibility, and a playful engagement with high and low culture (Featherstone 1995: 120). Post-tourists are well aware that the 'authentic' experiences and landscapes which are presented by local 'tourism industries' tend to be socially constructed in order to fit with tourist expectations. Thus, the particular tastes of post-tourists are very much in line with the broader habitus of the new middle classes. Finally, the rise of the post-tourist does not mean the end for the modern, mass forms of tourism in the most popular and populous resorts.

We might transfer these distinguishing features of the post-tourist into the field of sport spectatorship in order to reveal the 'post-fan' (Giulianotti 1999). In this sense, the 'post-fan' is a spectator who adopts a playful, ironic, detached attitude towards the social construction of sport. At sports tournaments, she may playfully enjoy public events that are stage-managed by the organizing authorities. She may recognize too that debates and issues within sport are heavily 'spun' by public relations employees; indeed, partly as a response, she is liable to produce her own media (such as through fanzines or blogs) and to engage actively in social media, providing content that is satirical and sharply critical. Again, like the post-tourist, the post-fan appears to be closely associated with the broader, postmodern habitus of the new middle classes. Finally, the 'post-fan' does not abolish older, modern types of spectator identity, such as the 'supporter' or 'fan'. Thus, supporters or fans continue, for example, to rely mainly on mainstream mass media for sport information.

In the next section, I turn to explore the deeper political economic forces that underpin the emergence of postmodern society, with regard both to new types of capitalism and how these processes may be identified within the realm of sport.

Postmodern sport and the new capitalism

According to some analysts, postmodern societies are marked by 'post-Fordist' and 'disorganized' relations of production (see, for example, Amin 1994; Lash and Urry 1994). Conversely, modern, organized capitalism in the twentieth century had been built around the 'Fordist' model of production, as pioneered by the Ford Motor Company. In its ideal form, Fordist factories involved the highly efficient, mass production of goods by long assembly lines of workers. Complex divisions of labour in Fordist factories featured high levels of employee specialization and routinization of work, the maximization of productive efficiency, and the systematic reduction of worker autonomy and creativity in return for higher wages and job security. Large, highly efficient, corporate organizations oversaw the entire factory-to-buyer process, through manufacturing, marketing and sales (Gramsci 1971: 310–13; Grint 1991: 294–7). Based in part on the 'economies of scale' principle, Fordist factories also produced the maximum number of units 'just in case' any surplus products might be sold on to mass markets.

Post-Fordism is viewed as contrasting strongly with these features of Fordist production. In post-Fordist businesses, there is far greater 'flexible specialization' in production, marketing and consumption. Products are rapidly introduced, redesigned and dropped, in order to fit 'just in time' with particular fluctuations and idiosyncrasies in market demand. Moreover, post-Fordism places a greater emphasis on service-sector input, notably through sales and marketing, as well as research and design; thus, for example, products are wrapped in lifestyle meanings that connect with the shifting consumer habits, tastes and identities of diverse market segments (Amin 1994). Post-Fordist working units are markedly smaller than those in Fordist environments and feature a greater focus on cross-task working and short-term contracts. In culture industries such as popular music or sport, post-Fordism is knowledge-intensive and reflexive (Lash and Urry 1994: 121–3). Sports media programming requires software specialists and sharp media analysts in order to upgrade production techniques and to monitor audience interests and responses on a continual basis.

In broader terms, as I argued earlier, sport showcases the co-existence and interplay between the modern and the postmodern, in this case with regard to Fordist and post-Fordist forms of production and consumption. We might consider the case of the production and sale of sport merchandise. Until the 1970s, sport merchandise tended to follow rather Fordist principles in production and design: for example, sport kit tended to be relatively uniform and functional in style, with comparatively few variations except in basic colour. Since then, post-Fordist principles have become far more prominent in the design and marketing of sport merchandise: aestheticized sport shirts have come to be packaged as general leisurewear, and a highly diverse range of models and styles are continually redesigned and subsequently endorsed by the latest celebrity athletes. Nevertheless, these post-Fordist products also rely heavily on Fordist techniques, most notably through mass manufacturing in large factories in the developing world, particularly South-East Asia and Central America.

The neo-Marxist social theorists Fredric Jameson and David Harvey have argued that processes of postmodernization are closely connected to changes in organized capitalism. Jameson (1991: 400) has defined postmodernism as the 'cultural logic of late capitalism' or, following Mandel (1975), as the post-war 'third stage' of capitalism. Postmodernism is characterized by the commodification of culture and media, ranging from the high arts through to television entertainment (Jameson 1991: 276–8). Harvey (1991) traced the origins of postmodern society to the early 1970s, when flexible accumulation arose alongside cultural fragmentation and unpredictable societal changes. For Harvey, postmodern social theory highlights the significance of difference, social complexity and time–space compression, such as in the global flows of information and human travel. However, postmodern social theories are criticized for being too dismissive towards the 'meta-narratives' of modernity (notably Marxism) and for placing too much emphasis on aesthetic issues rather than the economic base of society, as well as ethical questions.

Overall, Jameson and Harvey enable us to examine critically how postmodern social and cultural trends may serve to advance deeper political-economic forces and interests. For example, Jameson (1991: 406–7) has indicated that the 'ethos' and 'lifestyles' of the new middle classes represent a dominant ideological and cultural project within postmodern capitalism. In sport, as in other fields, this involves commercialization processes becoming 'normalized', while sales and marketing personnel within sport clubs are employed to instruct and guide potential consumers on how merchandise and other products contribute to a consumerist lifestyle.

For Lash and Urry (1987, 1994), the new stage of capitalism has really been about *dis*organization. This 'disorganized capitalism' connects in particular to processes of globalization, as marked by international flows of labour, capital, images and technology; the emergence of global cities and financial structures; the growing significance of global 'risks'; transnational communication networks (notably mass media); the dissolution of hierarchical class structures; the decline of the nation-state; and the rise of 'cosmopolitan' postmodern individuals (Lash and Urry 1994: 323).

If we look at the totality of global sport, there is certainly evidence of a substantial contribution to disorganized capitalism. As we discuss more fully in the next chapter, contemporary elite sport has come to be characterized by the transnational circulation and flow of images, capital, people (whether spectators or athletes) and commodities. International media networks – such as those controlled by Rupert Murdoch's various corporations – facilitate the rapid circulation (and the global consumption) of sporting images. The development of a postmodern sport culture is evidenced here, through the dizzying media-driven compression of time and space. In the next section, I explore how the contemporary mass media and consumerism were examined by Jean Baudrillard in distinctive ways that had substantial influence upon debates on the postmodern.

Extreme postmodern culture: Jean Baudrillard and hyperreality

The controversy surrounding the late French social theorist Jean Baudrillard begins with the very issue of his relevance to debates on the postmodern. On the one hand, some commentators point out that he personally rejected the idea of the postmodern, and thus should not be discussed with regard to this subject (Gane 1991: 46–8). On the other hand, it is pretty obvious that Baudrillard's provocative concepts and arguments have been highly influential in shaping theories of postmodern society and culture (Bauman 1992; Connor 1989; Kellner 1989; Lash 1990: 238). Here, with that latter observation in mind, I explore how Baudrillard's imaginary enables us to advance some key claims and observations with regard to postmodern culture.

To begin, Baudrillard's work directs us towards the basic proposition that postmodern cultures prioritize consumption and 'seduction' over modern production (cf. Baudrillard 1998, 2006). Consumer societies place greater emphasis on image over reality; thus, the symbolism and wrapping of the object, and its relationship to other objects, become more important than that object's actual use-value. In sport, we witness this triumph of the 'exchange-value' in how sport-related commercial items – such as sport shoes, tennis polo-shirts, football tops and baseball caps – have become more meaningful as fashion items, within a system of brand labels, rather than for their 'use-value', in terms of simply facilitating and maximizing sport performance. A similar process is sometimes identified in how, for some heavily marketed elite professional athletes, their 'seductive' appeal to consumer markets seems far to outweigh their actual 'use-values' as participants in sporting competition.

Baudrillard's concepts of *simulacrum* and *hyperreality* help to explain the simulated and virtual components of postmodern culture. Strictly defined, a simulacrum is a particular copy of something that does not actually exist (Jameson 1991: 18). It might be argued that our fake, postmodern culture is increasingly filled by simulacra, such as theme parks or recently constructed 'olde worlde' pubs, which include the 're-creation' of idealized, imagined places from the past (Baudrillard 1994a: 6). In extreme cases, sports events and identities are rooted in the logics of the simulacra. For example, 'virtual' horse-racing – a sport created by computer software – is devoid of everyday problems, such as steward inquiries into results or gamblers' suspicions over the efforts of losing jockeys.

The term 'hyperreality' refers to a media-saturated world that combines aspects of the simulated and artificial while also appearing to be 'realer than real'. For instance, large-screen 3-D sport video games are artificial but also have the effect of bringing the competitors closer to the simulated action than is possible in 'real' games. In broader terms, sport is presented by television in hyperreal form: offensive background noise is removed, while surround-sound audio systems amplify and simulate crowd 'atmosphere' to levels that do not arise in real stadiums. Meanwhile, 'interactive' devices allow viewers to watch the same sport incident from multiple camera angles; in this way, viewers may experience an excess of visual reality that is not available to participants or spectators in real life (Baudrillard 1995: 104; 1996b: 29; 1991: 31–6).

Hyperreality is further characterized by the dominance or pre-eminence of the virtual over the actual. Among elite athletes, 'virtual' personas and images seem to be followed or imitated in order to create the 'actual' identities of these individuals; part of this process may be attributed to public relations and marketing experts (step forward, members of the postmodern new middle classes), who advise sport celebrities on how to create and to cultivate their public image or 'brand' in a televisual age. A similar virtual-then-actual process occurs among sport subcultures. For example, we find that football hooligans are presented in particular virtual ways by the mass media, in films, novels and sensationalized press stories; we then find some football hooligan formations appearing to follow these images, in terms of their practices and identities (Poster 1988; Redhead 1991).

Perhaps the most striking way in which Baudrillard's insights on virtual culture may be applied to sport relates to the emergence and rapid growth of video gaming and electronic sports. These 'e-sports' involve individual or multiple individuals playing a wide range of video games, including specialized sport games (football, basketball, baseball, athletics, and so on) that are licensed by sport clubs and governing bodies. Major e-sport events, such as the World Cyber Games, feature the world's leading games players as competitors; and these purely virtual games are often contested on giant screens and watched by large numbers of actual spectators.

One of Baudrillard's (1994b) most provocative statements on virtual culture and hyperreality centred on his claim that the 'Gulf War did not take place'. His point here was that, for most audiences, as well as for many combatants, the Gulf War (1990–1) was experienced largely as a virtual event, as a hyperreal television moment (Gane 1993: 185). Indeed, much of the film footage from the war that was released by US forces resembled images from virtual war games, showing on-screen targets being targeted and destroyed.

In more peaceful contexts, we might make a similar point to argue that sports are increasingly experienced as 'virtual' events, to the extent that television companies dictate when mega-events are allowed to take place (Baudrillard 1993: 79–80; 1995: 98). Television units 'make' the event, for example by inciting peaceable groups of spectators to 'sing for the cameras', thereby simulating an actual social occasion; meanwhile, spectators wave messages, banners and flags, not to influence sports events but to attract television cameras; sport fans in the stadium also come to spend more time watching the 'virtual' action on giant television screens rather than the 'actual' events on the field of play. Indeed, in the case of e-sports, the virtual action on the screen *is* where the 'real' action is taking place.

Overall, Baudrillard advanced some sharp and incisive observations on the extreme phenomena and trends within contemporary culture: in the sport context, we may point to the hyperreality of sport theme parks and television coverage; the rapid rise of video-gaming and e-sports; and the steady stream of banal, xeroxed sport celebrities who continue to circulate across popular culture. Arguably, it is best to use Baudrillard's work in a heuristic way, in terms of comparing and contrasting how close contemporary culture is to his analyses of these extreme trends and images. His approach also encourages us to investigate the extent to which virtual, hyperreal culture will become increasingly embedded within mainstream sport. For example, we may consider whether e-sports will come to be recognized and integrated within major sport institutions and competitions, so that Olympic sport disciplines may in future include video-game events.

Concluding comments

I have argued that, while they have significantly less academic presence compared to the 1990s, the concepts of postmodernity and postmodernism do help to explain significant changes that have occurred within advanced societies since the 1980s. To summarize, the most insightful contributions from postmodern thinking help to probe the relationships between Western power, modern knowledge systems and science; to reveal the breaking down or dedifferentiation of many modern boundaries, categories and divisions; to register the rise of more fluid social and cultural identities, retro and pastiche cultures, and the broad aestheticization of everyday life; to highlight the growing prevalence and significance of the new middle classes; to examine 'disorganized' or 'third-stage' capitalism vis-à-vis postmodern culture; and to identify the emergence and spread of virtual, hyperreal cultures. As I have argued through this chapter, these wider processes and developments are all evidenced within the specific field of sport.

To conclude, I advance two interconnected points on the postmodern. First, as I have indicated at different points through this chapter, we should highlight the different ways in which the modern and the postmodern are interrelated and co-exist rather than standing in adversarial, 'either/or' relationships. We see this, for example, in how sport spectator identities feature modern subcultures, supporters and fans, as well as postmodern neo-tribes, *flâneurs* and post-fans. We also see this at sport events which feature live activities inside stadiums and in virtual, postmodern coverage in the mass media. On sport merchandise, we find that modern Fordist forms of factory production co-exist with post-Fordist types of marketing and consumption. Finally, in the political economy of sport, the basic model of modern capitalist accumulation combines with the postmodern entry of sport into more areas of business. In all of these cases and more, we find modern and postmodern processes are entwined.

Second, following from the above, we may probe the extent to which theories and arguments on postmodernity and postmodernism enable us to advance a critical sociological perspective on sport. That is, do these postmodern standpoints permit us to examine power inequalities and social divisions, to identify forms of social opposition and resistance, and to explore alternative models for the future organization of sport?

To answer that question, I would recommend a qualified engagement with postmodern and poststructuralist approaches. On the positive side, these perspectives remind us of the need to examine the complex and problematic interrelationships between power and knowledge; we are thus required, as Westerners, to exercise substantial self-criticism and caution when engaging with non-Western societies, for example when using sport as an educational tool for development purposes. In addition, these standpoints should also remind us to examine the sharpening of social divisions and inequalities through processes of post-industrialization. Some influential standpoints also suggest that we may identify some postmodern forms of social resistance in both familiar and unfamiliar places: Baudrillard (1993) points to how, in a media-driven age, we may still find that the most socially marginalized groups may resort to staging their own spectacles of disorder, as we sometimes witness in sport riots; in a more unfamiliar context, he locates senses and sentiments of public opposition in how consumers and voters toy with opinion pollsters and marketing people.

Yet, more critically, when we turn to consider how alternative models of sport might be envisioned or developed, the full postmodernist standpoint comes up short. The reluctance of postmodernists to advance any kind of future ideal for sport may be consistent with the core tenets of their social theory. But such a standpoint would leave us unable to respond effectively in the long term to the social divisions, injustices and harm that we continue to find within sport at local, national and global levels.

Questions for discussion

1 In what ways might it be argued that contemporary sport is postmodern?
2 Have forms of sport identification (such as supporting particular sport teams) become postmodern, in terms of being more fluid, complex and short-lived than in the past?
3 What roles are played by the media and other communications technologies in the making of postmodern sport?
4 Overall, what are the strengths and limitations of theories of the postmodern for explaining contemporary sport?

12

Globalization and Sport: Political Economy, Cultural Creativity and Social Development

Globalization has become a prominent research theme within sociology as well as a subject of major public and political debate over the past two decades. The sociology of sport has contributed substantially to this 'global turn', while sport has been a highly important driver of globalization processes, for example through the staging of mega-events such as the Olympics that have worldwide television audiences.

The sociologist Roland Robertson is arguably the founding figure of globalization studies within the social sciences (Robertson 1990, 1992, 1994, 1995). In this chapter, my analysis of globalization and sport is underpinned by three key aspects of Robertson's approach. First, I follow his definition of globalization as a concept that 'refers both to the compression of the world and the intensification of consciousness of the world as a whole' (Robertson 1992: 8). In other words, global processes are marked by greater transnational connections (such as in telecommunications) and greater awareness and reflexivity about the world as a 'single place' (such as in environmental politics).

Second, globalization should be understood as a long-term, complex and multi-faceted process, extending at least as far back as the fifteenth century, and featuring various cultural, social, political and economic dimensions (Robertson 1992; Giulianotti and Robertson 2009). This position contrasts directly with more simplified standpoints which view globalization in terms of the spread of Western modernization or neoliberal capitalism (cf. Bourdieu 1998a; Giddens 1990; Scholte 2005; Wolf 2004).

Third, there is the common assumption that 'the local' and 'the global' stand in direct opposition to each other. However, with

Robertson (1992), we should move beyond this dualism to recognize instead that the local and the global are interdependent. Hence, rather than always 'destroying' the local, globalization may also intensify forms of local or national particularity; for example, global sport tournaments allow and encourage particular club or national teams to project their identities in distinctive ways.

In this chapter, I explore three main aspects of the interconnections between sport and globalization. First, I discuss key political-economic issues and arguments within global sport. Second, I consider the socio-cultural aspects of sport and globalization with specific reference to debates on cultural convergence and cultural divergence. Third, I examine the emergence of the sport for the development and peace (SDP) sector, which represents the most significant field of activity in recent years for using sport to shape global change.

Political-economic aspects of global sport

In this section, I explore in turn two major issues with regard to the political economy of globalization that are relevant to sport and global processes. These relate to the growing range and complexity of political actors and the nature of the global economy.

Political actors in global sport

Over the past century or so, globalization has been marked by a growing number and diversity of important political actors. For example, since the end of the Second World War, one of the most significant political actors has been the United Nations and its many associated agencies, such as the International Labour Organization (ILO), UNESCO and the World Health Organization (WHO). The United Nations itself has expanded, from an initial meeting in 1946 involving fifty-one nations, into a highly complex global political body with 193 national members by the year 2011.

Similarly, the globalization of sport has been marked by a sharp rise in the volume and variety of political actors or stakeholders, particularly since the commercial expansion of sport from the late 1980s onwards. These political actors and stakeholders tend to have different interests and policies and to exercise different influences over the politics of global sport.

To make some sense of these diverse political stakeholders, we may position them within an 'ideal-type' model that features four categories.[30] As an ideal type, the model is intended to highlight the main tendencies and elements of these political stakeholders without necessarily capturing all of their features (Weber [1922] 1978: 23–4). Each category within the model is associated with a particular set of political priorities and ideologies relating to sport.

1 There are 'individual' or market-based political actors which are associated with *neoliberal* policies in global sport. Neoliberal policies have dominated global politics and economics since the late 1970s, and they promote free markets, income tax reductions, the privatization of state assets, cuts in welfare state provisions, and the implementation of social policies centred on individualism, self-reliance and self-responsibility (Harvey 2005; Smith 2005). In sport, the strongest proponents or beneficiaries of free-market policies include the largest and richest sport clubs (such as Barcelona, Chelsea, the Dallas Cowboys, the Los Angeles Dodgers, Manchester United, the New York Yankees, Real Madrid); top athletes and their agents; media corporations that operate pay-TV systems for sport coverage; corporate sponsors of sport organizations and events; and wealthy consumerist spectators who can afford to purchase sport tickets and products.

2 There are 'national' or nation-centred political actors associated particularly with *neo-mercantile* policies, which are intended to maintain the governance of sport at national level and to represent 'the national interest' within global sport. The strongest exponents of neo-mercantile policies are national sport governing bodies and associations (such as different national football associations and different national Olympic committees), national sport departments, the nation-state *per se*, and public-sector nation-based media (such as the BBC in the UK, CBC in Canada and ABC in Australia).

3 There are international political actors associated with policies that maintain and enhance the influence of formal structures of *international governance*. The main political actors here are international sport governing bodies and associations (such as UEFA, FIFA, IOC, ICC and IRB World Rugby) and also international governmental organizations (such as the EU and the United Nations).

4 There are political actors associated with 'humankind', with policies centred on the making of *global civil society*. The main political actors tend to be NGOs, campaign groups, social movements, and critical journalists and other intellectuals. These political actors tend to prioritize 'progressive' social causes, such as the use of

sport to promote human development, peace-building, human rights, social justice, and the combatting of racism, sexism, homophobia and corruption. I discuss the diversity of these political actors and policies later in this chapter with regard to the 'sport for development and peace' sector.

Three main points follow from this fourfold model of political actors. First, as an ideal type, this model underrepresents the substantial differences and schisms that occur *within* each category. For example, at the national level, different nations compete with each other to host mega-events or to attract corporate sponsorships. In addition, many organizations move beyond their 'home' categories in this model and seek to influence other categories or policy areas. As I explain later in this chapter, the 'global civil society' also features strong involvement by international organizations (such as the UN and EU), national governments and corporations.

Second, the politics and governance of global sport tend to emerge from the partnerships, interconnections and interrelations of organizations across these different categories. The most influential partnerships involve the first three categories – that is, elite sport clubs and athletes, wealthy sport consumers, corporations, and national and international sport and governmental organizations. These partnerships have tended to promote neoliberal or pro-market policies, which have advanced the 'hypercommodification' of sport, as discussed in earlier chapters.

Third, correlatively, some political actors within global sport have been relatively marginalized. These actors have tended to be located in the fourth category, which centres on 'global civil society'; but they also include weak groups within the other three categories, such as small sport clubs, nations, sport associations and communities. In many ways, these forms of political marginalization and domination have been openly contested, for example in regard to movements against racism, sexism and homophobia in sport. But this overall framework of global sport politics is reflected and sustained through the global economy of sport, to which I now turn.

The global economy and global sport

In order to understand the contemporary global economy, we need to consider the long-term impacts of Western imperialism and colonialism. From at least the sixteenth century, Western European nations systematically colonized other continents – the Americas,

Africa, Australasia and large parts of Asia; the indigenous populations were subjugated and, in many cases, annihilated, while vast
natural resources were plundered. In turn, as discussed in chapter 5,
sport played a key role in the racial stratification of these colonized
societies.

In much of Africa and Asia, from the 1950s onwards, the colonized
populations gradually won their hard-fought battles for political independence. However, a form of *neo-colonialism* then took hold, as many
nations came under the hegemony of Western corporations, governments, and financial institutions such as the IMF and World Bank
(Bah 2014; Leys 1974). One critical Marxist perspective here would
contend that systematic *underdevelopment* occurred, as rich nations
were able to develop more rapidly at the expense of poorer nations;
for example, African and Latin American nations were pressed by
Western institutions to maintain low-wage, low-technology agricul-
tural economies (producing cash crops such as fruits, tea, coffee or
sugar) which best served Western interests (cf. Kiely 2007: 16–17).

Theories of neo-colonialism, dependency and underdevelopment
may be applied to sport to examine the position of 'developing' nations
within global sporting economies. World baseball, for instance, is
dominated by the North American professional league (MLB); in
scouting and recruiting players, many MLB clubs organize baseball
academies in Latin America, which are run like Western-owned sugar
plantations. Thus, these American-controlled academies gather the
best local resources (young baseball players), conduct basic 'refining'
of local products (such as through initial coaching and assessment),
send the very best products to North America for final refining and
consumption by American markets (MLB fans) and leave the inferior
residue (weaker players) to be consumed by local people (Klein 1989;
1994: 193–4). This neo-colonial system of production and consumption is also highly wasteful: just as American consumers discard much
hard-produced sugar, so many Latino baseball players are wasted
by disappearing into lower-level American leagues; underdevelopment of young players also occurs, as the academies focus on honing
baseball skills to suit the interests of MLB clubs instead of providing
a wider education for their young pupils (Marcano and Fidler 1999).
Similar theories of neo-colonialism may be used to explain the international division of labour in other sports, such as in how African
football players or track and field athletes are recruited and trained by
European clubs and North American colleges respectively.

The 'world system theory' pioneered by Immanuel Wallerstein
(1974, 2000, 2002) provides the most systematic critical analysis of

the political economic aspects of globalization. Wallerstein has argued that the world system features three main types of nation-state:

- *core*, rich, strongly governed, well-established and dominant nation-states such as the United States, Japan or those in Western Europe;
- *semi-peripheral* nation-states, which have undergone substantial financial expansion, with relatively modest government powers and limited technological development or commodity diversity; among contemporary semi-peripheral nations are the 'Asian tigers' (such as Singapore and South Korea), post-Communist European transition societies (such as Poland, Hungary) and the 'BRICS' (Brazil, Russia, India, China, South Africa);
- *peripheral* nation-states which have weak government, contested borders and structural dependencies on 'core' nations and corporations; examples include many African and Latin American countries.

World system theory's basic model may be applied to sport in two broad ways. First, the global sport system directs the best resources from poor to rich nations; for example, African or Latin American football players join 'core' and 'semi-peripheral' leagues in Western or Eastern Europe respectively (Dejonghe 2001). Many football clubs in peripheral and semi-peripheral nations depend on revenues received through player transfer fees to clubs in core nations. Second, world system theory helps to explain the global production chains for sport merchandise, wherein transnational corporations based in core nations establish manufacturing plants in low-wage semi-peripheral and peripheral nations.

Wallerstein (2002) latterly explored how the world capitalist system has become stuck in a prolonged economic crisis, which intensified from 2007 onwards. The crisis may lead to the collapse of the world capitalist system, with a '50/50' chance of a better system appearing in its place.[31] Arguably, the economic crisis affects sport in uneven ways: on the one hand, in semi-peripheral or peripheral contexts, elite sport events and clubs are liable to lose spectators, sponsorship, advertising, athletes, and thus revenues; on the other hand, at least in core nations, leading sport leagues appear to have largely evaded the crisis, notably as television revenues remain strong or have grown in top European football competitions and the major North American sports.

Leslie Sklair's neo-Marxist model of the 'global system' has a greater emphasis on class and ideology in shaping the world economy. For Sklair (1995: 61), the global system is dominated by the 'transnational capitalist class' (TCC), which is a kind of 'international managerial bourgeoisie' characterized by a global outlook and self-identification, diverse national origins, and high consumption levels, notably in luxury goods and services. The TCC is comprised largely of corporate decision-makers, 'globalizing state bureaucrats', 'capitalist-inspired politicians and professionals' and 'consumerist groups' (for example, in business and media). For Sklair, the TCC advances a 'culture-ideology of consumerism', promoting 'induced wants' and a 'buying mood' for consumer items; this 'consumerist worldview' now permeates most societies.

Sklair's model invites exploration of how the TCC controls sport, whether in developed and developing nations or at the transnational level. For example, the Indian cricket league, the IPL, is dominated by upper- and middle-class elites in its management and governance, ownership of participating teams, external financing (such as through business executives with satellite broadcasters or team sponsors), patronage (by local and national politicians) and target audiences (that is, India's growing middle classes). Extensive advertising of consumer products inside stadiums and on television serves to wrap the IPL in a 'culture-ideology of consumerism'.

Other critical perspectives on the global economy have centred on the worldwide spread of right-wing neoliberal economic and social policies since the late 1970s. Neoliberalism, as noted earlier, is associated with individualistic, market-based political actors and with deregulated forms of transnational capitalism, rapid rises in upper-class wealth, and growing levels of social inequality. These negative social impacts of neoliberalism have been particularly evident in developing nations, and in Latin America have resulted in the counter-rise of popular left-wing political movements and governments, which have sought to resist free-market policies and the deeper influence of Western corporations and governments.

Global neoliberalism is broadly associated with hypercommodification in elite global sport, such as 'free markets' in the sale of television rights for elite events and the movement of professional athletes, leading to greater financial and competitive inequalities in sport, as the richest clubs recruit the best athletes and dominate major competitions. Thus, in European football, clubs from the richest leagues (notably England, Spain, Italy and Germany) have monopolized the most prestigious competition, the Champions League, since the mid-1990s. Neoliberalism also drives the commercial transformation of sport institutions. For example, elite clubs such as Manchester United in England or Corinthians in Brazil have been sold to more commercially focused owners. At the same time, these elite clubs form collective groupings primarily to press for further neoliberal 'reforms' that will increase their commercial growth; illustrations in football are the former Clube dos 13 cartel of leading clubs in Brazil and the former G14 of leading European clubs (Dubal 2010). At the everyday level, neoliberal policies have also led to reductions in state financial support for sport, with particularly negative effects on the provision of sporting facilities and education in developing countries.

Transnational corporations (TNCs) are prominent advocates and beneficiaries of neoliberal policies. TNCs are large businesses with production plants, sales points, investments and advertising campaigns that operate across the world. Market deregulation enables TNCs to benefit from the free flows and movements of capital, labour, media and marketing images, and commodities beyond all national borders. In the world economy, leading TNCs include financial companies such as J. P. Morgan and HSBC; oil and gas companies such as Exxon, Shell and BP; retail companies such as WalMart; and technology companies such as Microsoft, Apple, Sony and Samsung.

In a neoliberal context, TNCs have become significant players in elite level sport in three main ways. First, in line with Sklair's points, major sport clubs, tournaments and events are wrapped in TNC advertising images and backed by corporate 'partnerships' and sponsorships. Second, many leading TNCs have drawn heavily on sport in order to construct their global businesses; the most prominent illustrations are media TNCs such as News Corporation (including Sky and Fox television networks), which rely heavily on exclusive broadcasting of elite sports, and also sport merchandise TNCs such as Nike and Adidas. Third, we might view the world's largest elite sport clubs or 'franchises' as TNCs in their own right. Thus, clubs such as Manchester United, the Dallas Cowboys, Barcelona, the Boston Red Sox and the Los Angeles Lakers resemble TNCs in their transnational recruitment of players, global supporter or consumer profiles, and overall 'branding' (Giulianotti and Robertson 2004, 2009). These 'TNC sports clubs' resemble many other TNCs in maintaining some aspects of their distinctive or popular identity, for instance in their 'home' settings (their host stadium and city) (cf. P. Smith 1997).

Finally, the neoliberalization of sport is neither a uniform nor an uncontested process. As I noted earlier, in the area of 'global civil society', there are various grassroots movements at local, national and international level which criticize or campaign against free-market influences in sport; for example, the NGO War on Want has waged campaigns against the social clearing of poor communities to build sport facilities and the exploitation of sport merchandise workers in developing nations. At the institutional level, national sport governing bodies take different approaches to how free-market policies are introduced or accommodated. In some European and Latin American football systems, clubs tend to be partially or fully governed as 'membership associations' rather than as privately owned businesses. In leading American sports leagues, almost all teams are privately owned, but some key rules – such as the player 'draft system' or the partial sharing of television revenues – are in place partly to counteract the free market and to assist competitive balance.[32]

To sum up this section on the political economy of global sport, I have argued that there are four main categories of political actor: individual or market-based, national or nation-centred, international, and groups and movements centred on 'humankind'. Market-based individuals, groups and institutions are evidenced particularly among transnational corporations and global elites, which play critical roles in shaping the global sport economy. Accordingly, neoliberalism remains the dominant set of political and economic policies in global sport. Nevertheless, neoliberal policies are contested, adapted and implemented in diverse ways. In the next section, I explore how these frameworks and relationships of power in global sport are played out in socio-cultural terms.

Socio-cultural aspects of global sport

To understand the socio-cultural aspects of global sport, we need to examine a crucial underlying debate on the problem of 'convergence–divergence' (or 'homogenization–heterogenization'). The debate is essentially premised on two opposing positions. On the one side, theories of convergence or homogenization contend that globalization involves most societies sharing the same cultural values, beliefs, forms, identities, tastes and experiences. On the other side, theories of divergence or heterogenization argue that globalization is marked by forms of cultural creativity, variation, differentiation and divergence across different societies. Here, I shall consider the two approaches in turn and then move towards adopting a combined perspective through the theory of 'glocalization'.

Cultural convergence approaches

In turning to examine cultural convergence or homogenization arguments, I begin by making two important preliminary remarks. First, social scientists who argue that cultural convergence is taking place tend to be strongly critical rather than supportive of this process; that is, they are critical of how some societies come to dominate the cultures of other societies. Second, and following from this, the main convergence theorists tend to identify forms of *cultural imperialism* as underlying the broad global movements towards cultural homogenization. The basic premise of the cultural imperialism thesis is that the economic and political power of particular societies (such as Wallerstein's 'core' nations) enables them to define, to shape and to dominate global culture.

Convergence theorists advance different keywords and types of argument to explain cultural imperialism. Here, I outline briefly five of these approaches. First, some scholars have viewed cultural imperialism as essentially a form of *Americanization*, wherein the political and economic power of the United States enables American 'culture industries' (such as in film, television, music, fashion and food) to dominate global culture (cf. Marling 2006). In sport, Americanization is evidenced by the transnational spread of American sport leagues and merchandise; the copying of American sport culture, such as cheerleaders, dancers and other crowd 'entertainment' at sports events; the global marketing of American sport celebrities such as Michael Jordan; and the rise of American-styled advertising and sponsorship within sport.

Second, the American sociologist George Ritzer (2004) has coined the keyword *grobalization* to capture how, in his view, cultural homogenization is driven by three 'grobal' forces: capitalism, as led by expansionist transnational corporations; Americanization, featuring US corporations and their culture products; and 'McDonaldization', involving the highly efficient production and sale of mass cultural products. In sport, grobalization is at play in how, for example, American sport-related institutions such as the NBA and Nike have worked assiduously since the 1980s to promote basketball and basketball-related products in different nations, through carefully planned and highly rationalized marketing campaigns. Arguably, however, Ritzer's theory of grobalization places too much emphasis on market-based cultural products and commodities and pays too little attention to cultural meanings, interpretations, identities and aesthetics.

Third, some scholars have argued that media corporations play a critical role in enabling dominant societies (primarily, Western nations) to influence and control the cultures of weaker societies (Schiller 1976; McPhail 1981; Hamelink 1995). Western media corporations generate vast volumes of media content, particularly in films and television programmes; most profits are then generated in the 'home' nations, enabling these companies to sell cheaply or even to 'dump' their media products in developing societies. In sport, these forms of media-based colonialism are illustrated in the critical relationships between leading Western sport leagues (such as the EPL, NFL and NBA) and Western media corporations (such as Sky and Fox). Most television revenues within these leagues are generated by national markets which in part enable television rights to be sold cheaply abroad. In turn, large audiences in developing nations watch these glamorous Western sport leagues on television; one important consequence is a marked decline in interest or involvement in local sport clubs.

Fourth, the French economist Serge Latouche (1996) has been a polemical proponent of the theory of *Westernization*. For Latouche, the West constitutes the dominant global political force, which uses the language and practices of 'development' and modernization in order to destroy other, non-Western, non-industrial societies and cultures. Arguably, Westernization has been evidenced in sport by the marginalization or destruction of non-Western movement and body cultures and by the global imposition and spread of Western sporting disciplines and techniques. Given his critical comments on development as a Western construct, if we followed Latouche's arguments, we would view 'sport development' programmes as further examples of Western cultural imperialism within non-Western societies.

Finally, there is the subtle theory of *Orientalism*, advanced by the late Edward Said (1995; see also 1994). Drawing substantially on Foucault's poststructuralist approach, Said argued that power and knowledge are intertwined; thus, since at least the 1800s, the powerful Occident (in other words, the Western world) has created a set of dominant discourses which portray the West as 'rational, developed, humane and superior' and the Orient as the opposite, as irrational, 'aberrant, undeveloped, inferior' (Said 1995: 300). These powerful Orientalist discourses determine how 'Orientals' define and understand themselves. Said also noted that popular culture in the East is dominated by the West, notably the United States, whose products are 'consumed unthinkingly', giving rise to a 'vast standardization of taste' (ibid.: 354). Though Said focused on the Middle East and

North Africa, these arguments may be extended to encompass other non-Western cultures in Asia, Latin America, the Caribbean and Africa.

Orientalist discourses are frequently evident in Western portrayals of non-Western athletes, sport teams and cultures – for example, in how Australian sport and media discourses presented Pakistani cricket and the wider society as endemically corrupt, evasive towards direct questions of fact, impossible to understand rationally, and stuck in the alien environment of 'dirt, dust and dysentery' (Jaireth 1995). In football, the West has tended to portray Brazilian players in Orientalist terms, as natural, flamboyant, expressive, rhythmic, carefree and even erotic in contrast to the presentation of European professionals as scientific, methodical, watchful, well-drilled and predictable. Moreover, as an aspect of these self-Orientalizing processes, many of these themes have been celebrated by Brazilians as central to their football and thus their national culture (Giulianotti and Robertson 2009).

Overall, these diverse theories of cultural convergence help to capture the 'top-down' ways in which powerful political-economic forces may shape the formation and experience of global sport at the everyday level. However, these approaches do have some critical weaknesses. First, these theories often exaggerate the extent to which cultural homogenization has occurred; rather, we continue to see a wide diversity of cultural forms, styles, meanings and techniques in sport, art, dance, literature, music and other cultural fields, as I shall argue later below.

Second, convergence theories tend to fall into the trap of 'economic determinism', in assuming that the cultural structure of any society is essentially dominated and determined by an economic 'base'. As a result, these theories present individuals and social groups in different societies as passive consumers of American or Western cultural products and discourses. Conversely, we need to recognize more fully the everyday critical engagement of social actors in diverse cultural forms and processes, particularly in 'peripheral' societies. For example, Orientalism fails to account for how non-Western societies seek to ignore, resist or move beyond their 'Orientalist' representations. Thus, Gulf, Arab and Asian states such as Qatar have sought to host major sports events in part to replace negative, Orientalist images of these nations and regions with more positive images associated with modernity (Amara 2005). Moreover, to highlight how peripheral societies empower themselves in sport, we might point to numerous cases of cultural reversal, when athletes and teams from peripheral societies develop their own techniques and styles of play in order to defeat opponents from core societies. Examples here are Kenyan runners, West Indian cricketers and Latin American footballers.

Third, each convergence theory has specific weaknesses. The Americanization thesis, for instance, may exaggerate the global cultural power of the United States: outside of the United States, sports fans prefer to watch non-American sports, teams and events and to celebrate non-American sport icons, particularly in football.

These critical observations on cultural convergence and cultural imperialism lead us to consider the alternative approach, centring on cultural divergence.

Cultural divergence approaches

There are a variety of theories of heterogenization, divergence and differentiation which centre on specific keywords that have been deployed by various social scientists.

First, theories of *indigenization* help to explain the emergence and increasing importance of indigenous rights and identities in recent years. For example, there is greater recognition of the distinctive national and cultural identities of native or First Nation peoples in Australasia and North America, although, particularly in the case of Australia, we find that many Aboriginal peoples continue to live in Apartheid-like conditions (Friedman 1999). Second, the concepts of hybridity and *hybridization* register the diverse and vibrant ways in which cultural blending or mixing occurs across different societies – in dance, music and sport (Burke 2009; Nederveen Pieterse 1995, 2007). Cultural hybridization is evidenced particularly in post-colonial societies where diverse forms of migration and cultural interchange have taken place. Third, the theory of *creolization* helps us to examine how peoples in peripheral societies engage critically and selectively with the cultural phenomena of other societies, including 'core' nations in the Global North, in order to produce creolized cultural forms and practices (Hannerz 1992). Fourth, the concept of *vernacularization* helps to explain how, through language, aspects of global culture may be adapted and reinterpreted by local populations (Appadurai 1995).

Sport may be used to illustrate these various theories and keywords on cultural heterogenization. On indigenization, indigenous peoples in North America and Australia have used sport to project and to advance their specific national identities. For example, First

Nations peoples have put on their own sporting events, such as the Inuit Games, featuring sport disciplines derived from traditional forms of physical culture or labour. Some First Nations populations have also staged prominent protests at major sporting events – such as Australian Aboriginals at the Sydney 2000 Olympics – in order to challenge their denial of key civil and human rights (Lenskyj 2002; Rowe 2012). Moreover, in Europe, 'folk games' and 'traditional sports' – such as the Scottish Highland Games, the Basque *pelota* and the Breton Games – are often staged or discussed in ways that have strong indigenist overtones; references are made to the pre-modern histories of these sporting events and to the celebration of particular regional or national identities, as also expressed through distinctive music, dance, cuisine, songs, flags and general pageantry (cf. Eichberg 1994; Jarvie 1991; Abrisketa 2012).

The concept of hybridization was employed by Archetti (1998) to explain the cultural history and identity of Argentinian football. Archetti argued that, through the early twentieth century, Argentina was an emerging nation with a mix of old and new European migrants; football represented a highly popular cultural arena in which these diverse influences might be 'hybridized'. The result was a distinctive Argentinian style of play that reflected an emerging form of male national identity within a hybrid, increasingly urban society.

Processes of creolization may be identified in how peripheral societies have adapted different sport cultures to beat athletes and teams from 'core' societies. In cricket, different national teams from India, Pakistan and Sri Lanka have scored notable successes over England and Australia, while developing distinctive skills and techniques. India also 'vernacularizes' cricket – for example in television and radio commentaries on the game which blend English and Hindi words and phrases (Appadurai 1995).

Thus, overall, heterogenization theories such as indigenization and creolization help to capture the 'bottom-up' aspects of globalization in sport – that is, the dynamic and processual ways in which different meanings, identities, techniques and values within sport are created and re-created at the everyday level by social actors. In social science, the heterogenization approach is broadly associated with interpretive standpoints and the use of qualitative research methods, which focus heavily on the meanings, motives and identities of social actors. In sociology, heterogenization approaches have close links to anthropological standpoints which highlight the cultural creativity and distinctiveness of non-industrial and developing societies. Heterogenization theories also help to reveal the deep interconnections between 'the local' and 'the global', for example as global sports provide ideal cultural environments for different forms of 'local' identity to be explored and expressed before worldwide audiences.

I turn now to consider how the most persuasive aspects of homogenization and heterogenization theory may be combined, through the overarching theory of glocalization.

Glocalization

The theory of *glocalization* may be introduced to register the dual possibilities of homogenization *and* heterogenization within global sport and to capture the most persuasive features of convergence and divergence theories respectively. The term 'glocalization' is derived from the Japanese word *dochakuka*, which refers to the distinctive micro-marketing methods used by East Asian corporations in diverse international contexts (Robertson 1992: 173–4; Giulianotti and Robertson 2012b). Robertson (1990, 1992, 1995) introduced the term glocalization to examine the social and cultural dynamics of globalization, and since then it has been widely applied and discussed across social science, including in relation to sport (cf. Andrews and Ritzer 2007; Giulianotti and Robertson 2004, 2005, 2007a, 2007b, 2007c, 2007d, 2009, 2012b). In many debates, the term glocalization is often used to refer specifically to processes of cultural divergence; understandably, this usage helps to challenge oversimplistic claims on cultural convergence. However, as the word itself suggests, glocalization actually refers to the *interdependence* and interpenetration of the local and the global (Robertson 1992: 173–4; 1995, 2001). As a consequence, glocalization theory registers what we have termed the *duality of glocality* – that is, the processes of convergence *and* divergence within global sport and more generally in global culture (Giulianotti and Robertson 2007b, 2012b).

How is the duality of glocality evidenced in sport? I would argue that, in broad terms, processes of convergence or homogenization are more apparent in regard to specific sporting *forms*, which are associated particularly with 'top-down' global developments. Conversely, processes of divergence or heterogenization are more obvious in relation to sporting *contents*, notably in the bottom-up making of sport at everyday level.

For example, many sports – such as football, cricket, rugby union, baseball, basketball – were spread worldwide through the late nineteenth and twentieth centuries. In most locations, the key *form* of the sport has remained largely intact – that is, the rules and regulations of the sport, and how it is institutionalized and organized (such as through national associations that feature specific office-holders), have stayed in place. There are, of course, some significant exceptions to this 'homogenization of sport forms' – for example, in the Trobriand Islands, where the indigenous people transformed the game of cricket into a distinctive local male ritual with a very different set of rules and customs (Leach and Kildea 1976), and in the United States in the nineteenth century, when the English games of rounders and rugby were transformed to create the distinctive sports of baseball and American football. But, overall, when most sports are spread internationally and taken on by new societies, the broad forms of those sporting disciplines tend to remain in place in different contexts.

Alternatively, processes of divergence and heterogenization are evidenced more in sport *content* – that is, the meanings, techniques, aesthetic codes, identities, norms and values within sport tend to be creatively interpreted, adapted and transformed by different societies. In football, Latin American societies tend to place relatively high value on individual artistry in comparison with football cultures in Northern Europe. More generally, at sport mega-events, we are able to see how teams and their supporters identify and differentiate themselves from each other in strong symbolic ways, such as through distinctive anthems, songs, flags, team colours and techniques of play.

In broader terms, the duality of glocality is evidenced in the marketing of sport clubs and in the staging of sport mega-events. Leading sports clubs may deploy similar marketing structures and formats, such as tours, media appearances, billboard advertising and established public relations companies, to reach different audiences, yet sport clubs will substantially vary the content of these marketing strategies, such as in their choice of images, narratives and themes. For sport mega-events, host cities or nations are required to provide the same core structures, facilities and formats, for example in terms of specific event venues, types of athlete accommodation, and even event mascots and logos; diversity is evidenced in the event content, such as in stadium architecture, design of the athlete village, cultural and geographical backdrop, and the types of event narratives and symbols that give colour to the particular event.

We might also point to processes of *reverse glocalization* in sport. Reverse glocalization is based on the apparent reversal of earlier flows of cultural exchange – that is, where the cultural practices or techniques of a secondary, peripheral or 'receiving' society flow back to influence the 'core' or 'original' society. Cricket, for instance, originated in England and then underwent substantial popularization and glocalization in South Asia and elsewhere. In turn, reverse glocalization has occurred, as some Asian practices and techniques have come to influence English cricket – in the use of new techniques by slow bowlers or the highly aggressive methods of opening batsmen for shortened formats of the game. Reverse glocalization is also evidenced in some aspects of sport athlete migration, such as in how the nations which established specific sports come to recruit foreign professionals to improve their play: in the United States, the home of baseball, we find MLB teams hiring many Latin and East Asian baseball players while, in Canada, the home of ice-hockey, Scandinavian and East European players are hired by NHL teams (Giulianotti and Robertson 2012b).

Overall, glocalization is a highly adaptable keyword that enables us to explore and explain how processes of homogenization and heterogenization are manifested in the globalization of sport. We should also underline that glocalization theory enables us to examine and to explain political-economic as well as socio-cultural processes in the globalization of sport. Thus, we may certainly recognize significant aspects of convergence in how the global sport economy is strongly shaped by neoliberal policies and interests, to the clear benefit of 'core' sport teams, leagues and nations. Divergence is evidenced in how different political and economic models are selectively introduced, adapted or rejected by diverse sport individuals, groups and organizations – for example, elite sport clubs may be owned as private property by individuals or companies, as mutual associations by supporters, or in ways that combine the two models.

Sport for development and peace

In the final section of this chapter, I turn now to discuss the 'Sport for Development and Peace' (SDP) sector.[33] Since the late 1990s, the SDP sector has been one of the fastest growing aspects of the globalization of sport. By way of definition, I understand the SDP sector as featuring a wide diversity of programmes, campaigns and organizations which use sport as a site or tool of intervention in order to promote different kinds of social development and peace-making across the world. Hence, it represents a critical shift in emphasis, from 'the development *of* sport' to 'social development *through* sport'. To recall our opening definition of globalization, the emergence of the SDP sector also reflects a growing consciousness of the world as a shared single place.

The main types of organization within the SDP sector are:

- intergovernmental organizations, such as the United Nations (which has its own SDP office, the UNOSDP), European Commission and Commonwealth Secretariat;
- national governments and their ministries of education, international development and sport; also government-financed sport and development agencies, such as UK Sport, Canadian Heritage and Norad (Norway's development agency);
- sport governing bodies which support development work, such as the IOC and the world volleyball governing body (FIVB);
- private corporations and individual donors who support SDP work – e.g., Nike, Coca-Cola, McDonalds;
- NGOs which coordinate or implement SDP programmes at international, national and local levels; examples here are street-footballworld in Germany, the Sport for Development platform in Switzerland and Nowspar in Zambia;
- campaigning NGOs and social movements which focus on SDP-related issues – e.g., Play the Game, War on Want.

The United Nations have played a crucial role in building the SDP sector, notably through advocating and seeking to legitimize the use of sport to promote development and, more formally, by establishing its own office for SDP (the UNOSDP).

Most international SDP work is conducted in developing countries by NGOs, which implement projects with the aim of meeting critical social needs, such as building peace in divided societies; educating young people on health issues such as HIV/AIDS; facilitating the wider education of young people; and promoting the basic social rights and empowerment of girls and women. The SDP sector also includes significant activity in the Global North, for example in aiming to reduce crime and gang violence in inner-city areas, to draw young people into education, employment and training, and to assist the homeless.

The most influential stakeholders within the SDP sector are national and international governmental organizations, private donors and sport governing bodies. These stakeholders have the greatest financial, political and organizational resources and are thus able to set the aims and objectives for SDP projects. In a markedly weaker position are NGOs, which tend to rely on financial and other support from these other stakeholders in order to implement projects (and thus, in effect, to continue to function). Some commentators have argued that, as a result, most SDP activity tends to have a 'neoliberal' or pragmatic focus, for instance in terms of seeking to develop young people into being compliant, competitive and self-reliant individuals, or in attempting to meet immediate needs (such as in combatting HIV/AIDS) rather than pursuing work that will lead to long-term structural change (cf. Darnell 2012).

Conversely, more 'critical' approaches to SDP tend to be advocated instead by campaigning NGOs and social movements and by some academic researchers. As I indicated earlier in this chapter, these critical stakeholders are most 'at home' in focusing on civil and human rights within the broad field of 'global civil society'. Their general concern is with challenging the underlying structural causes of underdevelopment, conflict and oppression. Accordingly, these approaches criticize the roles of Global North institutions – including sport governing bodies, sport-related corporations, and national and international organizations – in actually creating and maintaining these structural problems and injustices. Illustrations of these critical approaches are campaigns by social movements against the exploitation of workers in sport merchandise plants in developing nations; by human rights groups over freedom of speech in China around the Beijing 2008 Olympics; or by various critical NGOs, international trade unions and journalists against the abuse of migrant workers employed in Qatar for the 2022 World Cup finals (some official reports have estimated that up to 4,000 workers would die in Qatar in the build-up to the event; *Business Insider*, 18 March 2014). The Qatar case highlights how these campaigns may impact more widely on sport and society: the future World Cup hosts were quickly placed in the global spotlight and needed to be seen to be responding to international criticism.

Overall, these critical forces in the SDP sector are in a relatively weak position; thus they are usually on the margins of the main meetings, networks and partnerships that otherwise involve different SDP stakeholders. One challenge for the sector lies in engaging more effectively with these critical stakeholders, in part to enable new fields of SDP activity to be pursued.

Concluding comments

The interface between globalization and sport has been one of the most important issues in the sociology of sport since the early 1990s. In political-economic terms, the globalization of sport has been marked by the growing number and diversity of stakeholders; the continuing significance, and partial transformation, of national identity and the nation-state; and the development of a substantially stratified, neoliberal global economy. In socio-cultural terms, global sport has featured a mix of convergence and divergence, notably in the imposition or sharing of cultural forms and in the creative differentiation of sport content (such as aesthetics, identities, styles and techniques). The concept of glocalization helps to register and to explain these dual processes. The SDP sector, which has expanded very quickly in recent years, is part of a growing global civil society, and, while pragmatic or neoliberal SDP activity seems to be most prevalent, there is significant scope for the pursuit of more critical SDP work which aims at deeper structural changes.

Arguably, global sport should be focused on securing the critical agency and participation of social actors in different cultural settings. The powerful role of neoliberalism in the making of global sport tends to undermine those objectives. At the same time, globalization processes facilitate greater levels of connectivity with different cultures and thus enable in turn greater public experience and understanding of how sport has been organized and interpreted in alternative ways in diverse contexts. Accordingly, three key reforms in global sport might be suggested.

First, explicit constraints on the role of the free market in global sport should be introduced. Such measures would, for example, seek to ensure that sport clubs are at least partly owned by their local communities; that sport clubs and systems in developing nations are accorded some protection; that the market-based exploitation of athletes from peripheral and semi-peripheral countries is directly challenged; and that competitive inequalities between clubs and nations in elite sport are markedly reduced. In implementing such reforms at the transnational level, there is much to be learnt from different national sport systems which have their own measures to protect against some of the pathologies of the free market.

Second, the political structure of global sport systems needs to be significantly reformed. The contribution of national and international governing bodies in shaping the politics of sport requires to be reasserted. However, such interventions may only be achieved and legitimized if these governing bodies are fully democratic, inclusive, transparent and accountable in all of their political, financial and other activities. In this sense, governing bodies need to be entirely open to public scrutiny, including by investigative journalists.

Third, I outlined at the outset of this chapter a fourth category of political stakeholders which features radical NGOs, campaign groups, social movements, investigative journalists and critical academics. The progressive politics of this category centre on advancing civil and human rights, social democracy and social justice. This category is largely on the political margins of global sport politics. The reform of different areas of global sport should engage fully with these progressive forces. The SDP sector is a case in point: by working alongside campaign groups, for example, SDP activity might be directed more effectively towards long-term social and structural changes in developing societies, say, in improving industrial conditions or gaining greater gender equality. Through such reforms, global sport may become far more politically democratic, economically balanced, socially inclusive and culturally compelling.

Questions for discussion

1 What are the main types of actor in the politics of world sport?
2 How is the world sport economy organized to benefit 'core' sport nations or leading sport clubs?
3 How might it be argued that sports in different societies are becoming increasingly similar or are retaining important differences?
4 How is sport used to promote development and peace in different social contexts?
5 How might global sport be reorganized in order to become more democratic, inclusive, balanced and socially just?

Epilogue:
Towards a Critical Sociology
of Sport

I conclude by drawing upon my various arguments to outline how a critical sociological perspective should approach the study of sport. To recap, I argued at the start of this book that a critical sociology should correct errors and misunderstandings; highlight power inequalities, divisions and interests that lie behind existing social arrangements and relations; and explore alternative forms of social organization and experience that are premised on the principles of democracy, social inclusion and social justice. These concluding observations and recommendations are intended to elaborate such a critical standpoint.

My opening comments are on the theoretical approach to be favoured by a critical sociology of sport. I have endeavoured here to highlight the benefits of a sociological perspective which strikes an appropriate theoretical balance between structure and agency. Such a position recognizes fully the structural conditions and contexts of social actors, notably in regard to power inequalities, social divisions, divergent life chances and distribution of resources, and also engages with the critical reflexivity of social actors and the open-endedness of social actions. In the main, this position is rooted in a critical analysis of the complex and conflicting interplays between top-down, primarily political-economic frameworks of power and domination and bottom-up, socio-cultural forms of creative practice and empowerment at the everyday level.

This position is not mono-theoretical but, instead, engages critically and selectively with a wide range of theories and perspectives discussed in this book. Indeed, as I have argued at several points here, the selective development and combination of theories to produce 'neo'-theoretical positions is particularly beneficial. The

most substantial critical theoretical influences throughout this text
have emanated from early Cultural Studies approaches on resistance,
transgression and the carnivalesque and Foucauldian positions on
discipline and governmentality. This broad critical mixture is further
registered in critical theories of 'race' and gender; the analysis of the
body and sporting spaces that is provided by scholars such as Archetti,
Bale, Eichberg and Wacquant; my critical extension of Bourdieu's
work, which widens the meaning of 'capital' and our appreciation of
the cultural creativity of social actors; and, in globalization, through
theories such as glocalization that recognize the interplay of sameness
and difference in global culture. My approach has also been to recognize the insights of, variously, functionalist theories, on sport's role
in building powerful social solidarities and *communitas*; Weberian
theories, to explore how sport facilitates the construction of social
identities while also being subjected to powerful forces of rationalization; and postmodern social theories, to examine how sport connects
both to contemporary consumer and media cultures and to major
changes within the class structures of late capitalist societies. Finally,
a critical sociological theory must also be a normative theory: in that
regard, my commitment has been to sustain and to advance the scope
of social actors to engage creatively, critically and democratically with
sport, while evading, resisting and reducing forms of domination,
such as in the 'hypercommodification' or the oppressive 'regulation'
of sport. This normative position emerges from my critical reading
of several social theorists, notably Bourdieu, Foucault, Gramsci and
Habermas.

The critical sociological study of sport benefits greatly from the
use of strongly comparative approaches across time (historically)
and space (cross-culturally). Historical approaches enable us to
understand the emergence and development of sport with reference
to political-economic and socio-cultural factors. As I have indicated
in earlier chapters, particularly useful in this regard are the broad
insights of Gramsci (on the making and remaking of hegemony),
Williams (through his 'dominant-emergent-residual' model), Marx
(as in his studies of Bonapartism) and Foucault (on the making of
disciplinary institutions and governing of populations).

Cross-cultural studies enable us to understand how sport is
adapted, experienced, interpreted and structured by different social
formations. They also provide the basis for explorations of some
alternative possibilities for the organization and understanding of
sport in our own societies. For example, we might look at the different ways in which supporter groups or local communities par-

ticipate in sport clubs or are engaged in sport leagues or explore the particular cultural aesthetics and bodily techniques that are evident in how some societies practise particular sports. Such historical and cross-cultural approaches strengthen crucial areas of inquiry within sport studies, notably in regard to the critical investigation of 'race' and ethnicity (such as through sport's relationship to colonialism and post-colonialism) and, more broadly, in relation to globalization and sport.

Turning to research methods, the sociology of sport is most effective when blending empirical research (particularly fieldwork) with theoretical analysis. Fieldwork revitalizes the Cultural Studies mission to connect interpretivist insights into the complexity of social roles, identities, meanings and practices, with critical readings of the structural conditions and contexts in which individuals and social groups are living. Theories of globalization are increasingly valuable here in enabling these research groups to be located within their full global context. Fieldwork should be a dialogical process wherein research objectives, hypotheses and tentative conclusions are constantly reformulated through ongoing research and communication with relevant social groups. With Bourdieu and others, I agree that researchers should engage in self-critical reflexivity to negate research biases and should seek to produce critical (or 'para-doxal') studies that challenge dominant assumptions, discourses and ideologies which are rooted in the structural inequalities of gender, ethnicity, class and age.

If we turn to the relationship of the sociology of sport to the wider academic field, an important aim should be to enhance our subdiscipline by sharpening our theories, methods and substantive focus, particularly with reference to issues of originality, diversity, impact, overall quality and (far from the least important) intellectual stimulation. On that broad platform, we might begin to advocate the sociology of sport's much fuller engagement with mainstream sociology and other social sciences, as well as cross-disciplinary research with colleagues in the natural sciences. Working with, and within, mainstream sociology must serve to register the broader social significance of sport and to challenge any tendencies for the sociology of sport to slide into a more marginal academic position or self-referential culture of debate.

As this book has highlighted, extensive and highly fruitful collaborative work has been undertaken by sociologists of sport with colleagues in other established social sciences, particularly in anthropology, economics, geography, history, law, philosophy, political science and social policy. The meta-discipline of Cultural Studies – which encompasses *inter alia* both ethnic and racial studies and gender studies – has provided one important domain for such cross-disciplinary activity. While research fields become more problem- or theme-focused, there is much greater scope for such collaborative work to be conducted, investigating, for example, sport for development and peace initiatives, the impacts of hosting sport mega-events, or the ethical reform of sport governance. Given that many sociologists of sport share departments, schools, faculties and colleges with colleagues in the natural sciences, we might say that collaborative research activities have been unduly limited and, instead, tend to reinscribe the division of the 'two cultures' between the humanities and the sciences that was long ago criticized by C. P. Snow (1959). Conversely, we might point to several broad research themes – such as on the body, health and injury, sport buildings and infrastructure, or sport technology – where there is a compelling case for the normalizing of such collaborative work within sport. Overall, the critical sociology of sport is greatly strengthened by this openness to working with scholars beyond our subdiscipline. Such activity would also underwrite the normative position of the critical sociology of sport, in terms of a commitment to positive dialogue with those who might otherwise appear as 'different' or as 'others' to ourselves.

If this is what the critical sociology of sport might look like, what issues and problems might it address in order to reform and transform global sport? Here, I would suggest four illustrative fields of research activity which indicate how sport at local, national and global levels might become more democratic, participatory and socially just.

First, we might redouble our focus on the political economy of elite sport in order to examine how we might challenge and remove the negative social influences and impacts of the free market and processes of hypercommodification. Thus, public issues in sport ripe for examination include the more extreme cases of finance-based competitive advantage in team sports; the alternative ways in which sport clubs and associations are or may be owned and controlled, particularly by local communities and fan groups; the routes through which different social groups are 'priced out' of sport, and what measures might be implemented to reform the distribution of access; the exploitation (including the trafficking) of athletes, particularly people who are young and/or from developing countries; and how these and other areas of hypercommodification in sport impact negatively upon the experiences of different social groups, particularly those historically marginalized with reference to 'race', gender and class.

Second, we might investigate the politics of sport with a particular focus on the fundamental reform of governing bodies, to become democratic, transparent in their policies and financial activities, accountable for their actions, and open to public question and scrutiny. We might thus examine how the governance of sport may embrace a full array of stakeholders, including grassroots sport organizations and movements, amateur athletes and officials, and spectator groups, as well as those groups that are historically marginalized along the lines of 'race', gender and class. We might also explore how the ethical overhaul of sport's governing bodies may provide an illustrative case study for the effective reform of other, much larger frameworks of transnational governance.

Third, alongside this political-economic inquiry, we need to redouble our focus on the everyday phenomenological experience and socio-cultural making of sport by diverse individuals and social groups. Such research, particularly through the application of qualitative methods, enables social scientists to develop a deeper, richer understanding of the aesthetics, communications, conflicts, identities, meanings, roles and rituals of sport. All of these aspects of everyday sport should be viewed as fluid and processual and as situated within the global context, particularly as they are marked at least in part by transnational social relations. Research with these social groups is valuable in and of itself, not least for revealing the complex interdependencies of local and global processes in sport – for example in the making of sport fan identities. Additionally, these areas of research also enable social scientists to acquire deeper understandings of how sport may be most advantageously and specifically reformed in order to empower social actors particularly in more marginalized social positions.

Fourth, one burgeoning area of research in recent years has been in the field of 'sport for development and peace' (SDP), and as this sector continues to expand we might reasonably anticipate that its sociological study will similarly grow. The focus of these studies should be extended more fully, into how SDP initiatives are implemented and experienced at the everyday level; on how user groups may be empowered to improve their quality of life in relevant communities; and on challenging the wider social structures and power arrangements that serve to marginalize and to oppress diverse individuals and social groups. More broadly, this field of inquiry should be realistic in recognizing that sports cannot 'act alone' and so must depend upon a much wider array of fundamental societal reforms, particularly in the political and economic spheres, in order for meaningful, structural changes to occur in the most difficult social contexts.

These four areas of research are, of course, far from constituting an exhaustive list; many other subjects demand sociological investigation. But they do, in my view, point to the key types of social issue that a critical sociology needs to address in order for sport at local, national and global levels to become more democratic, participatory and socially just.

Notes

1 An early analysis developed the work of Durkheim to explain how American baseball enhanced social solidarity (Cohen 1946: 334–6). This kind of study reflects the breadth of interpretation that is possible in examining the social functions of religion (Robertson 1970: 17–18).

2 Luhmann was also significantly influenced by the German phenomenologist Edmund Husserl, notably through the latter's concept of 'intentionality'. For a study of how this influence in Luhmann's work may be applied to sport (in this case, photographs of sport stadiums), see Tangen (2014).

3 Of course, this discussion is necessarily selective. I do not have space to elaborate Weber's other arguments relating to the scientific procedures of sociology.

4 In addition, many nations direct their sport policies towards providing funds (such as for coaches, athletes, facilities) for those sports which are 'efficient' in producing medal returns; according to this rationalized model, sports which do not provide measurable returns on these investments usually have their funding reduced (cf. De Bosscher et al. 2008).

5 See *The Sport Market: Major Trends and Challenges in an Industry Full of Passion* (A. T. Kearney, 2011), www.atkearney.co.uk/documents/10192/6f46b880-f8d1-4909-9960-cc605bb1ff34.

6 As Marx ([1845] 1965: 35) put it, 'The class which has the means of material production at its disposal, has control at the same time over the means of mental production, so that in consequence the ideas of those who lack the means of mental production are, in general, subject to it.' It should be added that Marx's conception of ideology went through several stages.

7 Marcuse (1964: 5) added that 'Most of the prevailing needs to relax, to have fun, to behave and consume in accordance with the advertisements, to love and hate what others love and hate, belong to this category of false needs.'

8 The Frankfurt School's broad contempt for mass culture has had notable political and cultural allies. In the UK, Keir Hardie, a founding father

of the Labour Party, described sport as 'degrading' and football as an 'abomination' (Smith and Williams 1980: 121). In the early post-war era, popular working-class pastimes such as wrestling or greyhound racing were excluded from coverage by the state-controlled BBC, as they did not fit its bourgeois ethics and sense of cultural 'responsibility' towards its preferred audience. The post-war Labour government, with its own version of 'puritan socialism', adopted a similarly discriminatory stance towards greyhound racing, which in turn prompted a significant public backlash (Baker 1996).

9 Rowe (1995: 20) aptly described Adorno and colleagues as 'Left Leavisites'.

10 Adorno (2001: 163) was critical of how modern mass culture is fixed to 'the almost unchanged ideology of early middle-class society' and so is out of date with the ideas of consumers. He illustrated this comment with reference to the anachronistic Puritanism of mass culture in post-war England.

11 McCree (2000) employed Williams's historical model to examine struggles over football's professionalization in the Caribbean.

12 My thanks to the Norwegian sociologist Tommy Langseth for drawing my attention to this issue in snowboarding and surfing subcultures.

13 There are ambiguities. In one passage, Gramsci (1971: 208) argued that the state (as the 'political society') and civil society are in balance; elsewhere, he suggests the two are 'one and the same'.

14 See, for example, the paintings and sketches by Bruegel, Hogarth and Beckmann that deal with scenes of carnival and excessive folk culture. On carnival generally, see Bakhtin (1968).

15 See the University of Central Florida's MS in Sport Business and Management at http://web.bus.ucf.edu/sportbusiness/?page=1445.

16 The militarist regime in pre-1945 Japan founded women's sports organizations and promoted female participation at national and international tournaments. One brilliant athlete, Hitomi Kinue, produced world-class performances in the 100 and 400 metres and the long jump, although not in Olympic competition (Guttmann and Thompson 2001: 120–1).

17 African-American boxers tie the slave metaphor partly to their ancestors' racialized subjugation; indeed, some slaves fought brutal, often lethal contests at their owners' behest.

18 Elite gymnastic careers are concentrated into childhood and adolescence, lasting generally from around twelve to eighteen years of age. Most girls abandon gymnastics after entering adulthood, not by choice but because their bodies 'expire' through unchecked regimens of work (Ryan 1996: 31).

19 See, for example, Bale (1982, 1989, 1992, 1994; Vertinsky and Bale 2004).

20 The disaster occurred through crowd crushing inside one ground 'pen'; fearing a violent invasion of supporters, police initially had refused to allow fans to escape onto the field of play.

21 See, for example, Giulianotti and Klauser (2011) and the special issue of *Urban Studies*, 48(15) (2011).

22 For a critical review of figurational sociology which draws on diverse criticisms by many social scientists, see Giulianotti (2004a).

23 Informalization refers to apparent relaxations of standards of self-control and bodily discipline which occur among social groups that have experienced the formalization of the civilizing process; the concept also registers aspects of convergence between working-class and middle-class codes of conduct (Wouters 1977: 449). In the context of football hooliganism, the concept may help to explain how 'respectable' social groups may slip into relatively instrumental violence with rivals while continuing to engage with 'established' groups in other social fields, such as in employment and family life.

24 'Genetic structuralism' received earlier development – for example by the French sociologist Lucien Goldmann (Williams 1981: 144).

25 As he argued elsewhere, 'the sociology of sociology is a fundamental dimension of sociological epistemology' (Bourdieu and Wacquant 1992: 68).

26 Witness those occasions when elite athletes seek to show their versatility in other sports, only to find their lack of technical skills being criticized by media experts while established professionals seek to 'teach the rookies a lesson' in the new game.

27 See, for example, the report *Olympism and the Olympic Movement*, www.olympic.org/Documents/Reports/EN/en_report_670.pdf.

28 Obviously Bourdieu was not the first social analyst to explore how social classes distinguish themselves through cultural preference. See, for example, Veblen ([1899] 1970) on class dynamics, materialism and conspicuous consumption in the United States.

29 By way of comparison, see *Otobiographies*, in which Derrida (1984) develops a deconstructionist analysis of the American constitution.

30 See Giulianotti and Robertson (2012a) for an application of this model to football.

31 See Immanuel Wallerstein, 'Crisis of the capitalist system: where do we go from here?', Harold Wolpe lecture, University of KwaZulu-Natal, 5 November 2009, http://mrzine.monthlyreview.org/2009/wallerstein121109.html.

32 Under the 'draft system', clubs with the weakest performance records are given first choice of young players emerging from college sports. Television revenue-sharing involves the sport league distributing money from television deals across all competing teams; the alternative model, allowing individual teams to negotiate entirely their own deals, would lead to far greater financial inequalities between the largest and smallest teams.

33 On the SDP sector in general, see Coalter (2013), Darnell (2012), Giulianotti (2011b) and Schulenkorf and Adair (2014).

References

Abrisketa, O. G. (2012) *Basque Pelota*, Reno: Center for Basque Studies.

Adler, P. A., and P. Adler (1991) *Backboards and Blackboards*, New York: Columbia University Press.

Adorno, T. W. (1982) *Prisms*, Cambridge, MA: Harvard University Press.

Adorno, T. W. (2001) *The Culture Industry*, London: Routledge.

Adorno, T. W., and M. Horkheimer ([1944] 1979) *Dialectic of Enlightenment*, London: Verso.

Agger, B. (2000) *Public Sociology*, Boston: Rowman & Littlefield.

Alegi, P. (2010) *African Soccerscapes*, London: Hurst.

Alexander, J. C. (1992) 'Citizen and enemy as symbolic classification', in M. Fournier and M. Lamont (eds), *Where Culture Talks: Exclusion and the Making of Society*, Chicago: University of Chicago Press.

Alomes, S. (1994) 'Tales of a dreamtime', in I. Craven (ed.), *Australian Popular Culture*, Melbourne: Cambridge University Press.

Alt, J. (1983) 'Sport and cultural reification', *Theory, Culture & Society*, 1(3): 93–107.

Althusser, L. (1971) *Lenin and Philosophy and Other Essays*, London: New Left Books.

Amara, M. (2005) '2006 Qatar Asian Games: a 'modernization' project from above?', *Sport in Society*, 8(3): 493–514.

Amin, A. (1994) *Post-Fordism: A Reader*, Oxford: Wiley.

Anderson, B. (1983) *Imagined Communities*, London: Verso.

Anderson, E. (2005) *In the Game: Gay Athletes and the Cult of Masculinity*, New York: SUNY Press.

Anderson, E. (2011) 'Masculinities and sexualities in sport and physical cultures: three decades of evolving research', *Journal of Homosexuality*, 58(5): 565–78.

Andrews, D. L. (1997) 'The [Trans]National Basketball Association', in A. Cvetovitch and D. Kellner (eds), *Articulating the Global and the Local*, Boulder, CO: Westview Press.

Andrews, D. L. (2001) 'The fact(s) of Michael Jordan's blackness', in D. L. Andrews (ed.), *Michael Jordan, Inc.*, New York: SUNY Press.

Andrews, D. L. (2008) 'Kinesiology's inconvenient truth and the physical cultural studies imperative', *Quest* 60(1): 45–60.

Andrews, D. L., and B. Carrington (eds) (2013) *A Companion to Sport*, Oxford: Wiley.

Andrews, D. L., and M. Silk (eds) (2011) *Physical Cultural Studies*, Philadelphia: Temple University Press.

Andrews, D. L., and M. Silk (2015) 'Physical Cultural Studies', in R. Giulianotti (ed.), *Routledge Handbook of the Sociology of Sport*, London: Routledge.

Andrews, D. L., R. Pitter, D. Zwick and D. Ambrose (1997) 'Soccer's racial frontier', in G. Armstrong and R. Giulianotti (eds), *Entering the Field*, Oxford: Berg.

Appadurai, A. (1995) 'Playing with modernity: the decolonization of Indian cricket', in C.A. Breckenridge (ed.), *Consuming Modernity*, Minneapolis: University of Minnesota Press.

Apter, M. J. (1982) *The Experience of Motivation*, London: Academic Press.

Archetti, E. (1998) *Masculinities*, Oxford: Berg.

Archetti, E. (1999) 'The spectacle of heroic masculinity', in A. M. Klausen (ed.), *Olympic Games as Performance and Public Event*, Oxford: Berghahn.

Aristotle (1981) *The Politics*, Harmondsworth: Penguin.

Armstrong, G. (1998) *Football Hooligans: Knowing the Score*, Oxford: Berg.

Armstrong, G., and R. Giulianotti (1998) 'From another angle: police surveillance and football supporters', in C. Norris, G. Armstrong and J. Moran (eds), *Surveillance, CCTV & Social Control*, Aldershot: Gower/Ashgate.

Armstrong, G., and R. Giulianotti (eds) (2004) *Football in Africa*, Basingstoke: Palgrave.

Aronowitz, S. (1973) *False Promises*, New York: McGraw-Hill.

Atkinson, M. (2000) 'Brother can you spare a seat?', *Sociology of Sport Journal*, 17(2): 151–70.

Atkinson, M., and K. Young (2005) 'Reservoir dogs', *International Review for the Sociology of Sport*, 40(3): 335–56.

Atkinson, M., and K. Young (2008) *Deviance and Social Control in Sport*, Champaign, IL: Human Kinetics.

Back, L., T. Crabbe and J. Solomos (2001) *The Changing Face of Football*, Oxford: Berg.

Bah, C. A. M. (2014) *Neocolonialism in West Africa*, Bloomington: iUniverse.

Bain-Selbo, E. (2009) *Game Day and God*, Macon, GA: Mercer University Press.

Baker, N. (1996) 'Going to the dogs – hostility to greyhound racing in Britain: puritanism, socialism and pragmatism', *Journal of Sport History*, 23: 97–119.

Baker, W. J. (1992) 'Muscular Marxism and the Chicago Counter-Olympics of 1932', *International Journal of the History of Sport*, 9: 397–410.

Bakhtin, M. (1968) *Rabelais and his World*, Cambridge, MA: MIT Press.

Bale, J. (1982) *Sport and Place*, London: Hurst.

Bale, J. (1989) *Sports Geography*, London: Spon.

Bale, J. (1990) 'In the shadow of the stadium', *Geography*, 75(4): 324–34.

Bale, J. (1991a) 'Playing at home', in J. Williams and S. Wagg (eds), *British Football and Social Change*, Leicester: Leicester University Press.

Bale, J. (1991b) *The Brawn Drain*, Champaign: University of Illinois Press.

Bale, J. (1992) *Sport, Space and the City*, London: Routledge.

Bale, J. (1994) *Landscapes of Modern Sport*, London: Leicester University Press.

Bale, J. (1995) 'Cricket', in K. Raitz (ed.), *Theater of Sport*, Baltimore: Johns Hopkins University Press.

Bale, J. (1998) 'Virtual fandoms', in A. Brown (ed.), *Fanatics!*, London: Routledge.

Bale, J. (2000) 'Sport as power', in J. P. Sharp, P. Routledge, C. Philo and R. Paddison (eds), *Entanglements of Power*, London: Routledge.

Bale, J., and J. Sang (1996) *Kenyan Running*, London: Frank Cass.

Banton, M. (1988) *Racial Consciousness*, London: Longman.

Baudrillard, J. (1991) *Seduction*, Basingstoke: Palgrave.

Baudrillard, J. (1993) *The Transparency of Evil*, London: Verso.

Baudrillard, J. (1994a) *The Illusion of the End*, Cambridge: Polity.

Baudrillard, J. (1994b) *The Gulf War Did Not Take Place*, Sydney: Power Institute.

Baudrillard, J. (1995) 'The virtual illusion', *Theory, Culture & Society*, 12: 97–107.

Baudrillard, J. (1996a) 'Disneyworld Company', *Liberation*, 4 March.

Baudrillard, J. (1996b) *The Perfect Crime*, London: Verso.

Baudrillard, J. (1998) *The Consumer Society*, London: Sage.

Baudrillard, J. (2006) *The System of Objects*, London: Verso.

Bauman, Z. (1992) *Intimations of Postmodernity*, London: Routledge.

Beamish, R. (1993) 'Labor relations in sport', in A. G. Ingham and J. W. Loy (eds), *Sport in Social Development*, Champaign, IL: Human Kinetics.

Beck, U. (1992) *Risk Society*, London: Sage.

Becker, G. S. (1964) *Human Capital*, Chicago: University of Chicago Press.

Beckles, H., and B. Stoddart (eds) (1995) *Liberation Cricket*, Manchester: Manchester University Press.

Bélanger, A. (2000) 'Sport venues and the spectacularization of urban spaces in North America', *International Review for the Sociology of Sport*, 35(3): 378–97.

Bellah, R. (1975) *The Broken Covenant*, New York: Seabury Press.

Benedict, J. (1998) *Public Heroes, Private Felons*, Boston: Northeastern University Press.

Bennett, T. (1998) *Culture: A Reformer's Science*, London: Sage.

Bentham, J. ([1791] 2010) *Panopticon, or the Inspection House*, London: Kessinger.

Berger, P., and T. Luckmann (1966) *The Social Construction of Reality*, New York: Anchor.

Best, S., and D. Kellner (1991) *Postmodern Theory*, New York: Guilford Press.

Bette, K. H. (1999) *Systemtheorie und Sport*, Frankfurt am Main: Suhrkamp.

Birrell, S. (1978) 'Sporting encounters', Unpublished doctoral dissertation, University of Massachusetts, Amherst.

Birrell, S. (1981) 'Sport as ritual', *Social Forces*, 60: 354–76.

Bischoff, A. (2012) 'Between me and the other there are paths: on paths, people and the experience of nature', unpublished PhD thesis, Department of Mathematical Sciences and Technology, Norwegian University of Life Sciences.

Blake, A. (1995) *The Body Language*, London: Lawrence & Wishart.

Bloyce, M., A. Smith, R. Mead and J. Morris (2008) 'Playing the game plan', *European Sport Management Quarterly*, 8(4): 359–78.

Boltanski, L. (2011) *On Critique: A Sociology of Emancipation*, Cambridge: Polity.

Booth, D. (1998) *The Race Game*, London: Routledge.

Booth, D. (2001) *Australian Beach Cultures*, London: Frank Cass.

Booth, D., and C. Tatz (1994) 'Swimming with the big boys', *Sporting Traditions*, 11(1): 3–23.

Booth, D., and C. Tatz (2000) *One-Eyed: A View of Australian Sport*, St Leonards, NSW: Allen & Unwin.

Bottenburg, M. van (2001) *Global Games*, Urbana: University of Illinois Press.

Bourdieu, P. (1978) 'Sport and social class', *Social Science Information*, 17(6): 819–40.

Bourdieu, P. (1984) *Distinction*, London: Routledge.

Bourdieu, P. (1990a) *In Other Words*, Stanford, CA: Stanford University Press.

Bourdieu, P. (1990b) *The Logic of Practice*, Cambridge: Polity.

Bourdieu, P. (1993) *Sociology in Question*, London: Sage.

Bourdieu, P. (1998a) *Acts of Resistance*, New York: New Press.

Bourdieu, P. (1998b) 'The state, economics and sport', *Culture, Sport, Society*, 1(2): 15–21.

Bourdieu, P. (2000) *Pascalian Meditations*, Cambridge: Polity.

Bourdieu, P., and J.-C. Passeron (1977) *Reproduction in Education, Society and Culture*, London: Sage.

Bourdieu, P., and L. J. D. Wacquant (1992) *An Invitation to Reflexive Sociology*, Cambridge: Polity.

Bourdieu, P., et al. (1999) *The Weight of the World: Social Suffering in Contemporary Society*, Cambridge: Polity.

Boyd, T. (1997) 'The day the niggaz took over', in A. Baker and T. Boyd (eds), *Out of Bounds*, Bloomington: Indiana University Press.

Brackenridge, C. (2001) *Spoilsports*, London: Routledge.

Bradbury, S. (2013) 'Institutional racism, whiteness and the under-representation of minorities in leadership positions in football in Europe', *Soccer and Society*, 14(3): 296–314.

Brailsford, D. (1985) 'Morals and maulers', *Journal of Sport History*, 2: 126–42.

Brannagan, P., and R. Giulianotti (2014) 'Soft power and soft disempowerment: Qatar, global sport, and football's 2022 World Cup finals', *Leisure Studies*, doi: 10.1080/02614367.2014.964291.

Brohm, J.-M. (1978) *Sport: A Prison of Measured Time*, London: Pluto Press.

Bromberger, C. (1995) 'Football as world-view and as ritual', *French Cultural Studies*, 6: 293–311.

Brophy, J. (1997) 'Carnival in Cologne', *History Today*, July.

Brownell, S. (1995) *Training the Body for China*, Chicago: University of Chicago Press.

Bruce, S. (2000) 'Comparing Scotland and Northern Ireland', in T. M. Devine (ed.), *Scotland's Shame?*, Edinburgh: Mainstream.

Buch, E. (2003) *Beethoven's Ninth*, Chicago: University of Chicago Press.

Burawoy, M. (2005) 'For public sociology', *American Sociological Review*, 70(1): 4–28.

Burdsey, D. (2006) 'If I ever play football, dad, can I play for England or India?', *Sociology*, 40(1): 11–28.

Burdsey, D. (2010) 'British Muslim experiences in English first-class cricket', *International Review for the Sociology of Sport*, 45(3): 315–34.

Burdsey, D. (2011) *Race, Ethnicity and Football*, London: Routledge.

Burke, P. (2009) *Cultural Hybridity*, Cambridge: Polity.

Burns, T. (1992) *Erving Goffman*, London: Routledge.

Butler, J. (1990) *Gender Trouble*, London: Routledge.

Cachay, K., and A. Thiel (2000) *Soziologie des Sports: zur Ausdifferenzierung und Entwicklungsdynamik des Sports der modernen Gesellschaft*, Weinheim: Juventa.

Calhoun, C. (1995) *Critical Social Theory*, Oxford: Wiley.

Canclini, N. G. (1995) *Hybrid Cultures*, Minneapolis: Minnesota University Press.

Carrington, B. (2010) *Race, Sport and Politics*, London: Sage.

Carter, T. (2008) *The Quality of Home Runs*, Durham, NC: Duke University Press.

Cashman, R. (1995) *Paradise of Sport*, Oxford: Oxford University Press.

Cashmore, E. (1982) *Black Sportsmen*, London: Routledge & Kegan Paul.

Cashmore, E. (2008) 'Tiger Woods and the new racial order', *Current Sociology*, 56(4): 621–34.

Cashmore, E., and J. Cleland (2012) 'Fans, homophobia and masculinities in association football', *British Journal of Sociology*, 63(2): 370–87.

Caudwell, J. (2006) *Sport, Sexualities and Queer/Theory*, London: Routledge.

Clarke, A. (1992) 'Figuring a brighter future', in E. Dunning and C. Rojek (eds), *Sport and Leisure in the Civilizing Process*, Toronto: University of Toronto Press.

Clarke, J. (1976) 'Style', in S. Hall and T. Jefferson (eds), *Resistance through Rituals*, London: Hutchinson.

Clément, J.-P. (1985) 'Etude comparative de trois sports de combat et de leurs usages sociaux', unpublished PhD thesis, Université Paris III.

Clément, J.-P. (1995) 'Contributions of the sociology of Pierre Bourdieu to the sociology of sport', *Sociology of Sport Journal*, 12: 147–57.

Coakley, J. (2001) *Sport in Society*, 7th edn, Boston: McGraw-Hill.

Coalter, F. (2013) *Sport for Development*, London: Routledge.

Cohen, M. B. (1946) *The Faith of a Liberal*, New Brunswick, NJ: Transaction.

Cohen, S., and L. Taylor (1976) *Escape Attempts*, London: Routledge.

Connell, R. W. (1987) *Gender and Power*, Stanford, CA: Stanford University Press.

Connell, R. W. (1990) 'An iron man', in M. Messner and D. Sabo (eds), *Sport, Men and the Gender Order*, Champaign, IL: Human Kinetics.

Connell, R. W. (1995) *Masculinities*, Cambridge: Polity.

Connell, R. W. (2000) *The Men and the Boys*, Cambridge: Polity.

Connor, S. (1989) *Postmodernist Culture*, Oxford: Blackwell.

Cornelissen, S. (2011) 'More than a sporting chance? Appraising the sport for development legacy of the 2010 FIFA World Cup', *Third World Quarterly*, 32(3): 503–29.

Cox, B., and S. Thompson (2001) 'Facing the bogey: women, football and sexuality', *Football Studies*, 4(2): 7–24.

Crenshaw, K. W. (1989) 'Demarginalizing the intersection of race and sex', *University of Chicago Legal Forum*, 139–67.

Critcher, C. (1979) 'Football since the war', in J. Clarke, C. Critcher and R. Johnson (eds), *Working Class Culture*, London: Hutchinson.

Crossley, N. (1995) 'Merleau-Ponty, the elusive body and carnal sociology', *Body and Society*, 1(1): 43–63.

Cruikshank, B. (1999) *The Will to Empower: Democratic Citizens and Other Subjects*, Ithaca, NY: Cornell University Press.

Csikszentmihalyi, M. (1975) *Beyond Boredom and Anxiety*, San Francisco: Jossey-Bass.

Csikszentmihalyi, M., and I. S. Csikszentmihalyi (1988) *Optimal Experience*, Cambridge: Cambridge University Press.

Cunningham, G. (2012) 'Occupational segregation of African Americans in intercollegiate athletics administration', *Wake Forest Journal of Law & Policy*, 2: 165–78.

Da Matta, R. (1991) *Carnivals, Rogues and Heroes*, Notre Dame, IN: University of Notre Dame Press.

Darnell, S. (2012) *Sport for Development and Peace*, London: Bloomsbury.

David, P. (2005) *Human Rights in Youth Sport*, London: Routledge.

Davis, L. R. (1997) *The Swimsuit Issue and Sport*, New York: SUNY Press.

De Bosscher, V., J. Bingham, S. Shibli, M. van Bottenburg and P. De Knop (2008) *The Global Sporting Arms Race*, Oxford: Meyer & Meyer.

Dean, P. (2002) '"Dear sisters" and "hated rivals"', in P. B. Miller (ed.), *The Sporting World of the Modern South*, Urbana: University of Illinois Press.

Debord, G. (1984) *The Society of the Spectacle*, New York: Black & Red.

Defrance, J. (1976) 'Esquisse d'une histoire sociale de la gymnastique', *Actes de la Recherche en Sciences Sociales*, 6: 22–46.

Defrance, J. (1987) *L'Excellence corporelle*, Rennes: Presses Universitaires de Rennes.

Defrance, J. (1995) 'The anthropological sociology of Pierre Bourdieu', *Sociology of Sport Journal*, 12: 121–31.

Degen, M. (2004) 'Barcelona's games: the Olympics, urban design, and global tourism', in M. Sheller and J. Urry (eds), *Tourism Mobilities: Places to Play, Places in Play*, London: Routledge.

Dejonghe, T. (2001) 'The place of sub-Saharan Africa in the world sport system', *Afrika Focus*, 17(1): 79–111.

Delaney, K., and R. Eckstein (2003) *Public Dollars, Private Stadiums*, New Brunswick, NJ: Rutgers University Press.

deMause, N., and J. Cagan (2008) *Field of Schemes*, rev. edn, Lincoln, NE: Bison Books.

Derrida, J. (1978) *Writing and Difference*, Chicago: University of Chicago Press.

Derrida, J. (1984) *Otobiographies*, Paris: Galilée.

Donnelly, P. (1993) 'Subcultures in sport', in A. G. Ingham and J. W. Loy (eds), *Sport in Social Development*, Champaign, IL: Human Kinetics.

Donnelly, P., and L. Petherick (2006) 'Workers' playtime?', in D. McArdle and R. Giulianotti (eds), *Sport, Civil Liberties and Human Rights*, London: Routledge.

Donnelly, P., and K. Young (1988) 'The construction and confirmation of identity in sport subcultures', *Sociology of Sport Journal*, 5(3): 223–40.

Douglas, D. (2005) 'Venus, Serena, and the Women's Tennis Association (WTA): when and where "race" enters', *Sociology of Sport Journal*, 22: 256–82.

Dubal, S. (2010) 'The neoliberalization of football', *International Review for the Sociology of Sport*, 45(2): 123–45.

Duncan, M. (1994) 'The politics of women's body images and practices', *Journal of Sport and Social Issues*, 18: 48–65.

Duncan, M. C., and B. Brummett (1989) 'Types and sources of spectating pleasures', *Sociology of Sport Journal* 3: 195–211.

Dunning, E. (1977) 'Power and authority in the public schools (1700–1850)', in P. R. Gleichmann, J. Goudsblom and Hermann Korte (eds), *Human Figurations*, Amsterdam: Amsterdam Sociologisch Tijdschrift.

Dunning, E. (1999) *Sport Matters*, London: Routledge.

Dunning, E., and K. Sheard (1979) *Barbarians, Gentlemen and Players*, Oxford: Blackwell.

Dunning, E., P. Murphy and J. Williams (1988) *The Roots of Football Hooliganism*, London: Routledge.

Durkheim, E. ([1895] 1938) *The Rules of Sociological Method*, New York: Free Press.

Durkheim, E. ([1915] 1961) *The Elementary Forms of the Religious Life*, New York: Collier Books.

Durkheim, E. ([1893] 1964) *The Division of Labour in Society*, London: Routledge & Kegan Paul.

Durkheim, E. ([1897] 1970) *Suicide: A Study in Sociology*, London: Routledge & Kegan Paul.

Durkheim, E. ([1898] 1973) 'Individualism and the intellectuals', in *Emile Durkheim on Morality and Society*, Chicago: University of Chicago Press.

Durkheim, E. ([1924] 1974) *Sociology and Philosophy*. New York: Free Press.

Duru, N. J. (2011) *Advancing the Ball*, New York: Oxford University Press.

Dyck, N. (2012) *Fields of Play: An Ethnography of Children's Sports*, Toronto: University of Toronto Press.

Edelman, R. (1993) *Serious Fun*, New York: Oxford University Press.

Edwards, H. (1969) *Revolt of the Black Athlete*, New York: Free Press.

Eichberg, H. (1994) 'Travelling, comparing, emigrating', in J. Bale and J. Maguire (eds), *The Global Sports Arena*, London: Frank Cass.

Eichberg, H. (1995) 'Stadium, pyramid, labyrinth', in J. Bale and O. Moen (eds), *The Stadium and the City*, Keele: Keele University Press.

Eick, V. (2011) 'Lack of legacy? Shadows of surveillance after the 2006 FIFA World Cup in Germany', *Urban Studies*, 48(15): 3329–45.

Eitzen, D. S. (1999) *Fair and Foul*, Lanham, MD: Rowman & Littlefield.

Elias, N. ([1939] 1978a, 1982) *The Civilizing Process*, Vol. 1: *The History of Manners*; Vol. 2: *State Formation and Civilization*, Oxford: Blackwell.

Elias, N. (1978b) *What is Sociology?*, London: Hutchinson.

Elias, N. (1987) *Involvement and Detachment*, Oxford: Blackwell.

Elias, N. (1996) *The Germans*, Cambridge: Polity.

Elias, N., and E. Dunning (1986) *Quest for Excitement*, Oxford: Blackwell.

Entine, J. (2000) *Taboo*, New York: Public Affairs.

Euchner, C. C. (1993) *Playing the Field*, Baltimore: Johns Hopkins University Press.

Featherstone, M. (1991) *Consumer Culture and Postmodernism*, London: Sage.

Featherstone, M. (1995) *Undoing Culture*, London: Sage.

Feifer, M. (1985) *Going Places*, Macmillan: London.

Finn, G. P. T (1990) 'Prejudice in the history of Irish Catholics in Scotland', paper given at the 24th History Workshop conference, Glasgow Polytechnic, November.

Finn, G. P. T. (1994a) 'Football violence', in R. Giulianotti, N. Bonney and M. Hepworth (eds), *Football, Violence and Social Identity*, London: Routledge.

Finn, G. P. T. (1994b) 'Sporting symbols, sporting identities', in I. S. Wood (ed.), *Scotland and Ulster*, Edinburgh: Mercat Press.

Finn, G. P. T. (1999) 'Scottish myopia and global prejudices', *Culture, Sport, Society*, 2(3): 54–99.

Finn, G. P. T. (2000) 'A culture of prejudice', in T. M. Devine (ed.), *Scotland's Shame?*, Edinburgh: Mainstream.

Fiske, J. (1993) *Power Plays, Power Works*, London: Verso.

Fletcher, R. (2008) 'Living on the edge: the appeal of risk sports for the professional middle class', *Sociology of Sport Journal*, 25(3): 310–30.

Foley, D. (1990) 'The great American football ritual', *Sociology of Sport Journal*, 7(2): 111–35.

Forney, C. A. (2007) *The Holy Trinity of American Sport: Civil Religion in Football, Baseball and Basketball*, Macon, GA: Mercer University Press.

Foucault, M. (1977) *Discipline and Punish*, London: Penguin.

Foucault, M. (1979) *The History of Sexuality*, Vol. 1, London: Penguin.

Foucault, M. (1980) *Power/Knowledge*, Brighton: Harvester Press.

Foucault, M. (1983) 'The subject and power', in H. L. Dreyfus and P. Rabinow, *Michel Foucault*, Chicago: University of Chicago Press.

Foucault, M. (1985) *The Use of Pleasure*, New York: Vintage Books.

Fowler, B. (1997) *Bourdieu and Cultural Theory*, London: Sage.

Freyre, G. (1964) 'O negro no futebol brasileiro', in M. Filho (ed.), *O Negro no Futebol Brasileiro*, Rio de Janeiro: Civilização Brasileira.

Freyre, G. (1967) *Sociologia*, Rio de Janeiro: José Olympio.

Friedman, J. (1999) 'Indigenous struggles and the discreet charm of the bourgeoisie', *Journal of World-Systems Research*, 5(2): 391–411.

Frisby, W. (1982) 'Weber's theory of bureaucracy and the study of voluntary sports organizations', in A. O. Dunleavy, A. W. Miracle and C. R. Rees (eds), *Studies in the Sociology of Sport*, Fort Worth: Texas Christian University Press.

Gaffney, C. (2013) 'Virando o jogo: the challenges and possibilities for social mobilization in Brazilian football', *Journal of Sport and Social Issues*, doi: 10.1177/0193723513515887.

Gane, M. (1991) *Baudrillard: Critical and Fatal Theory*, London: Routledge.

Gane, M. (1993) *Baudrillard Live*, London: Routledge.

Gans, H. J. (1999) *Popular Culture and High Culture*, New York: Basic Books.

Gartman, D. (1991) 'Culture as class symbolization or mass reification? A critique of Bourdieu's *Distinction*', *American Journal of Sociology*, 97(2): 421–47.

Gavora, J. (2002) *Tilting the Playing Field*, New York: Encounter Books.

Geertz, C. (1973) *The Interpretation of Cultures*, New York: Basic Books.

Gems, G. R. (1995) 'Blocked shot', *Journal of Sport History*, 22(2): 135–48.

Giddens, A. (1971) *Capitalism and Modern Social Theory*, Cambridge: Cambridge University Press.

Giddens, A. (1990) *The Consequences of Modernity*, Cambridge: Polity.

Giulianotti, R. (1991) 'Scotland's Tartan Army in Italy', *Sociological Review*, 39(3): 503–27.

Giulianotti, R. (1995) 'Football and the politics of carnival', *International Review for the Sociology of Sport*, 30(2): 191–224.

Giulianotti, R. (1999) *Football*, Cambridge: Polity.

Giulianotti, R. (2002) 'Supporters, followers, fans and *flâneurs*', *Journal of Sport and Social Issues*, 26(1): 25–46.

Giulianotti, R. (2004a) 'Civilizing games: Norbert Elias and the sociology of sport', in R. Giulianotti (ed.), *Sport and Modern Social Theorists*, Basingstoke: Palgrave.

Giulianotti, R. (2004b) 'Human rights, globalization and sentimental education: the case of sport', *Sport in Society*, 7(3): 355–69.

Giulianotti, R. (2005) 'Sport supporters and the social consequences of commodification', *Journal of Sport and Social Issues*, 29: 386–410.

Giulianotti, R. (2011a) 'Sport mega-events, urban football carnivals and securitized commodification: the case of the English Premier League', *Urban Studies*, 48(15): 3293–310.

Giulianotti, R. (2011b) 'The sport, development and peace sector: a model of four social policy domains', *Journal of Social Policy*, 40(4): 757–76.

Giulianotti, R., and G. Armstrong (2002) 'Avenues of contestation', *Social Anthropology*, 10(2): 211–38.

Giulianotti, R., and F. Klauser (2010) 'Security governance and sport mega-events', *Journal of Sport and Social Issues*, 34(1): 49–61.

Giulianotti, R., and F. Klauser (2011) 'Security and surveillance at sport mega-events', *Urban Studies*, 48(15): 3157–68.

Giulianotti, R., and R. Robertson (2004) 'The globalization of football: a study in the glocalization of the "serious life"', *British Journal of Sociology*, 55(4): 545–68.

Giulianotti, R., and R. Robertson (2005) 'Glocalization, globalization and migration: the case of Scottish football supporters in North America', *International Sociology*, 21(2): 171–98.

Giulianotti, R., and R. Robertson (2007a) 'Forms of glocalization: globalization and the migration strategies of Scottish football fans in North America', *Sociology*, 41(1): 133–52.

Giulianotti, R., and R. Robertson (2007b) 'Recovering the social: globalization, football and transnationalism', *Global Networks*, 7(2): 144–86.

Giulianotti, R., and R. Robertson (2007c) 'Sport and globalization: transnational dimensions', *Global Networks*, 7(2): 107–12.

Giulianotti, R., and R. Robertson (2007d) *Globalization and Sport*, Oxford: Wiley-Blackwell.

Giulianotti, R., and R. Robertson (2009) *Globalization and Football*, London: Sage.

Giulianotti, R., and R. Robertson (2012a) 'Mapping the global football field: a sociological model of transnational forces within the world game', *British Journal of Sociology*, 63(2): 216–40.

Giulianotti, R., and R. Robertson (2012b) 'Glocalization and sport in Asia', *Sociology of Sport Journal*, 29: 433–54.

Giulianotti, R., G. Armstrong, G. Hales and D. Hobbs (2014a) 'Global sport mega-events and the politics of mobility: the case of the London 2012 Olympics', *British Journal of Sociology*, doi: 10.1111/1468-4446.12103.

Giulianotti, R., G. Armstrong, G. Hales and R. Hobbs (2014b) 'Sport mega-events and public opposition: a sociological study of the London 2012 Olympics', *Journal of Sport and Social Issues*, doi: 10.1177/0193723514530565.

Gmelch, G., and P. M. San Antonio (1998) 'Groupies and American baseball', *Journal of Sport and Social Issues*, 22(1): 32–45.

Goffman, E. (1959) *The Presentation of Self in Everyday Life*, Harmondsworth: Penguin.

Goffman, E. (1967) *Interaction Ritual*, Harmondsworth: Penguin.

Goffman, E. (1971) *Relations in Public*, London: Allen Lane.

Goldblatt, D. (2014) *Futebol Nation*, London: Penguin.

Goody, J. (2002) 'Elias and the anthropological tradition', *Anthropological Theory*, 2(4): 401–12.

Gorn, E. J., and W. Goldstein (1993) *A Brief History of American Sports*, New York: Hill & Wang.

Gottdiener, M. (1995) *Postmodern Semiotics*, Oxford: Blackwell.

Goulstone, J. (1974) *Modern Sport*, Bexleyheath: Goulstone.

Goulstone, J. (2000) 'The working-class origins of modern football', *International Journal of the History of Sport*, 17: 135–43.

Gramsci, A. (1971) *Selections from the Prison Notebooks*, London: Lawrence & Wishart.

Griffin, P. (1998) *Strong Women, Deep Closets*, Champaign, IL: Human Kinetics.

Grindstaff, L., and E. West (2006) 'Cheerleading and the gendered politics of sport', *Social Problems*, 53(4): 500–18.

Grint, K. (1991) *The Sociology of Work*, Cambridge: Polity.

Grossberg, L. (1988) *It's a Sin*, Sydney: Power.

Grossberg, L. (1992) *We Gotta Get Out of This Place*, London: Routledge.

Grossman, M. (1972) 'On the concept of health capital and the demand for health', *Journal of Political Economy*, 80(2): 223–55.

Grosz, E. (1995) 'Women, *chora*, dwelling', in S. Watson and K. Gibson (eds), *Postmodern Cities and Spaces*, Oxford: Blackwell.

Grundlingh, A. (1994) 'Playing for power?', in J. Nauright and T. J. L. Chandler (eds), *Making Men*, London: Frank Cass.

Gruneau, R. (1999) *Class, Sports and Social Development*, Champaign, IL: Human Kinetics.

Guelke, A. (1993) 'Sport and the end of Apartheid', in L. Allison (ed.), *The Changing Politics of Sport*, Manchester: Manchester University Press.

Guttmann, A. (1978) *From Ritual to Record*, New York: Columbia University Press.

Guttmann, A. (1988) *A Whole New Ball Game*, Chapel Hill: University of North Carolina Press.

Guttmann, A. (1991) *Women's Sports*, New York: Columbia University Press.

Guttmann, A. (1994) *Games and Empires*, New York: Columbia University Press.

Guttmann, A. (1996) *The Erotic in Sports*, New York: Columbia University Press.

Guttmann, A., and L. Thompson (2001) *Japanese Sports*, Hawaii: University of Hawaii Press.

Habermas, J. (1970) *Toward a Rational Society*, Boston: Beacon Press.

Habermas, J. (1987a) *The Philosophical Discourse of Modernity*, Cambridge: Cambridge University Press.

Habermas, J. (1987b) *The Theory of Communicative Action*, Vol. 2, Boston: Beacon Press.

Habermas, J. (1989) *The Structural Transformation of the Public Sphere*, Cambridge: Polity.

Hagemann, A. (2010) 'From the stadium to the fan zone', *Soccer and Society*, 11(6): 723–36.

Haggerty, K. D., and R. V. Ericson (2000) 'The surveillant assemblage', *British Journal of Sociology*, 51(4): 605–22.

Hakim, C. (2011) *Honey Money: The Power of Erotic Capital*, London: Allen Lane.

Hall, C. M. (2006) 'Urban entrepreneurship, corporate interests and sports mega-events', *Sociological Review*, 54(2): 59–70.

Hall, M. A. (2002) *The Girl and the Game*, Toronto: Broadview Press.

Hall, S. (1977) 'Re-thinking the "base and superstructure" metaphor', in J. Bloomfield (ed.), *Class, Hegemony and Party*, London: Lawrence & Wishart.

Hall, S., and T. Jefferson (eds) (1976) *Resistance through Rituals*, London: Hutchinson.

Hallinan, C. (1991) 'Aborigines and positional segregation in the Australian rugby league', *International Review for the Sociology of Sport*, 12(1): 69–82.

Hamelink, C. J. (1995) *World Communication: Disempowerment and Self-Empowerment*, London: Zed Books.

Hannerz, U. (1992) *Cultural Complexity*, New York: Columbia University Press.

Hannigan, J. A. (1998) *Fantasy City*, London: Routledge.

Hardy, S. (1986) 'Entrepreneurs, organizations and the sports marketplace', *Journal of Sport History*, 13: 14–33.

Hargreaves, Jennifer (1993) 'Gender on the sports agenda', in A. G. Ingham and J. W. Loy (eds), *Sport in Social Development*, Champaign, IL: Human Kinetics.

Hargreaves, Jennifer (1994) *Sporting Females*, London: Routledge.

Hargreaves, Jennifer (2000) *Heroines of Sport: The Politics of Difference and Identity*, London: Routledge.

Hargreaves, Jennifer (2002) 'The Victorian cult of the family and the early years of female sport', in S. Scraton and A. Flintoff (eds), *Gender and Sport: A Reader*, London: Routledge.

Hargreaves, Jennifer, and P. Vertinsky (eds) (2007) *Physical Culture, Power and the Body*, London: Routledge.

Hargreaves, John (1986) *Sport, Power and Culture*, Cambridge: Polity.

Harpalani, V. (1998) 'The athletic dominance of African Americans', in G. Sailes (ed.), *African Americans in Sport*, New Brunswick, NJ: Transaction.

Harris, O. (1998) 'The role of sport in the black community', in G. Sailes (ed.), *African Americans in Sport*, New Brunswick, NJ: Transaction.

Harrison, A. K. (2013) 'Black skiing, everyday racism and the racial spatiality of whiteness', *Journal of Sport and Social Issues*, 37(4): 315–39.

Harvey, A. (1999) 'Football's missing link', in J. A. Mangan (ed.), *Sport in Europe*, London: Frank Cass.

Harvey, D. (1991) *The Condition of Postmodernity*, Oxford: Blackwell.

Harvey, D. (2005) *A Brief History of Neoliberalism*, Oxford: Oxford University Press.

Hawkins, M. (1997) *Social Darwinism in European and American Thought, 1860–1945*, Cambridge: Cambridge University Press.

Hayhurst, L. (2013) 'Girls as the new agents of social change?', *Sociological Research Online*, 18(2).

Hebdige, D. (1979) *Subculture*, London: Methuen.

Hebdige, D. (1988) *Hiding in the Light*, London: Routledge.

Heinilä, K. (1998) *Sport in Social Context*, Jyväskylä: University of Jyväskylä Press.

Henderson, R. (1995) 'Is it in the blood?' *Wisden Cricket Monthly*, July.

Henderson, R. W. (2001) *Ball, Bat and Bishop*, Champaign: University of Illinois Press.

Herrnstein, R. J., and C. Murray (1994) *The Bell Curve*, Glencoe, IL: Free Press.

Hess, R. (1998) 'The Victorian football league takes over, 1897–1914', in R. Hess and B. Stewart (eds), *More than a Game*, Melbourne: Melbourne University Press.

Hill, D. (2010) *The Fix: Soccer and Organized Crime*, London: McClelland & Stewart.

Hoberman, J. M. (1984) *Sport and Political Ideology*, Austin: University of Texas Press.

Hoberman, J. M. (1997) *Darwin's Athletes*, Boston: Houghton Mifflin.

Hoberman, J. M. (2001) *Mortal Engines: The Science of Performance and the Dehumanization of Sport*, Caldwell, NJ: Blackburn Press.

Hoch, P. (1972) *Rip Off the Big Game*, Garden City, NY: Doubleday.

Hochschild, A. R. (1983) *The Managed Heart*, Berkeley: University of California Press.

Hockey, J., and J. Allen-Collinson (2007) 'Grasping the phenomenology of sporting bodies', *International Review for the Sociology of Sport*, 42(2): 115–31.

Hofmeyer, J. (ed.) (2012) *The Youth Divided*, Cape Town: Institute for Justice and Reconciliation.

Hoggart, R. (1958) *The Uses of Literacy*, London: Penguin.

Holt, R. (1991) 'Women, men and sport in France, c.1870–1914', *Journal of Sport History*, 18(1): 121–34.

Hong, F. (1997) 'Iron bodies: women, war and sport in the early communist movement in China', *Journal of Sport History*, 1: 1–22.

Houlihan, B., and R. Giulianotti (2012) 'Politics and the London 2012 Olympics: the (in)security games', *International Affairs*, 88(4): 701–17.

Howe, D. (2001) 'An ethnography of pain and injury in professional rugby union', *International Review for the Sociology of Sport*, 36(3): 289–304.

Howe, D. (2004) *Sport, Professionalism and Pain*, London: Routledge.

Howe, D. (2008) *The Cultural Politics of the Paralympic Movement*, London: Routledge.

Howe, D. (2011) 'Cyborg and supercrip', *Sociology*, 45(5): 868–82.

Huizenga, R. (1995) *You're OK, It's Just a Bruise*, New York: St Martin's Press.

Humphreys, D. (2003) 'Selling out snowboarding: the alternative response to commercial co-optation', in R. E. Rinehart and S. Sydnor (eds), *To the Extreme: Alternative Sports, Inside and Out*, New York: SUNY Press.

Hunter, D. W. (1998) 'Race and athletic performance', in G. Sailes (ed.), *African Americans in Sport*, New Brunswick, NJ: Transaction.

Hylton, K. (2008) *Race and Sport*, London: Routledge.

ICSS/Sorbonne (2014) *Protecting the Integrity of Sport Competition*, Paris: International Centre for Sport Security/Université Paris 1 Panthéon Sorbonne.

Ingham, A. G. (1975) 'Occupational subcultures in the work world of sport', in D. Ball and J. Loy (eds), *Sport and Social Order*, Reading, MA: Addison-Wesley.

Ingham, A. G. (and Friends) (1997) 'Toward a department of Physical Cultural Studies and an end to tribal warfare', in J.-M. Fernández-Balboa (ed.), *Critical Postmodernism in Human Movement, Physical Education, and Sport*, New York: SUNY Press.

Jaireth, S. (1995) 'Tracing Orientalism in cricket', *Sporting Traditions*, 12(1): 103–20.

James, C. L. R. (1963) *Beyond a Boundary*, London: Paul.

Jameson, F. (1979) 'Reification and utopia in mass culture', *Social Text*, 1: 130–48.

Jameson, F. (1981) *The Political Unconscious*, Ithaca, NY: Cornell University Press.

Jameson, F. (1991) *Postmodernism, or, The Cultural Logic of Late Capitalism*, London: Verso.

Jarvie, G. (1991) *Highland Games*, Edinburgh: Edinburgh University Press.

Jenkins, R. (1992) *Pierre Bourdieu*, London: Routledge.

Jhally, S., and J. Lewis (1992) *Enlightened Racism*, Boulder, CO: Westview Press.

Johns, D. P., and J. S. Johns (2000) 'Surveillance, subjectivism and technologies of power', *International Review for the Sociology of Sport*, 35(2): 219–34.

Kay, J., and S. Laberge (2002) 'The "new" corporate habitus in adventure racing', *International Review for the Sociology of Sport*, 37(1): 17–36.

Kellner, D. (1989) *Jean Baudrillard*, Cambridge: Polity.

Kellner, D., and S. Best (2001) *The Postmodern Adventure*, New York: Guilford Press.

Kelly, W. W. (2004) 'Sense and sensibility at the ballpark', in W. W. Kelly (ed.), *Fanning the Flames*, New York: SUNY Press.

Kennedy, P., and D. Kennedy (eds) (2012) *Football Supporters and the Commercialization of Football*, London: Routledge.

Kerry, D. S., and K. M. Armour (2000) 'Sport sciences and the promise of phenomenology', *Quest*, 52: 1–17.

Kiely, R. (2007) *The New Political Economy of Development*, Basingstoke: Palgrave.

Kimmel, M. S. (1990) 'Baseball and the reconstitution of American masculinity, 1880–1920', in M. A. Messner and D. F. Sabo (eds), *Sport, Men and the Gender Order*, Champaign, IL: Human Kinetics.

King, S. (2008) 'What's queer about (queer) sport sociology now? A review essay', *Sociology of Sport Journal*, 25: 419–42.

Klausen, A. M. (1999) 'Norwegian culture and Olympism', in A. M. Klausen (ed.), *Olympic Games as Performance and Public Event*, Oxford: Berghahn.

Klauser, F. (2008) 'Spatial articulations of surveillance at the FIFA World Cup 2006 in Germany', in K. Aas, H. Oppen and H. Mork (eds), *Technologies of Insecurity*, London: Routledge.

Klein, A. (1989) 'Baseball as underdevelopment', *Sociology of Sport Journal*, 6: 95–112.

Klein, A. (1991) *Sugarball*, New Haven, CT: Yale University Press.

Klein, A. (1993) *Little Big Men*, New York: SUNY Press.

Klein, A. (1994) 'Transnational labor and Latin American baseball', in J. Bale and J. Maguire (eds), *The Global Sports Arena*, London: Frank Cass.

Koppett, L. (1981) *Sports Illusion, Sports Reality*, Urbana: University of Illinois Press.

Korr, C., and M. Close (2009) *More Than Just a Game: Football v Apartheid*, London: Collins.

Laberge, S., and D. Sankoff (1988) 'Physical activities, body *habitus* and lifestyles', in J. Harvey and H. Cantelon (eds), *Not Just a Game*, Ottawa: University of Ottawa Press.

Laclau, E., and C. Mouffe (1985) *Hegemony and Socialist Strategy*, London: Verso.

Laderman, S. (2014) *Empire in Waves: A Political History of Surfing*, Berkeley: University of California Press.

LaFeber, W. (2002) *Michael Jordan and the New Global Capitalism*, New York: W. W. Norton.

Langseth, T. (2011) 'Risk sports', *Sport in Society*, 14(5): 629–44.

Lasch, C. (1979) *The Culture of Narcissism*, London: Abacus.

Lash, S. (1990) *Sociology of Postmodernism*, London: Routledge.

Lash, S., and J. Urry (1987) *The End of Organized Capitalism*, Cambridge: Polity.

Lash, S., and J. Urry (1994) *Economies of Signs and Space*, London: Sage.

Latouche, S. (1996) *The Westernization of the World*, Cambridge: Polity.

Le Breton, D. (2000) 'Playing symbolically with death in extreme sports', *Body & Society*, 6: 1–11.

Leach, J., and G. Kildea (1976) *Trobriand Cricket: An Ingenious Response to Colonialism*, Papua New Guinea: Office of Information.

Lenin, V. I. ([1916] 1997) *Imperialism*, New York: International.

Lenin, V. I. ([1902] 1998) *What is to be Done?*, Harmondsworth: Penguin.

Lenskyj, H. (2000) *Inside the Olympic Industry*, New York: SUNY Press.

Lenskyj, H. (2002) *The Best Olympics Ever?*, New York: SUNY Press.

Lenskyj, H. (2003) 'The Olympic industry and civil liberties', in R. Giulianotti and D. McArdle (eds), *Sport and Human Rights*, London: Frank Cass.

Lenskyj, H. (2008) *Olympic Industry Resistance*, New York: SUNY Press.

Leonard, D. J., and C. R. King (eds) (2011) *Commodified and Criminalized*, Lanham, MD: Rowman & Littlefield.

Levine, P. (1992) *Ellis Island to Ebbets Field*, Oxford: Oxford University Press.

Lewis, R. W. (1996) 'Football hooliganism in England before 1914', *International Journal of the History of Sport*, 13(3): 310–39.

Leys, C. (1974) *Underdevelopment in Kenya*, Los Angeles: University of California Press.

Liston, K. (2005) 'Established–outsider relations between males and females in male-associated sports in Ireland', *European Journal for Sport and Society*, 2(1): 25–35.

Loland, S. (2000) 'Justice and game advantage in sporting games', in T. Tännsjö and C. Tamburrini (eds), *Values in Sport*, London: E. & F. N. Spon.

Long, J., and K. Hylton (2002) 'Shades of white', *Leisure Studies*, 21: 87–103.

Long, J. G. (2012) *Public/Private Partnerships for Major League Sports Facilities*, London: Routledge.

Loy, J. W., and J. F. McElvogue (1970) 'Racial segregation in American sport', *International Review for the Sociology of Sport*, 5: 5–24.

Luhmann, N. (1986) 'The autopoiesis of social systems', in F. Geyer and J. van der Zouwen (eds), *Sociocybernetic Paradoxes: Observation, Control and Evolution of Self-Steering Systems*, London: Sage.

Luhmann, N. (1995) *Social Systems*, Stanford, CA: Stanford University Press.
Luhmann, N. (2000) *Organisation und Entscheidung*, Wiesbaden: Westdeutscher.
Lukács, G. ([1923] 1967) *History and Class Consciousness*, London: Merlin.
Lüschen, G. (1967) 'The interdependence of sport and culture', *International Review of Sport Sociology*, 2(1): 27–41.
Lynch, R. (1992) 'A symbolic patch of grass: crowd disorder and regulation on the Sydney Cricket Ground Hill', *ASSH Studies in Sports History*, 7: 10–49.
Lyng, S. (1990) 'Edgework', *American Journal of Sociology*, 95(4): 851–86.
Lyotard, J.-F. (1984) *The Postmodern Condition*, Manchester: Manchester University Press.
Lyotard, J.-F. (1993) *The Postmodern Explained*, Minneapolis: Minnesota University Press.
McCall, L. (2005) 'The complexity of intersectionality', *Signs*, 30(3): 1771–800.
McCree, R. (2000) 'Professional soccer in the Caribbean', *International Review for the Sociology of Sport*, 35(2): 199–218.
McCrone, K. E. (1988) *Sport and the Physical Emancipation of Women, 1870–1914*, London: Routledge.
McDonald, I. (2009) 'One dimensional sport', in B. Carrington and I. McDonald (eds), *Marxism, Cultural Studies and Sport*, London: Routledge.
McInman, A. D., and J. R. Grove (1991) 'Peak moments in sport', *Quest*, 43: 333–51.
McKay, J. (1997) *Managing Gender*, New York: SUNY Press.
McKay, J., and M. Roderick (2010) 'Lay down Sally', *Journal of Australian Studies*, 34(3): 295–315.
McLean, R., and D. Wainwright (2009) 'Social networks, football fans, fantasy and reality', *Journal of Information, Communication and Ethics in Society*, 7(1): 54–71.
McPhail, T. (1981) *Electronic Colonialism: The Future of International Broadcasting and Communication*, London: Sage.
McPherson, B. D., J. E. Curtis and J. W. Loy (1989) *The Social Significance of Sport*, Champaign, IL: Human Kinetics.
McRobbie, A. (2005) *The Uses of Cultural Studies*, London: Sage.
Maffesoli, M. (1996) *The Time of the Tribes*, London: Sage.
Maguire, J. (1991) 'Sport, Racism and British Society', in G. Jarvie (ed.) *Sport, Racism and Ethnicity*, London: Falmer.
Maguire, J. (1999) *Global Sport*, Cambridge: Polity.
Majors, R. (1990) 'Cool pose', in M. Messner and D. Sabo (eds), *Sport, Men and Gender Order*, Champaign, IL: Human Kinetics.
Malcolm, D. (2013) *Globalizing Cricket*, London: Bloomsbury.
Malfas, M., E. Theodoraki and B. Houlihan (2004) 'Impacts of the Olympic Games as mega-events', *Municipal Engineer*, 157: 209–20.

Mandel, E. (1975) *Late Capitalism*, London: Humanities Press.

Mangan, J. A. (1981) *Athleticism in the Victorian and Edwardian Public School*, Cambridge: Cambridge University Press.

Mangan, J. A. (1986) *The Games Ethic and Imperialism*, London: Viking.

Mangan, J. A. (1987) 'Ethics and ethnocentricity', in W. J. Baker and J. A. Mangan (eds), *Sport in Africa*, London: Holmes & Meier.

Mangan, J. A. (1998) 'Sport in society', in H. Meinander and J. A. Mangan (eds), *The Nordic World*, London: Frank Cass.

Manning, F. (1981) 'Celebrating cricket', *American Ethnologist*, 8(3): 616–32.

Marcano, A. J., and D. P. Fidler (1999) 'The globalization of baseball', *Global Legal Studies Journal*, 6: 511–77.

Marcuse, H. (1964) *One Dimensional Man*, London: Ark.

Markula, P. (1995) 'Firm but shapely, fit but sexy, strong but thin', *Sociology of Sport Journal*, 12: 424–53.

Markula, P., and R. Pringle (2006) *Foucault, Sport and Exercise*, London: Routledge.

Marling, W. H. (2006) *How American Is Globalization?*, Baltimore: Johns Hopkins University Press.

Marqusee, M. (1994) *Anyone but England*, London: Verso.

Martin, P. (1995) *Leisure and Society in Colonial Brazzaville*, Cambridge: Cambridge University Press.

Marx, K. ([1852] 1934) *The Eighteenth Brumaire of Louis Bonaparte*, Moscow: Progress.

Marx, K. ([1875] 1938) *Critique of the Gotha Programme*, New York: International.

Marx, K. ([1845] 1965) *The German Ideology*, London: Lawrence & Wishart.

Marx, K. ([1844] 1973) *Economic and Philosophical Manuscripts of 1844*, London: Victor Kamkin.

Marx, K. ([1867] 1999) *Capital*, Oxford: Oxford University Press.

Marx, K., and F. Engels ([1848] 1998) *The Communist Manifesto*, Oxford: Oxford University Press.

Mason, A. (1980) *Association Football and English Society, 1863–1915*, Brighton: Harvester.

Mason, C., and R. Roberts (1991) 'The spatial externality fields of football stadiums', *Applied Geography*, 11: 251–66.

Maton, K. (2005) 'A question of autonomy', *Journal of Education Policy*, 20(6): 687–704.

Mead, G. H. (1934) *Mind, Self and Society*, Chicago: University of Chicago Press.

Mennesson, C. (2000) 'Hard women and soft women', *International Review for the Sociology of Sport*, 35(1): 21–33.

Merleau-Ponty, M. (1962) *Phenomenology of Perception*, London: Routledge & Kegan Paul.

Merrett, C. (1994) 'Sport, racism and urban policy in South Africa', *Sporting Traditions*, 11(2): 97–122.

Merton, R. K. (1938) 'Social structure and anomie', *American Sociological Review*, 3(6): 672–82.

Merton, R. K. (1968) *Social Theory and Social Structure*, New York: Free Press.

Messner, M. A. (1992) *Power at Play*, Boston: Beacon Press.

Messner, M. A. (1994) 'AIDS, homophobia and sport', in M. A. Messner and D. F. Sabo (eds), *Sex, Violence and Power in Sports*, Freedom, CA: Crossing Press.

Messner, M. A. (2007) *Out of Play: Critical Essays on Gender and Sport*, New York: SUNY Press.

Messner, M. A. (2009) *It's All for the Kids: Gender, Families and Youth Sports*, Berkeley: University of California Press.

Messner, M. A., M. Dunbar and D. Hunt (2000) 'The televised sports manhood formula', *Journal of Sport and Social Issues*, 24(4): 380–94.

Messner, M. A., M. C. Duncan and C. Cooky (2003) 'Silence, sports bras, and wrestling porn', *Journal of Sport and Social Issues*, 27(1): 38–51.

Miliband, R. (1977) *Marxism and Politics*, Oxford: Oxford University Press.

Miller, A. (2006) *Ancient Greek Athletics*, New Haven, CT: Yale University Press.

Miller, P. (1998) 'The anatomy of scientific racism', *Journal of Sport History*, 24(1): 119–51.

Mills, C. W. (1959) *The Sociological Imagination*, Harmondsworth: Penguin.

Møller, V. (2007) 'Walking the edge', in M. McNamee (ed.), *Philosophy, Risk and Adventure Sports*, London: Routledge.

Møller, V. (2015) 'Doping in elite sport', in R. Giulianotti (ed.), *Routledge Handbook of the Sociology of Sport*, London: Routledge.

Morgan, W. J. (1988) 'Adorno on sport', *Theory and Society*, 17: 813–38.

Morgan, W. J. (1993) *Leftist Theories of Sport*, Urbana: University of Illinois Press.

Morgan, W. J. (1998) 'Hassiba Boulmerka and Islamic green', in G. Rail (ed.), *Sport and Postmodern Times*, New York: SUNY Press.

Morgan, W. J. (2002) 'Social criticism as moral criticism', *Journal of Sport and Social Issues*, 26(3): 281–99.

Morgan, W. J. (2004) 'Habermas on sports', in R. Giulianotti (ed.), *Sport and Modern Social Theorists*, Basingstoke: Palgrave.

Morgan, W. J. (2015) 'Why sport philosophy and sport sociology need each other', in R. Giulianotti (ed.), *Routledge Handbook of the Sociology of Sport*, London: Routledge.

Muchembled, R. (1985) *Popular Culture and Elite Culture in France, 1400–1750*, Baton Rouge: Louisiana State University Press.

Müller, A. F. (2002) 'Sociology as a combat sport: Pierre Bourdieu (1930–2002) – admired and reviled in France', *Anthropology Today*, 18(2): 5–9.

Murphy, P., E. Dunning and J. Williams (1990) *Football on Trial*, London: Routledge.

Nadel, D. (1998) 'The league goes national, 1986–1997', in R. Hess and B. Stewart (eds), *More than a Game*, Melbourne: Melbourne University Press.

Nederveen Pieterse, J. (1995) 'Globalization as hybridization', in M. Featherstone, S. Lash and R. Robertson (eds), *Global Modernities*, London: Sage.

Nederveen Pieterse, J. (2007) *Ethnicities and Global Multiculture*, Lanham, MD: Rowman & Littlefield.

Nixon, H. L. (1993) 'Accepting the risks of pain and injury in sport', *Sociology of Sport Journal*, 10: 183–96.

Noll, R. G., and A. S. Zimbalist (1997) *Sports, Jobs and Taxes*, Washington, DC: Brookings Institution Press.

Novak, M. ([1976] 1993) *The Joy of Sports*, rev. edn, Lanham, MD: Madison Books.

Numerato, D. (2009) 'Revisiting Weber's concept of disenchantment: an examination of the re-enchantment with sailing in the post-communist Czech Republic', *Sociology*, 43: 439–56.

O'Donnell, H. (1994) 'Mapping the mythical', *Discourse & Society*, 5(3): 345–80.

O'Neill, M. (2003) 'The policing of football spectators', unpublished PhD thesis, University of Aberdeen.

Oriard, M. (1993) *Reading Football*, Chapel Hill: University of North Carolina Press.

Oriard, M. (2001) *King Football*, Chapel Hill: University of North Carolina Press.

Parsons T. (1951) *The Social System*, New York: Free Press.

Parsons, T. (1966) *Societies*, Englewood Cliffs, NJ: Prentice-Hall.

Pearson, G. (2013) *An Ethnography of English Football Fans*, Manchester: Manchester University Press.

Perelman, M. (2012) *Barbaric Sport*, London: Verso.

Perkin, H. (1989) 'Teaching the nations how to play: sport and society in the British Empire and Commonwealth', *International Journal of the History of Sport*, 6(2): 145–55.

Pfister (2002) 'Sport for women', in R. Naul and K. Hardman (ed.), *Sport and Physical Education in Germany*, London: Routledge.

Phillips, J. (1994) 'The hard man', in J. Nauright and T. J. L. Chandler (eds), *Making Men*, London: Frank Cass.

Polsky, N. (1969) *Hustlers, Beats and Others*, Garden City, NY: Anchor Books.

Poster, M. (1988) *Jean Baudrillard*, Cambridge: Polity.

Poster, M. (1990) *The Mode of Information*, Cambridge: Polity.

Prasad, D. (1999) 'Environment', in R. Cashman and A. Hughes (eds), *Staging the Olympics*, Sydney: University of New South Wales Press.

Presner, T. S. (2007) *Muscular Judaism*, London: Routledge.

Preuss, H. (2006) *The Economics of Staging the Olympics*, Cheltenham: Edward Elgar.

Pye, G. (1986) 'The ideology of Cuban sport', *Journal of Sport History*, 13(2): 119–27.

Rabinow, P., and N. Rose (2003) 'Thoughts on the concept of biopower today', unpublished paper, available at: www.lse.ac.uk/sociology/pdf/ RabinowandRose-BiopowerToday03.pdf.

Rail, G. (1998) 'Seismography of the postmodern condition', in G. Rail (ed.), *Sport and Postmodern Times*, New York: SUNY Press.

Ranger, T. (1987) 'Pugilism and pathology', in W. J. Baker and J. A. Mangan (eds), *Sport in Africa*, London: Holmes & Meier.

Real, M. (1999) 'Aerobics and feminism', in R. Martin and T. Miller (eds), *SportCult*, Minneapolis: University of Minnesota Press.

Redhead, S. (1991) 'Some reflections on discourses on football hooliganism', *Sociological Review*, 39(3): 479–88.

Reiss, S. (1991) *City Games*, Urbana: University of Illinois Press.

Rigauer, B. (1981) *Sport and Work*, New York: Columbia University Press.

Rigauer, B. (2001) 'Marxist theories', in J. Coakley and E. Dunning (eds), *Handbook of Sports Studies*, London: Sage.

Rinehart, R., and S. Sydnor (eds) (2003) *To The Extreme*, New York: SUNY Press.

Riordan, J. (1976) 'Marx, Lenin and physical culture', *Journal of Sport History*, 2: 152–61.

Riordan, J. (1987) 'Soviet muscular socialism: a Durkheimian analysis', *Sociology of Sport Journal*, 4(4): 376–93.

Riordan, J. (1991) 'The rise, fall and rebirth of sporting women in Russia and the USSR', *Journal of Sport History*, 18(1): 183–99.

Ritzer, G. (1993) *The McDonaldization of Society*, Thousand Oaks, CA: Pine Forge Press.

Ritzer, G. (1996) *Modern Sociological Theory*, 4th edn, New York: McGraw-Hill.

Ritzer, G. (2004) *The Globalization of Nothing*, Thousand Oaks, CA: Pine Forge Press.

Ritzer, G., and T. Stillman (2001) 'The postmodern ballpark as leisure setting', *Leisure Sciences*, 23: 99–113.

Roberts, R., and J. Olsen (1989) *Winning is the Only Thing*, Baltimore: Johns Hopkins University Press.

Robertson, R. (1970) *The Sociological Interpretation of Religion*, Oxford: Blackwell.

Robertson, R. (1990) 'After nostalgia? Wilful nostalgia and the phases of globalization', in B. S. Turner (ed.), *Theories of Modernity and Postmodernity*, London: Sage.

Robertson, R. (1992) *Globalization*, London: Sage.

Robertson, R. (1994) 'Globalisation or glocalisation?', *Journal of International Communication* 1(1): 33–52.

Robertson, R. (1995) 'Glocalization', in M. Featherstone, S. Lash and R. Robertson (eds), *Global Modernities*, London: Sage.

Robertson, R. (2001) 'Globalization theory 2000+', in G. Ritzer and B. Smart (eds), *The Handbook of Social Theory*, London: Sage.

Robson, G. (2000) *Nobody Likes Us, We Don't Care*, Oxford: Berg.

Roderick, M. (1998) 'The sociology of risk, pain and injury: a comment on the work of Howard Nixon II', *Sociology of Sport Journal*, 15: 64–79.

Roderick, M. (2006) *The Work of Professional Football*, London: Routledge.

Rojek. C. (1985) *Capitalism and Leisure Theory*, London: Tavistock Press.

Rojek, C. (1993) 'Disney culture', *Leisure Studies*, 12: 121–35.

Rojek, C. (1995) *Decentring Leisure*, London: Sage.

Rojek, C. (2006) *Cultural Studies*, Cambridge: Polity.

Rorty, R. (1991) *Objectivity, Relativism and Truth*, Cambridge: Cambridge University Press.

Rosbrook-Thompson, J. (2013) *Sport, Difference and Belonging*, London: Routledge.

Rose, N. (1996) 'Governing advanced liberal democracies', in A. Barry, T. Osborne and N. Rose (eds), *Foucault and Political Reason*, London: UCL Press.

Rose, N. (1999) *Powers of Freedom*, Cambridge: Cambridge University Press.

Rosentraub, M. (1999) *Major League Losers*, New York: Basic Books.

Rowe, D. (1995) *Popular Cultures*, London: Sage.

Rowe, D. (2012) 'The bid, the lead-up, the event and the legacy', *British Journal of Sociology*, 63: 285–305.

Rowe, D., and P. McGuirk (1999) 'Drunk for three weeks', *International Review for the Sociology of Sport*, 34(2): 125–41.

Rumford, C. (2007) 'More than a game: globalization and the post-Westernization of world cricket', *Global Networks*, 7(2): 202–14.

Russell, D. (1999) 'Associating with football', in G. Armstrong and R. Giulianotti (eds), *Football Cultures and Identities*, Basingstoke: Macmillan.

Ryan, J. (1996) *Little Girls in Pretty Boxes*, London: Women's Press.

Sack, A., P. Singh and R. Thiel (2005) 'Occupational segregation on the playing field', *Journal of Sport Management*, 19: 300–18.

Said, E. (1994) *Culture and Imperialism*, London: Chatto & Windus.

Said, E. (1995) *Orientalism*, Harmondsworth: Penguin.

Sailes, G. A. (1998) 'The African American athlete', in G. Sailes (ed.), *African Americans in Sport*, New Brunswick, NJ: Transaction.

St Pierre, M. ([1995] 2008) 'West Indian cricket as cultural resistance', in M. A. Malec (ed.), *The Social Roles of Sport in Caribbean Societies*, Abingdon: Routledge.

Samatas, M. (2011) 'Surveillance in Athens 2004 and Beijing 2008', *Urban Studies*, 48(15): 3347–66.

Sammons, J. T. (1997) 'A proportionate and measured response to the provocation that is *Darwin's Athletes*', *Journal of Sport History*, 24(3): 378–88.

Sandiford, K., and B. Stoddart (1995) 'The elite schools and cricket in

Barbados', in H. M. Beckles and B. Stoddart (eds), *Liberation Cricket*, Manchester: Manchester University Press.

Sartore-Baldwin, M. (ed.) (2013) *Sexual Minorities in Sports*, Boulder, CO: Lynne Rienner.

Schiller, H. I. (1976) *Communication and Cultural Domination*, Armonk, NY: M. E. Sharpe.

Schimank, U. (2005) 'The autonomy of modern sport: dangerous and endangered', *European Journal for Sport and Society*, 2(1): 25–33.

Schimmel, K. (2011) 'From "violence-complacence" to "terrorist-ready"', *Urban Studies*, 48(15): 3277–91.

Scholte, J. A. (2005) *Globalization*, 2nd edn, Basingstoke: Palgrave.

Schulenkorf, N., and D. Adair (ed.) (2014) *Global Sport for Development*, Basingstoke: Palgrave.

Schutz, A. (1972) *Phenomenology of the Social World*, Chicago: Northwestern University Press.

Sennett, R. (1977) *The Fall of Public Man*, London: Faber & Faber.

Serazio, M. (2013) 'The elementary forms of sports fandom: a Durkheimian exploration of team myths, kinship, and totemic rituals', *Communication and Sport*, 1(4): 303–25.

Shamir R. (2008) 'The age of responsibilization: on market-embedded morality', *Economy and Society*, 37(1): 1–19.

Shehu, J. (ed.) (2010) *Gender, Sport and Development in Africa*, Dakar: Codesria.

Silva, C. F., and D. Howe (2012) 'The (in)validity of *supercrip* representation of Paralympian athletes', *Journal of Sport and Social Issues*, 36(2): 174–94.

Simon, R. (2005) *Sporting Equality: Title IX Thirty Years Later*, New Brunswick, NJ: Transaction.

Simpson, J. L. et al. (2000) 'Gender verification in the Olympics', *Journal of the American Medical Association*, 284(12): 1568–9.

Sklair, L. (1995) *Sociology of the Global System*, Baltimore: Johns Hopkins University Press.

Sklair, L. (2001) *The Transnational Capitalist Class*, Oxford: Blackwell.

Smith, C. (1997) 'Control of the female body', *Sporting Traditions*, 14(2): 59–71.

Smith, D., and G. Williams (1980) *Fields of Praise*, Cardiff: University of Wales Press.

Smith, D. (2001) *Norbert Elias and Modern Social Theory*, London: Sage.

Smith, N. (2005) *The Endgame of Globalization*, London: Routledge.

Smith, P. (1997) *Millennial Dreams*, London: Verso.

Snow, C. P. (1959) *The Two Cultures*, Cambridge: Cambridge University Press.

Sperber, M. (2000) *Beer and Circus: How Big-Time College Sports is Crippling Undergraduate Education*, New York: Henry Holt.

Spivey, D. (1985) 'Black consciousness and Olympic protest movement, 1964–1980', in D. Spivey (ed.) *Sport in America*, Westport, CT: Greenwood Press.

Sport Accord (2011) *Integrity in Sport*, Lausanne: Sport Accord.

Staurowsky, E. (2000) 'The Cleveland "Indians": a case study in American Indian cultural dispossession', *Sociology of Sport Journal*, 17(4): 307–30.

Stichweh, R. (1990) 'Sport: Ausdifferenzierung, Funktion, Code', *Sportwissenschaft*, 20: 373–89.

Sugden, J. (1987) 'The exploitation of disadvantage', in J. Horne, D. Jary and A. Tomlinson (eds), *Sport, Leisure and Social Relations*, London: Routledge & Kegan Paul.

Suttles, G. (1968) *The Social Order of the Slum*, Chicago: University of Chicago Press.

Suttles, G. (1972) *The Social Construction of Communities*, Chicago: University of Chicago Press.

Sykes, H. (1998) 'Turning the closets inside/out: towards a queer-feminist theory in women's physical education', *Sociology of Sport Journal*, 15(2): 154–73.

Symons, C. (2010) *The Gay Games: A History*, London: Routledge.

Tangen, J. O. (2004) 'Embedded expectations, embodied knowledge and the movements that connect', *International Review for the Sociology of Sport*, 39(1): 7–25.

Tangen, J. O. (2010) 'Observing sport participation: some sociological remarks on the inclusion/exclusion mechanism in sport', in U. Wagner, R. K. Storm and J. M. Hoberman (eds), *Observing Sport: Modern System Theoretical Approaches*, Schorndorf: Hofmann.

Tangen, J. O. (2014) 'Materiality, meaning and power', in I. Nalivaika and M. Tin (eds), *Phenomenology of the Everyday*, Oslo: Novus.

Taylor, I. (1970) 'Football mad: a speculative sociology of soccer hooliganism', in E. Dunning (ed.), *The Sociology of Sport*, London: Frank Cass.

Taylor, I. (1971) 'Soccer consciousness and soccer hooliganism', in S. Cohen (ed.), *Images of Deviance*, Harmondsworth: Penguin.

Theberge, N. (2008) 'Just a normal bad part of what I do', *Sociology of Sport Journal*, 25(2): 206–22.

Thiel, A., and H. Meier (2004) Überleben durch Abwehr: Zur Lernfähigkeit des Sportvereins, *Sport und Gesellschaft*, 1(2): 103–25.

Thompson, E. P. (1963) *The Making of the English Working Class*, London: Penguin.

Thompson, J. B. (1995) *The Media and Modernity*, Cambridge: Polity.

Thompson, S. M. (1999) 'The game begins at home', in J. Coakley and P. Donnelly (eds), *Inside Sports*, London: Routledge.

Thornton, S. (1995) *Club Cultures: Music, Media and Subcultural Capital*, Cambridge: Polity.

Thorpe, H. (2012) *Snowboarding: The Ultimate Guide*, Santa Barbara, CA: Greenwood.

Thorpe, H. (2014) *Transnational Mobilities in Action Sport Cultures*, Basingstoke: Palgrave.

Thrane, C. (2001) 'Sport spectatorship in Scandinavia', *International Review for the Sociology of Sport*, 36(2): 149–63.

Tomlinson, A. (2004) 'Pierre Bourdieu and the sociological study of sport', in R. Giulianotti (ed.), *Sport and Modern Social Theorists*, Basingstoke: Palgrave.

Tomlinson, J. (1999) *Globalization and Culture*, Cambridge: Polity.

Tordsson, B. (2010) *Friluftsliv, kultur og samfunn*, Kristiansand: Høyskoleforlaget.

Tranter, N. (1998) *Sport, Economy and Society in Britain, 1750–1914*, Cambridge: Cambridge University Press.

Trujillo, N. (1991) 'Hegemonic masculinity on the mound', *Critical Studies in Mass Communication*, 8: 290–308.

Tuan, Y.-F. (1974) *Topophilia*, Englewood Cliffs, NJ: Prentice-Hall.

Turner, B. (1999) 'The possibility of primitiveness', *Body & Society*, 5(2–3): 39–50.

Turner, V. (1974) *Dramas, Fields and Metaphors*, Ithaca, NY: Cornell University Press.

United Nations (2014) *Human Development Report*, New York: United Nations.

Urry, J. (1990) *The Tourist Gaze*, London: Sage.

Vaczi, M. (2014) 'Dangerous liaisons, fatal women', *International Review for the Sociology of Sport*, doi: 10.1177/1012690214524756.

Vamplew, W. (1994) 'Australians and sport', in W. Vamplew and B. Stoddart (eds), *Sport in Australia*, Melbourne: Cambridge University Press.

Vannini, A., and B. Fornssler (2007) 'Girl, interrupted: interpreting Semenya's body, gender verification testing, and public discourse', *Cultural Studies<=>Critical Methodologies*, 11(3): 243–57.

Veblen, T. ([1899] 1970) *The Theory of the Leisure Class*, London: Allen & Unwin.

Vertinsky, P., and J. Bale (eds) (2004) *Sites of Sport*, London: Routledge.

Vertinsky, P., and G. Captain (1998) 'More myth than history', *Journal of Sport History*, 25(3): 532–61.

Vigarello, G. (1995) 'The sociology of sport in France', *Sociology of Sport Journal*, 12: 224–32.

Vinnai, G. (1973) *Football Mania*, London: Ocean.

Wacquant, L. (1995a) 'Pugs at work', *Body & Society*, 1: 65–93.

Wacquant, L. (1995b) 'The pugilistic point of view', *Theory & Society*, 24: 489–535.

Wacquant, L. (2001) 'Whores, slaves and stallions', *Body & Society*, 7(2–3): 181–94.

Wacquant, L. (2002) 'The sociological life of Pierre Bourdieu', *International Sociology*, 17(4): 549–56.

Wacquant, L. (2004) *Body and Soul: Ethnographic Notes of an Apprentice Boxer*, Oxford: Oxford University Press.

Wacquant, L. (2005) 'Carnal connections', *Qualitative Sociology*, 28(4): 445–74.

Waddington, I. (2000) *Sport, Health and Drugs*, London: Routledge.

Wagner, U. (2009) 'The World Anti-Doping Agency', *International Journal of Sport Policy and Politics*, 1(2): 183–201.

Wagner, U., R. K. Storm and J. M. Hoberman (eds) (2010) *Observing Sport: Modern System Theoretical Approaches*, Schorndorf: Hofmann.

Walby, S. (1997) *Gender Transformations*, London: Routledge.

Wallerstein, I. (1974) *The Modern World System*, Vol. 1, London: Academic Press.

Wallerstein, I. (2000) *The Essential Wallerstein*, New York: New Press.

Wallerstein, I. (2002) *The Decline of American Power*, New York: New Press.

Walsh, A., and R. Giulianotti (2001) 'This sporting mammon', *Journal of the Philosophy of Sport*, 28: 53–77.

Walsh, A., and R. Giulianotti (2007) *Ethics, Money and Sport*, London: Routledge.

Wann, D., and N. Branscombe (1990) 'Die-hard and fair-weather fans', *Journal of Sport and Social Issues*, 14(2): 103–17.

Wearing, B. (1998) *Leisure and Feminist Theory*, London: Sage.

Weber, J. D., and R. M. Carini (2013) 'Where are the female athletes in *Sports Illustrated?*', *International Review for the Sociology of Sport*, 48(2): 196–203.

Weber, M. ([1922] 1978) *Economy and Society*, New York: Bedminster Press.

Westmarland, N., and G. Gangoli (ed.) (2011) *International Approaches to Rape*, Bristol: Policy Press.

Wiggins, D. K. (1989) '"Great speed but little stamina"', *Journal of Sport History*, 16(2): 158–85.

Wilkinson, R., and K. Pickett (2010) *The Spirit Level: Why Equality is Better for Everyone*, London: Penguin.

Williams, J. (1991) 'Having an away day', in J. Williams and S. Wagg (eds), *British Football and Social Change*, Leicester: Leicester University Press.

Williams, J. (2001) *Cricket and Race*, Oxford: Berg.

Williams, R. (1958) *Culture and Society*, New York: Columbia University Press.

Williams, R. (1961) *The Long Revolution*, New York: Columbia University Press.

Williams, R. (1975) *The Country and the City*, St Albans: Paladin.

Williams, R. (1977) *Marxism and Literature*, Oxford: Oxford University Press.

Williams, R. (1981) *The Sociology of Culture*, Chicago: University of Chicago Press.

Wilson, B., and B. Millington (2015) 'Sport and environmentalism in a post-political age', in R. Giulianotti (ed.), *Routledge Handbook of the Sociology of Sport*, London: Routledge.

Wilson, W. J. (1978) *The Declining Significance of Race*, Chicago: University of Chicago Press.

Wilson, W. J. (2009) *More Than Just Race*, New York: W. W. Norton.

Wolf, M. (2004) *Why Globalization Works*, New Haven, CT: Yale University Press.

Wouters , C. (1986) 'Formalization and informalization', *Theory, Culture & Society*, 3: 1–18.

Wouters, C. (1990) 'Social stratification and informalization in global perspective', *Theory, Culture & Society*, 7: 69–90.

Wray, A., and A. Newitz (eds) (1997) *White Trash: Race and Class in America*, New York: Routledge.

Wren-Lewis, J., and J. Clarke (1983) 'The World Cup: a political football', *Theory, Culture & Society*, 1: 123–32.

Young, K., W. McTeer and P. White (1994) 'Body talk: male athletes reflect on sport, injury, and pain', *Sociology of Sport Journal*, 11: 175–94.

Zaman, H. (1997) 'Islam, well-being and physical activity', in G. Clarke and B. Humberstone (eds), *Researching Women and Sport*, Basingstoke: Macmillan.

Index

44094